Physics and archaeology

BY

M. J. AITKEN

SECOND EDITION

CLARENDON PRESS · OXFORD
1974

Oxford University Press, Ely House, London W.1

GLASGOW NEW YORK TORONTO MELBOURNE WELLINGTON
CAPE TOWN IBADAN NAIROBI DAR ES SALAAM LUSAKA ADDIS ABABA
DELHI BOMBAY CALCUTTA MADRAS KARACHI LAHORE DACCA
KUALA LUMPUR SINGAPORE HONG KONG TOKYO

ISBN 0 19 851922 2

SECOND EDITION © OXFORD UNIVERSITY PRESS 1974

FIRST PUBLISHED BY INTERSCIENCE PUBLISHERS INC., NEW YORK, 1961

Text set in 10/12 pt. Monotype Times New Roman, printed by
letterpress, and bound in Great Britain at The Pitman Press, Bath

Preface

"And the next Day being otherwise imploy'd, I was fain to make use of a drowsie part of the Night to set down hastily in Writing what I had observ'd . .."

ROBERT BOYLE, 1663

THIS book describes some of the ways in which physics has been involved in archaeological research. For the physical scientist I hope that it will provide a window into unusual and stimulating fields of application, and for the archaeologist that it will provide guidance on topics that are becoming increasingly important to his profession. However, although there are several techniques from physics that are extremely powerful in archaeological application, notably radiocarbon dating, this does not imply any diminution in the role of conventional archaeological techniques—and, in general the new techniques are heavily reliant on the high quality of these. The new evidence should take its place with the other data that the archaeologist has to piece together, and in drawing a conclusion the archaeologist needs to know what weight to give the different types of information. He must bear in mind that a physicist is not a machine that regurgitates archaeological answers that are acceptable without qualification.

In the thirteen years that have elaspsed since the first edition of this book there has been an order of magnitude activity increase in this branch of *Archaeometry*—sometimes called *Archaeophysics*. There has been much crossing of barriers between disciplines and archaeologists have shown themselves as capable of this as physicists. This book does not attempt to spoon feed archaeologists by isolating technicalities but presumes on their ability to step back when they find themselves sinking, so that they may move on to drier land. For those that survive there are several relevant journals: *Archaeometry*,[1] *Prospezioni Archeologiche*,[2] and *The MASCA Newsletter*.[3] There is an annual Archaeometry Symposium, at Oxford usually in late March, organized by the Research Laboratory for Archaeology, and an annual course on Archaeological Prospecting, in Rome during April, organized by the Lerici Foundation.

In so far as this book records my own work at the Oxford University Research Laboratory for Archaeology and the History of Art, I record my debt to its director Dr. E. T. Hall for help and stimulation, as well as to past and present members of the Laboratory as a whole, and particularly to my research students. For my own enthusiasm in this field I owe much to the privilege of guidance from Professor C. F. C. Hawkes who together with the late Viscount Cherwell provided the initiative for the formation of the Research Laboratory in 1955.

In the production of this book, I am grateful to Miss J. A. Aitken, Dr. M. S. Baxter, Dr. R. Burleigh, Mr. A. Clark, Mr. A. Lonsdale, Dr. H. McKerrell, and Mr. R. Otlett for helpful discussions on various topics, to Dr. E. K. Ralph for kindly supplying radiocarbon calibration data, and to Toni Tattersall for translating my handwriting into typescript.

The Ofslang, Islip　　　　　　　　　　　　　　　　M. J. AITKEN
August 1973

1. Published by the Research Laboratory for Archaeology, 6 Keble Road Oxford OX1 3QJ, England.
2. Published by the Lerici Foundation, 00187 Roma, via Veneto 108, Italy.
3. Published by the University Museum, 33rd and Spruce Streets, Philadelphia, Pennsylvania 19104, U.S.A.

Contents

Contents

1 *Dating*

1.1. Introduction

THE earliest historical date is 3100 B.C.—the start of the First Dynasty in Egypt. This is derived from the recorded observation, more than a thousand years later, of a datable astronomical event in the ninth year of the reign of Sesostris III; this recording ties down the floating chronology provided by fragmentary lists of kings giving lengths of reigns and allows the date of the 1st Dynasty to be calculated. Prior to the third millennium B.C. archaeological chronology is almost entirely reliant on radiocarbon dating, a technique that reaches back to about 50 000 years. Even subsequent to the beginning of the third millennium there is a great need for radiocarbon dating because although the prehistoric cultures of contiguous regions can be reliability dated by reference to the Egyptian chronology, for remoter regions the linkage becomes tenuous and the dating unreliable. Accurate dating is important for two reasons. First, it allows an objective determination of the length of time required for a given cultural or technological development in a given environment. Secondly, absolute datings of similar developments in different parts of the world are vital in understanding how ideas diffused about the world, or alternatively, in establishing that they evolved in different areas independently.

Although radiocarbon dating is pre-eminent among the applications of physics in archaeology, it is not the only way in which evidence of age may be obtained from an object. This chapter outlines a number of methods both from physics and from other disciplines. In subsequent chapters three methods from physics—radiocarbon, thermoluminescence, and archaeomagnetism—are described in more detail. It will be seen that the techniques are complex ones, and that aside from their archaeological usage they are an integral part of geo-physics and geochemistry. The involvement of physics in archaeology is much more than as a technical aid; this is particularly the case with archaeomagnetism which has more importance in extracting geo-physical data from archaeological remains than as a dating method.

1.2. Methods from physics

Radiocarbon dating

In the carbon dioxide of the atmosphere, in living trees, plants, and animals, and in the dissolved carbonates of the ocean, there is a minute amount of the weakly radioactive isotope carbon-14. The concentration is about 1 part of carbon-14 per million million parts of natural carbon (carbon-12) and it is effectively uniform. The uni-formity occurs because of comparatively rapid mixing throughout the *carbon exchange reservoir*; this consists of the atmosphere, the bio-sphere, and the ocean. The concentration stays approximately con-stant because it represents the equilibrium level that is established on a global scale between loss by radioactive decay and production by cosmic rays. The latter generate neutrons in the upper atmosphere and these transmute nitrogen-14 atoms into carbon-14 atoms which then mix in with atmospheric carbon dioxide. Carbon is taken into oceans as dissolved carbonate, and it is incorporated into plant life by photosynthesis. In animals and plants that are preserved—and thereby removed from the exchange reservoir—the concentration diminishes by 1% every 83 years (as determined by the 5730-year half-life† of carbon-14), and by comparing the concentration found in such material with the concentration for living material the time that has elapsed since death can be evaluated.

The level of carbon-14 is obtained by measuring the beta-particle activity of the sample. The maximum age that can be measured is about 50 000 years; the limit is set by the difficulty of measuring the very low level of activity and by the risk that there has been incorpora-tion into the sample of more recent carbon—the level in a 50 000-year-old sample is only 0·2% of the level for living material. It is essential that the sample should be in a well preserved condition, since the assimilation of fresh carbon may accompany decomposition. Wood and charcoal are two of the best types of material and this is fortunate

† The time taken for the number of radioactive atoms to decrease to one half of the number present initially.

since they are widely associated with human occupation. Other materials are peat, reed, leaves, nuts, hair, skin, leather, paper, cloth, antler, bone and shell. For the last three special pre-treatments must be given and rather large samples are required—about a kilogram. For most other materials some tens of grams are enough, depending on the design of the measuring apparatus; for charcoal, wood, and peat the sample size can be reduced to a few grams if necessary. With charcoal and wood there is the possibility that the sample represents inner rings of a slow-growing tree and in such a case the radiocarbon date can be several hundred years earlier than the archaeological event of felling the tree; this is because when a ring is formed the carbon atoms are fixed in it and the carbon-14 activity is determined by the date of formation despite the presence of higher and lower activities on either side. This puts a premium on rapid-growth materials such as straw, seeds, nuts, grasses, twigs etc. Useful advice on sample collection will be found in Ralph (1971), and in Michels (1973).

The development of radiocarbon dating stems from research into the effects of cosmic rays on the earth's atmosphere by W. F. Libby and his group at the University of Chicago in the late 1940s. Widespread archaeological application took place during the 1950s and established its overwhelming importance for prehistoric chronology; today there are some 80 radiocarbon dating laboratories in operation serving not only archaeology but also other fields such as paleobotany and Pleistocene geology. Current research is mainly concerned with the degree to which the atmospheric carbon-14 concentration has been constant over past millennia; due to variations in this there are systematic deviations, on a worldwide basis, of radiocarbon ages from true calendar ages, and the *bristlecone pine calibration* has been developed to correct for such deviations. The effective accuracy after calibration is significantly worse than indicated by the error limit (typically ± 40 years, for 1 standard deviation) based only on experimental uncertainty in sample measurement, and in general it is more realistic to have ±150 years in mind as the effective error limit, though there may be occasions when the assumption of a smaller one is justified.

Although the need to apply a correction in order to obtain a precise date in calendar years means that the technique is less 'absolute' than had been assumed in early years of application, radiocarbon dating remains the backbone of prehistoric chronology. It would be surprising to find another radioisotope with the combination of properties that make carbon-14 suitable for archaeological dating: the half-life is of the right order, it has chemical properties that ensure its distribution throughout the biosphere, it is produced at an approximately constant rate, and it is fixed in materials associated with archaeological remains at a time that within limits is archaeologically significant.

Thermoluminescent dating

If a ground-up sample of ancient pottery is heated rapidly to 500°C there is a weak but measurable emission of light—see Fig. 1.1 curve

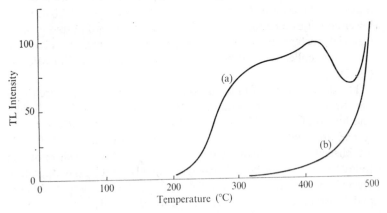

FIG. 1.1. TL glow-curve from ancient pottery. (a) 1st heating of sample. (b) 2nd heating of sample.

(a). For a second heating of the same sample the emission—curve (b) —consists only of thermal radiation (i.e. 'red-hot glow', or incandescence). The extra light in the first heating is *thermoluminescence* (TL); this comes from constituent minerals in the pottery and is due to the prolonged exposure they have had to the weak flux of nuclear radiation emitted by radioactive impurities in the pottery and the surrounding burial soil—uranium, thorium and potassium-40 at a concentration of a few parts per million. These radioisotopes have long half-lives (10^9 years or more) and so the radiation flux is constant; hence the amount of TL is proportional to the time that has elapsed since the pottery was fired by ancient man. The act of firing 'drains' the clay of all previously acquired TL thereby setting the 'clock' to zero.

The amount of TL depends not only on the age of the pottery but
also on its sensitivity to acquiring TL and to the concentration of
the radioactive impurities in the pottery and the soil. The sensitivity
is determined by measuring the TL induced by exposure to a known
amount of nuclear radiation from an artificial radioisotope source,
and the impurity concentration by radioactive and chemical analysis.
In principle the age can then be calculated.

In practice various factors make the determination much more
complicated and it is only since the late 1960s that reliable TL ages
have been obtained, although the idea was proposed more than a
decade earlier (Daniels *et al.*, 1953). At present (1973) an absolute
accuracy of somewhat better than ±10% of the age can be achieved;
with continued development of technique this should improve to
around ±5% but for various reasons this is likely to be the limit.
This is somewhat poorer than is usually quoted for radiocarbon
dating though for some periods it is no worse than indicated by a
realistic assessment of accuracy having regard to the short-term
carbon-14 variations (see section 2.9). The TL method has the
advantage that the event dated is the actual firing of the pottery,
whereas in the case of radiocarbon dating of wood or charcoal the
event dated may precede involvement with ancient man by several
hundred years. A further advantage is that the changing technique
and style of pottery often forms the basis of archaeological dating so
that TL dates are directly related to chronologically significant
objects.

A limitation with the TL technique is the need to have a sample
of the burial soil and to use only pottery coming from acceptable
burial circumstances. The nuclear radiation due to radioisotopes in
material surrounding the pottery usually amounts to 10–20% of the
effective total and is due to gamma-rays. The penetrating power of
these is such that if the sample has lain within a foot of, say, a wall
built of stones of higher or lower radioactivity than the soil, the value
for the gamma-ray flux derived from measurements on a sample of
the soil may differ significantly from the actual flux that was
experienced. This means that for good accuracy there must be careful
selection of samples while excavation is in progress.

Besides archaeological dating there is another important field of
application of TL and in this one the inaccuracy introduced by
uncertainty about burial circumstances (and unavailability of samples
of burial soil) usually does not matter. This is in testing ceramic

works of art and detecting which are modern forgeries. For such application a prime consideration is the minimization of damage to the object; a sample of about 20 milligrams obtained by drilling a small hole in an unobtrusive part of the object is usually adequate. For archaeological dating a fragment at least 5 millimetres thick and 2 or 3 centimetres across is required; it is desirable to have half-a-dozen or more such fragments from each context being dated, of a variety of fabric types if available.

In addition to pottery and terracotta, the technique has been applied to baked clay from hearths and ovens, to burnt stone, to enamel, and to burnt flint. There is some possibility of application to glass, volcanic lava, and shell. The age range of application depends on the material being dated. For baked clay the limit is probably around 50 000 years but for material of low radioactivity such as stone and shell it may well be half a million or more. Baked clay more recent than 500–1000 years cannot usually be dated with the conventional ('high temperature') technique, but when the 'pre-dose' method is applicable TL dating can be brought forward into the past century.

Archaeomagnetism

The time-dependent quantities in this case are the direction and intensity of the earth's magnetic field. When baked clay cools down from firing it acquires a weak permanent magnetization in the same direction as the field and of a strength proportional to the intensity of the field. To be a useful record of *direction* the clay must be part of a kiln, hearth, or oven so that it has exactly the same orientation today as when it cooled down. On the other hand information about *intensity* can be obtained from bricks and pottery fragments, as well as from kilns, hearths and ovens.

Direction changes appreciably from decade to decade and it was hoped initially that 'magnetic dating' would be a powerful technique. However its useful applications have been rather restricted. One difficulty is that the variation of direction does not follow any predictable law and calibration from samples of known date is an essential prerequisite; this calibration holds only for a region 500–1000 miles across. Another difficulty is that a given direction may recur after an interval of a few centuries. A practical difficulty is that in many structures the recorded direction is appreciably distorted by the magnetism of the baked clay itself. The foregoing comment is in respect of the small-scale *secular variation* of direction. From time to time in the geological past there has been a worldwide *reversal* of direction and there is evidence that this has occurred two or three times in the last 200 000 years; these reversals will be recorded in the hearths of some Mesolithic and Paleolithic levels and may provide useful time-marks.

Intensity variations are important in connection with radiocarbon dating. The earth's magnetic field acts as a shield against cosmic rays and during millennia when the intensity has been low the rate of radiocarbon production will have been high. Such study goes a long way towards explaining the known long-term systematic error in radiocarbon dating and may eventually allow prediction of the systematic error in earlier periods. Apart from this direct feedback into archaeology, archaeomagnetism has provided geophysical data, that is unobtainable except through archaeology, both in respect of intensity and of direction. This data is of interest for the light it throws on the mechanism by which the earth's magnetic field is produced.

Potassium–argon dating

The two preceeding methods rely on an unwitting act by ancient man for the event that is dated. On the time-scale relevant to the emergence of early man the association of skeletal remains with a geological event (such as a volcanic eruption) is sufficiently close that dating the latter is of interest. Potassium–argon dating is the first to be described of three geological techniques which are relevant in this context. It is simpler in concept than the radiocarbon method and does not utilize isotopes produced by cosmic rays. Its basis is the build-up of argon by the radioactive decay of potassium-40 in volcanic rocks, the amount present being a measure of the time that has elapsed since the rocks last cooled down. Natural potassium is present in rocks in the range 0–10% and in addition to the stable isotopes potassium-39 and potassium-41, contains 0·012% of the weakly radioactive isotope potassium-40. This has a half-life of $1·3 \times 10^9$ years and decays either to argon,

$$^{40}K \xrightarrow{11\%} {}^{40}Ar \tag{1.1}$$

or to calcium

$$^{40}K \xrightarrow{89\%} {}^{40}Ca \tag{1.2}$$

The age determination is based on argon rather than calcium because the former can be detected with very high sensitivity in a mass spectrometer, and because calcium-40 is already abundant in most rocks anyway. Also, since argon is a gas, it is less likely to exist in the material at the time of the event being dated—namely the volcanic eruption. Thereafter the argon builds up according to

$$N_2 = N_1 \frac{1 - \exp(-\lambda t)}{\exp(-\lambda t)} \qquad (1.3)$$

where N_1 and N_2 are the numbers of potassium-40 and argon-40 atoms in a given amount of sample, and λ is the disintegration rate. The potassium-40 content is determined either by measuring the total potassium content chemically (by flame photometry) or by measuring the potassium-39 content using neutron activation (Merrihue *and* Turner, 1966; Mitchell, 1968). In either case knowledge of the abundance ratio for the potassium isotopes allows derivation of the potassium-40 content itself.

The difficulty of using the method on rocks that are young enough to be of archaeological relevance is due to the very slow rate of formation of argon. For example, rocks with a potassium content of 2%, formed 10 000 years ago, have a fractional argon-40 content of only about 10^{-12}. Beside the need for high instrumental sensitivity there is also the difficulty of contamination by argon-40 from the atmosphere; this occurs by absorption on the sample material and on the walls of the measuring apparatus. The minimum age that can be measured depends on the condition of the minerals present as well as on the potassium content. The limit to which the method is considered generally useful is around 100 000 years though in special cases meaningful ages have been obtained for much younger rocks; for instance, Dalrymple (1967) has obtained ages in the range 6000 to 10 000 years for some potassium-rich lava flows (the measurements being made on potassium feldspar separated out from the lava).

The most notable examples of archaeological application are the dating of hominid remains in Africa. The Olduvai man (Zinjanthropus) has been dated to 1·75 million years by Evenden *and* Curtis (1965). Hominid remains and artefacts found near Lake Rudolf in Kenya have been dated to 2·6 million years by Fitch *and* Miller (1970). In both cases the dating is of the volcanic pumice with which the remains are associated. Mention of some other archaeological applications, as well as a fuller account of the technique, will be found in Gentner *and* Lippolt (1969); recent reviews have been given by Miller (1972) *and* by Fitch (1972).

The applicability of potassium–argon dating to volcanic lava makes it important for paleomagnetic studies of the remanent magnetization recorded in the lava. In particular it has been vital in establishing that in certain age ranges there is reversed magnetization in rocks all over the world and hence that there has been true reversal of the geomagnetic field itself.

Uranium-series dating (including ionium dating)

The uranium series (see Table 3.1) consists of about a dozen isotopes formed by successive radioactive decay; in a rock that is old enough these are in equilibrium, i.e.

$$\lambda_1 N_1 = \lambda_2 N_2 = \lambda_3 N_3 \dots \text{etc.} \tag{1.4}$$

where $\lambda_1, \lambda_2, \dots$ represent the disintegration rate of the successive decay products, and $N_1, N_2, \dots$ their equilibrium quantities. Thus the equilibrium amounts are inversely proportional to the decay constants—that is, directly proportional to the respective half-lives. If the equilibrium is disturbed by the chemical removal of all products subsequent to the nth member of the chain then the re-establishment to equilibrium of the $(n + 1)$th member is determined by the equation

$$\frac{dN_{n+1}}{dt} - \lambda_{n+1} N_{n+1} = (\lambda_n N_n)_{\text{eq}} \tag{1.5}$$

of which the solution is

$$N_{n+1} = \frac{(\lambda_n N_n)_{\text{eq}}}{n + 1} \{1 - \exp(-\lambda_{n+1} t)\} \tag{1.6}$$

This means that the $(n + 1)$th member builds up at a rate determined by its own half-life rather than that of the preceding member. Alternatively if the upset to equilibrium consists of removal of all preceding members, the $(n + 1)$th member is said to be *unsupported*, and it decays according to

$$N_{n+1} = \frac{(\lambda_n N_n)_{\text{eq}}}{n + 1} \exp(-\lambda_{n+1} t) \tag{1.7}$$

eventually reaching the new equilibrium value of zero. Uranium-series dating is based on measurement of the degree to which equilibrium has been re-established (according to either (1.6) or (1.7)) following an event that has upset the equilibrium.

The successive long-lived components of the uranium-238 series are

uranium-238	half-life, 4.5×10^9 years
uranium-234	half-life, 2.5×10^5 years
thorium-230	half-life, 75 200 years
radium-226	half-life, 1622 years
lead-206	stable

For simplicity the intervening short-lived members have been omitted; their short lives mean that the equilibrium amounts are very small and the rapidity with which they re-establish equilibrium makes them uninteresting from the geological point of view. The long-lived components of the actinium (uranium-235) series are:

uranium-235	half-life, 7×10^8 years
protactinium-231	half-life, 32 400 years
lead-207	stable

The thorium series has only two long-lived components, the initial parent and the final end-product:

thorium-232	half-life, 1.4×10^{10} years
lead-208	stable

The isotopes of interest in the present context are thorium-230 (ionium), radium-226, and protactinium-231.

The basis of the ionium method of dating ocean sediments is that, because of its chemical nature, this isotope tends to be precipitated from sea water whereas the parent uranium remains in solution. Hence in deposited sediment the thorium-230 is no longer supported and its concentration decays according to the half-life of 75 200 years. Consequently in sediment that has been deposited at a uniform rate the thorium-230 concentration decreases exponentially with depth, and the time that has elapsed since the sediment at a given depth was deposited can be determined. Error due to variation in rate of deposition can be avoided by measuring the ratio thorium-230/ thorium-232. Thorium-232 has a very much longer half-life but it is chemically identical so that its concentration is a measure of the deposition rate of the thorium-230. It is assumed of course that the uranium and thorium concentrations in sea water remain constant and that the inherent concentrations of each in the sediment are negligible.

These and other assumptions are not often strictly met in practice and more reliable results are obtained (Rosholt *et al.*, 1961) by measuring the ratio of thorium-230 to protactinium-231. This isotope has a half-life of 32 400 years and is similarly deposited in ocean sediments. Reasonable agreement has been obtained with radiocarbon dating. Such agreement was also obtained with the straightforward ionium technique for cores that were carefully selected as best fulfilling the necessary requirements (Volchok *and* Kulp, 1957).

Of more direct archaeological relevance is application to shell, stalagmite, and bone (e.g. Cherdyntsev, Kazachevskii, *and* Kuzmina, 1965; Broecker *et al.*, 1968; Fornaca-Rinaldi, 1968; Szabo *and* Rosholt, 1969; Szabo, Malde, *and* Irwin-Williams, 1969; Hansen *and* Begg, 1970; Turekian *et al.*, 1970; Turekian *and* Bada, 1972). If it is assumed that uranium is incorporated at formation (or shortly after) without any accompanying thorium-230 and protactinium-231, then measurement of the degree to which these isotopes have built up towards equilibrium can be used to determine the age on the basis of eqn (1.6). This equation assumes that after formation the system was 'closed' so that there was no subsequent incorporation (*diagenetic uptake*) of uranium, nor any leaching out. In this case the ages obtained independently from measurement of each isotope (relative to its parent uranium) should be concordant. The frequent occurrence of discordant ages indicates that for shell the closed system assumption is not valid, and attempts have been made to use the more complex 'open system' model in which the age is determined from the Pa-231/Th-230 ratio; it is assumed that there is a mobile uranium component which migrates through the shell and leaves it, whereas the decay products from this component are retained. Direct evidence for the mobile component is the occurrence of protactinium-231 in excess of equilibrium (when compared with the amount of retained uranium). In a recent review Broecker *and* Bender (1972) contrast the reliability of uranium-series dating when applied to coral with the general unreliability when applied to shell; the reason given for this is the much higher initial uranium content in coral ($\sim$3 ppm compared to $\sim$0·05 ppm for shell) which makes any subsequent uptake or loss of uranium much less important.

The uptake of uranium during burial is a chemical method of distinguishing old bone from new—as outlined in section 1.3. Hence one might expect that the ages obtained for bone by the above technique will be too young; however the results of Hansen *and* Begg suggest that when ground water has been present the uranium rapidly reaches its final value, and it is only in drier situations that the residence time of the uranium is significantly less than the true age. The number of measurements is as yet too limited to judge the general validity of application to bone but it is a development of high potential importance for the Paleolithic period since this is mostly beyond the range of radiocarbon dating. Turekian *et al.* have attempted to date bone by measuring the amount of helium that has accumulated from the emission of alpha particles in the uranium series, a technique which when applied to shell has given ages concordant with thorium-230 dating. The results for nine bone samples (estimated to be several million years old or more from other evidence) give ages that are much too young—presumably because there has been continuous loss of helium.

Measurement of the various isotopes relevant to uranium series dating is by the techniques of mass spectrometry, alpha-particle spectrometry, and neutron activation, in combination with chemical separation.

Fission-track dating

In minerals and glasses that contain traces of uranium, substantial damage to the lattice is caused by recoiling fragments from the spontaneous fission of uranium-238 nuclei. These damage tracks can be made visible under the microscope by etching with hydrofluoric acid, the damaged regions being less resistant to attack. The tracks so revealed are between 5 and 20 microns long and can be distinguished from etch pits due to dislocations. The tracks are sufficiently stable (a temperature of the order of 500 °C typically being needed to anneal them) for the number present to be used as a measure of age—in a similar way to the build up of thermoluminescence. The uranium concentration is conveniently evaluated by measuring the increase in track density that results from exposing the sample to a known dose of thermal neutrons in a nuclear reactor. Thermal neutrons induce fission in uranium-235 and knowing the cross-section for this, the present day abundance ratio of uranium-235/uranium-238, and the spontaneous fission decay constant, the age may be determined.

The technique is primarily of use for geological dating (Price *and* Walker, 1963), the event dated being the formation of the mineral concerned. Some archaeological application has been made but lack of sensitivity limits this technique to materials with a fairly high uranium content. In absolute terms the accuracy of the geological ages obtained is limited by the precision to which the decay constant for spontaneous fission is known—the values quoted in the literature from radio-chemical determinations show a considerable spread. The value used by Fleischer *and* Price (1964) is 7.0×10^{-17} year^{-1} and this gives concordance between fission-track ages and potassium–argon ages. An alternative way of evaluating this constant is by measuring the track density in fairly recent uranium-rich man-made glasses, the age of which is known exactly from documentary evidence. The contribution to fission events in natural materials by fission induced by the ambient neutron flux is negligible.

A useful review has been given by Fleischer *and* Hart (1972) who include discussion of techniques for use with minerals in which appreciable track fading occurs (Storzer *and* Wagner, 1969).

Archaeological application. Because of the very slow rate at which uranium-238 undergoes spontaneous fission the number of tracks per cm^3 for a 1000-year-old sample having a uranium content of 1 ppm is only about 500. In scanning a surface for tracks only those originating within a few microns of the surface are seen and the corresponding number of tracks seen per cm^2 is about 0.3. In practice it is difficult to work with samples containing less than several tracks per cm^2 and consequently for the method to be used on 1000-year-old samples it is necessary for the uranium concentration to be at least 10 ppm. Although the uranium contents of ancient man-made glasses is too low, in more recent glasses (of the past 150 years) uranium is sometimes used as a colourant at a level of a few per cent. Brill *et al.* (1964) have reported good agreement between the historical age and the fission-track age for five such specimens.

Although the average uranium content of ancient pottery may be too low, there are sometimes uranium-rich mineral inclusions. As long as the firing temperature is sufficient, the tracks acquired by these during geological time are annealed and the date obtained corresponds to the archaeological event. This has been demonstrated by Nishimura (1971) for some Japanese hearths, pottery, and tiles of the past two thousand years from which zircons (having uranium contents in the range 1000 to 10 000 ppm) have been extracted. Using the same principle Watanabe *and* Suzuki (1969) have dated a 4000-year-old ceramic vase by counting the tracks in an obsidian spearhead that was embedded in it. In this case the uranium content was only

3 ppm and diligent counting of repeatedly repolished surfaces was necessary.

An example of dating skeletal remains by association with a geological event is the fission-track dating (Fleishcher *et al.*, 1965) of volcanic pumice from Bed I of the Olduvai Gorge which has given an age of 2·03 ± 0·28 million years, in agreement with the potassium–argon age of 1·76 million years. The geologic age of formation of volcanic material used for prehistoric tools can also be used as an additional facet in identifying the geographic origin of the material; this has been used by Durrani *et al.* (1971) in respect of obsidian— on the basis that all obsidian of the same source should have the same age—as a complement to the existing techniques of trace element identification.

The barrier to using fission-track dating in archaeology is, as already emphasized, the low rate at which spontaneous fission occurs. The observation by Huang *and* Walker (1967), using phase-contrast microscopy, of fossil tracks in mica produced by the recoiling nuclei that accompany the alpha-particle decay of uranium and thorium suggested that a much more sensitive technique might be available, since the alpha decay rate is many orders of magnitude higher. However, the tracks are very much shorter (0·01 microns) and consequently rather difficult to identify with reliability, particularly against a natural background of similar pits from other causes (see, e.g., Turkowsky, 1969).

1.3. Chemical change

Analytical dating of bone: fluorine, uranium, and nitrogen

Apart from the technical difficulties in using radiocarbon to date bone, the period covering the anthropological development of man is outside the range of that method. However, some indication of the age of bone can be obtained by measuring the content of chemical elements which increase or decrease during prolonged burial. The fluorine and uranium contents increase because of incorporation of these elements in the phosphatic mineral (hydroxyapatite) of which bones are mainly composed. On the other hand, the nitrogen content decreases due to the disappearance of protein (collagen). Because of dependence on external conditions these methods are restricted to relative dating of bones found in the same deposit. Old bones can be distinguished from later intrusions, an example being the demonstration that the Piltdown Man was a hoax. The rate of acquisition depends on the contents of uranium and fluorine in the ground water which has percolated through the deposits; in limestone caves, for example, the fluorine content of ancient bones is anomalously low. The disappearance of nitrogen is severely attenuated by freezing conditions or by the exclusion of bacteria and air (e.g., by burial in clay). For further information the reader should consult Oakley (1969).

Amino-acid dating of bone

In some conditions the chemical changes referred to above may be completed in a comparatively short time after burial rather than continuing at a uniform rate until the present day. On the other hand it has been suggested that the conversion of amino acids is gradual enough to go on continuously, although still dependent on temperature and chemical conditions. Turekian *and* Bada (1972) have reported the utilization of the change of isoleucine to alloisoleucine and suggest that the limiting age would be about 200 000 years for an environmental temperature of 20°C and a million years for 10°C. The rate of change increases by the order of 20% per 1 °C so it is important to use burial contexts in which temperature variations have been damped out, such as deep caves in regions well beyond the zone of glacial ice cover.

Obsidian dating

Obsidian, a variety of volcanic glass, was widely used for prehistoric tools. A fresh surface (as made by ancient man in chipping the material to form the tool) slowly absorbs water and in the course of time there is a measurable hydration layer. The rate of growth depends on temperature, and consequently in using the thickness of the layer as a measure of age it is necessary to take this into account; typical growth rates for different climatic regions have been established. Rather surprisingly the rate of growth is independent of the wetness of the burial soil. The chemical composition influences the hydration rate but fortunately there are unlikely to be more than one or two effective types within a given region. The actual thickness of the layer for a 4000-year-old specimen (as an example) is about 7 microns for a hot region such as Egypt but only about 1 micron for the Arctic. On theoretical grounds the thickness is proportional to the square root of the age. The hydrated layer contains about 3% water—about ten times the water content of fresh obsidian.

Accounts of the method have been given by Michels *and* Bebrich (1971), and by Michels (1973). On a site for which the growth rate has been established by comparison with radiocarbon at one or two levels, the method can be used for interpolation and its cheapness then makes it extremely advantageous. It is particularly useful in testing the validity of the stratigraphy deduced for a site, or for segregating materials from a poorly stratified site into chronological groups. A complication with the technique is the possibility of archaeological re-use of old material; however it is sometimes possible to detect the separate hydration rims corresponding to different periods of burial.

The hydration technique gives the dates of utilization by ancient man irrespective of the geological age of the obsidian. The latter can be determined by fission-track dating and sometimes this is relevant to early human remains (see section 1.2).

Glass layer counting

Some ancient glass exhibits irridescence and studies of glasses from Nineveh by Brewster (1863) showed this to arise from diffraction effects associated with thin weathering layers on the surface. For glasses which have a poor corrosion resistance, and which have been buried in moist conditions, the weathering may be sufficient to give rise to a crust which is sometimes several millimetres in overall thickness. Study of some well-dated specimens by Brill *and* Hood (1961) revealed the remarkable fact that the number of layers within the crust was equal to the age, suggesting the possibility of 'layer counting' as a powerful method of dating. It is however only applicable to a rather restricted number of samples; Roman and Byzantine glasses are generally too resistant to become sufficiently weathered and Egyptian glasses are usually found in too arid an environment. On the other hand, when the weathering is heavy the poor quality of the glass often gives rise to layer structures that are too irregular for reliable results.

The validity of the technique has been questioned by Newton (1966, 1969, 1971) who points out that layered crusts can also be produced in accelerated weathering experiments in which the conditions (temperature, humidity) are kept constant. Also, layers are exhibited by ancient glasses which have been subject to negligible annual variation in environment, such as obtains on the bed of the sea. In some examples, the number of layers varies from place to place in the same piece, and although the number is equal to the age in one or two places, elsewhere it is less. Newton suggests that the layers are produced at a fairly constant rate which is generally rather less than one per year and that the examples of apparently 'annual' rings occur when the rate happens to be as fast as one per year.

The mechanisms that gives rise to the layers is not at all understood, but it seems possible that they result from internal strains set up by chemical change in which there is an associated expansion or contraction. Early studies (Newton, 1971) showed that in the weathering crusts the alkali of the glass had been replaced by water, the degree of hydration being about 20%. Periodic variations in the silicon and calcium concentrations have been observed with an electron probe micro-analyser (Shaw, 1965), the peak to peak spacing being approximately 6 to 8 microns. The layer thicknesses reported from microscopic examination by various workers in this field in general lie in the range 0·5 to 20 microns.

1.4. Climate

Dendrochronology (tree-ring dating)

The significance of the annual growth rings in the cross-section of a tree has been realized for a long time and the first archaeological application was made in 1811. In a recently-felled tree the date is established simply by counting backwards from the outermost ring, but by using the techniques of dendrochronology it is also possible to date the rings of trees that died in antiquity. This applies to trees grown under 'stress' conditions in the sense that their annual growth is mainly determined by climate; wet summers produce thick rings and dry summers narrow ones. Then, within one climatic region the pattern of varying ring widths is the same for all trees, and it is possible to match the pattern of the outer rings of an old tree with the pattern of the inner rings of a younger tree whose life span just overlapped the older tree. The overlapping is applied to successive younger trees until the present day is reached. Care must be taken to avoid error due to 'missing rings' and 'multiple rings'—by cross checking against contemporary trees grown in conditions that cause them to be sensitive to climate to a different degree.

Tree-ring studies are going on in various parts of the world and the species and climatic regions which are suitable for dendrochronology are gradually being established. Besides its direct archaeological use for remains that still carry beams and timbers, dendrochronology is of vital importance as a means of checking the accuracy of radiocarbon dating. The radiocarbon errors indicated by measurements on the 8000-year long sequence established by Ferguson (1968) for sequoia and bristlecone pine in California has had far-reaching implications for world archaeology as well as for geochemists concerned with the causes of fluctuations in the radiocarbon concentration of the atmosphere. Dendrochronology is also a tool for studying past climate (Fritts, 1966).

Sometimes on prehistoric sites there are beams available which give 'floating' tree-ring sequences. When such a sequence extends to a hundred rings or more, radiocarbon measurement of successive groups of rings can lead to very much more accurate dating than the same number of measurements on samples of the same age (see section 2.9).

Pollen analysis

The most obvious manifestation of the climate of a region is in the types of tree and plant which flourish there, though man's agricultural activities have an influence too. Pollen is preserved in acid soils and in peat bogs especially. When stratigraphic sequences of pollen types —identified by microscopic examination—are available, changes of climate can be studied in this way. The pollen zones following the last Ice Age are now well-defined and the boundaries of these zones have been dated by radiocarbon; hence archaeological remains having pollen in association can be ascribed to an age range on this basis alone. After 5000 B.C. boundaries between zones are separated by several thousand years but before that, closer in time to the Ice Age, climatic changes were more rapid. The first two warm periods, known as the Bølling and the Allerød, lasted for two or three centuries and eight centuries respectively, the first occurring just before 10 000 B.C. and the second during the ninth millennium B.C.

For discussion of the chronology of pollen zones with reference to radiocarbon corrections the reader should refer to Tauber (1970) and for application of pollen analysis in archaeology to Dimbleby (1969).

Varve Chronology

Analogous to tree-rings are the annual layers (*varves*) found in clays that originated in the beds of former lakes that had been fed by melting glaciers. The meltwater carries a fine suspension of sand and clay particles and if discharged into quiet water the clay bed formed on the bottom is laminated. Melting occurs mainly in the summer and the coarse particles settle out first followed by finer and finer material as the year goes on. The change of colour, from light to dark, associated with the change from coarse to fine grains makes each year's deposit visually distinguishable. The thickness of a layer, typically between a few millimeters and a few centimetres, reflects the amount of melting during that particular year, an exceptionally hot summer giving rise to an abnormally thick layer (which may reach several tens of centimetres) and a cold summer giving a layer which may only be a fraction of a millimetre. Hence, since the sequence of thin and thick layers is determined by climate, glacially deposited clay in different localities can be cross-dated. By linking a distinctive pattern in the lower part of one sequence with the same pattern in the upper part of a sequence from a more southerly locality, it has been possible (de Geer, 1940) to establish the chronology of the varved clays left behind by the glaciers as they retreated from Southern Sweden and Denmark at the end of the last Ice Age. The chronology shows the retreat to have taken 3600 years. It is linked to a 7500-year sequence of river estuary varves (formed by seasonal variations in annual flooding) of which the uppermost has been estimated to correspond to A.D. 900. This places the beginning of the glacier retreat at 10 500 B.C. and its conclusion at 6900 B.C. The date of the uppermost river varve is based on the estimated rate of land elevation since its formation—it is now 10 metres above sea-level. Reassessments of this rate suggest that the date of the uppermost varve is probably nearer to A.D. 700, with an uncertainty of one or two centuries (Fromm 1970; Tauber 1970).

The Swedish glacial varves have general importance both because they can be linked with pollen zones and used to define climatic change during the Late-Glacial periods and because they provide an independent means of checking the absolute accuracy of radiocarbon dating. During warm periods the rate of glacier retreat (as evidenced by the successively more recent dates for varves as one moves northward) is more rapid than in cold periods and this makes it possible to fix the pollen zones with respect to the varve chronology. Hence the radiocarbon chronology of pollen zones (obtained by dating peat bogs in which pollen is preserved) can be related to the varve chronology. As discussed in Chapter 2 this corroborates the general trend of radiocarbon errors indicated by the bristlecone pine measurements but suggests that from 6000 B.C. to 10 500 B.C. radiocarbon dates are close to true calendar dates.

Glacial varves have also been studied in North America but the situation there is complicated by gaps in the series and by simultaneous retreat and advance in different parts of the ice front (Antevs, 1955); in addition, no reliable linking up of the varve series with the present day has been established. For further information on varve chronology in general the reader is referred to the three references quoted and to Zeuner (1958).

Varves acquire a remanent magnetism on deposition and this provides a link with archaeomagnetism. Unfortunately the conditions of deposition can give rise to inaccurate recording and this limits their value as far as small-scale secular variation is concerned. However, like other forms of sedimentary deposit, they can be extremely valuable in recording geomagnetic reversals.

Oxygen isotope ratio

In the atmosphere and oceans the concentration of oxygen-18 relative to oxygen-16 is approximately 2 parts per thousand. Variations of this in various deposited materials can be used as an indication of the water temperature at the time of deposition. For instance when calcium carbonate is deposited, either inorganically or in the form of shell, the concentration of oxygen-18 decreases by approximately 10% for each 1°C increase in temperature. Thus measurement of the concentration in carbonate materials in cores taken from the ocean floor can be used to infer past climatic variations, the different levels of the core being dated by radiocarbon for the younger portions and uranium-series dating for the older portions (see Emiliani, 1969). The method is not absolute because the oxygen-18 concentration in sea water has not always been the same; however the variations in sea water are associated with the extent of the polar ice cap, and so do in fact correlate with glacial and interglacial phases. (Shackleton, 1967; Dansgaard *and* Tauber, 1969.) Its application with regard to past climate has been very powerfully illustrated by the results of measurements of a mile-long vertical core from the polar ice cap: this gives a detailed climatic record spanning the last 100 000 years (Dansgaard, Johnsen, *and* Møller, 1969; Johnson, Dansgaard, Clausen, *and* Langway, 1972); in this case an increased mean air temperature causes a higher oxygen-18 concentration (Dansgaard, 1964).

A more directly archaeological application has been made by Shackleton (1973) in determining whether a site was occupied all the year round or only seasonally. This is by analysis of shells from domestic refuse pits and middens, the variation in oxygen-18 concentration being sufficient to distinguish between growth in winter and growth in summer.

1.5. Astronomy

Solar radiation

In the earth's motion around the sun there are perturbations in the eccentricity of the ellipse describing the orbit, and in the obliquity of the ecliptic (the angle between the equatorial plane of the earth and the plane of the orbit). Also there is the precession of the equinoxes (due to a top-like wobble of the earth's axis of rotation). The periodicities are 92 000 years 40 000 years and 25 000 years respectively. These perturbations cause variation in the amount and distribution of solar radiation received by the earth and it has been suggested that the intensive phases of the last four Ice Ages are associated with minima in the level of summer solar radiation. However, variation in solar radiation cannot be the cause of Ice Ages as a whole since the minima have been recurring for a very long time whereas the Ice Ages have not.

The calculations of Milankovitch, as discussed and interpreted in Zeuner (1959), indicate nine outstanding minima during the last 600 000 years, of which the three most recent are 25 000, 72 000, and 115 000 years ago. The grouping of the minima matches well with the phases of the four recent Ice Ages. As regards absolute chronology, Zeuner points out that the actual climatic minima are likely to be retarded by several thousand years with respect to the radiation minima because of the time required for the climatic conditions to develop.

Stone circles

According to a monumental study by Thom (1967, 1971) the stone circles which abound in Britain, and particularly in Scotland, had astronomical observation as one primary purpose. Sight-lines, defined by standing stones in conjunction with natural foresights on the horizon, recorded the direction of rising and setting of certain bright stars, of the sun at midsummer, midwinter, etc., and of the moon at certain extremes of its motion. This interpretation implies a remarkable astronomical knowledge on the part of builders—in strong disagreement with the accepted view of their intellectual and technological development. The relevance to dating is that because of the wobble of the earth's axis and because of the much slower change in its angle of tilt, the expected direction for the events recorded changes very slightly from century to century. From the star data Thom derives dates in the range 2000–1770 B.C.; from the solar and lunar directions the mean dates are 1750 B.C. and 1650 B.C. The derivation of these dates, which are consistent with archaeological expectations, are a remarkable achievement requiring high precision of measurement and allowance for parallax, refraction, etc. In the case of solar and lunar directions the accuracy is estimated to be the order of ±100 years.

The most outstanding megalith in Britain is Stonehenge and it has been accepted for many years that an outlying stone to the East—the Heel stone—gave the direction of Midsummer sunrise when viewed from the altar stone. However the line is not sufficiently well-defined to give a reliable date, the change in direction being only 0·01 degrees per century. The lines used by Thom have natural foresights at a distance of some miles, thereby giving much higher precision; also, the same direction is defined on a number of different sites so that averaging and statistical analysis is possible.

The Egyptian calendar

An astronomical event noted from time to time in Egyptian records is the heliacal rising of the bright star Sothis (Sirius), occurring at about the same time as the beginning of the Nile inundation—around July 20 in our present calendar. The rising of Sothis is during daylight for a major portion of the year but since its rising gets progressively earlier, there comes a day on which it is just enough in advance of the sun to be visible. Because there were only 365 days in the Egyptian calendar and no leap year adjustment, the event moved forward by one day every four years, completing a full Sothic cycle in 1453 years. This cycle is tied in to the Christian calendar by the recording in the year A.D. 139, of a heliacal rising on New Year's Day in the Egyptian calendar. This is in agreement with another recording, dated by other means to 238–9 B.C., of a heliacal rising on the first day of the tenth month in the calendar. The earliest recording of a heliacal rising is on the sixteenth day of the eighth month of the seventh year of Sesostris III; given that this was during the Sothic cycle previous to the one that ended in A.D. 139, the calculated date for it is 1870 B.C. (±6). There are two other ancient recordings—dating to around 1530 B.C. and 1460 B.C.—and from these data historical records are complete enough to give Egyptian history a firmly based chronology back to 2000 B.C. Earlier than this the chronology is by extrapolation using the Turin canon (a list of kings that was not compiled until the thirteenth century B.C.) and the incomplete fragments of the Palermo stone covering the first to fifth dynasties. Differing interpretations place the start of the First Dynasty—the beginning of historic times—within the limits 3100 B.C. ± 100 (Edwards, 1970; Save-Soderburg, *and* Olsson, 1970). For later dynasties the uncertainty becomes less.

As already mentioned, apart from radiocarbon, the Egyptian chronology is the basis of prehistoric dating. It is also used as a check of the accuracy of radiocarbon dating; though not as precise as the bristlecone-pine chronology it does provide an independent judgement.

REFERENCES

ANTEVS, E. (1955). Varve and radiocarbon chronologies appraised by pollen data. *J. Geol.* **63**, 495–9.

BREWSTER, D. (1863). On the structure and optical phenomena of ancient decomposed glass. *Trans. R. Soc. Edin.* **23**, 193–204.

BRILL, R. H., FLEISCHER, R. L., PRICE, P. B., *and* WALKER, R. M. (1964). The fission-track dating of man-made glasses: preliminary results. *J. Glass Stud.* **7**, 151–6.

BRILL, R. H. *and* HOOD, H. P. (1961). A new method for dating ancient glass. *Nature*, **189**, 12–14.

BROECKER, W. S. *and* BENDER, M. L. (1972). Age determinations on marine strandlines. *Calibration of Hominid Evolution* (ed. W. W. Bishop *and* J. A. Miller), pp. 19–36. Scottish Academic Press, Edinburgh.

CHERDYNSTEV, V. V., KAZACHEVSKII, I. V., *and* KUZMINA, E. A. (1965). Dating of Pleistocene carbonate formations by the thorium and uranium isotopes. *Geochem. Internat.* **2**, 794–805.

DALRYMPLE, G. B. (1967). Potassium argon ages of recent rhyolites of the Mono and Inyo craters, California. *Earth Planet. Sci. Lett.* **3**, 289–98.

DANIELS, F., BOYD, C. A., *and* SAUNDERS, D. F. (1953). Thermoluminescence as a research tool. *Science*, **117**, 343–9.

DANSGAARD, W. (1964). Stable isotopes in precipitation. *Tellus*, **16**, 436–68.

DANSGAARD, W., JOHNSON, S. J., *and* MØLLER, J. (1969). One thousand centuries of climatic record from Camp Century on the Greenland ice sheet. *Science*, **166**, 377–80.

DANSGAARD, W. *and* TAUBER, H. (1969). Glacier oxygen-18 content and Pleistoscene ocean temperatures. *Science*, **166**, 499–502.

DIMBLEBY, G. W. (1969). Pollen analysis. In *Science in Archaeology* (Eds. D. Brothwell *and* E. Higgs), pp. 167–77. Thames and Hudson, London.

DURRANI, S. A., KHAN, H. A., TAJ, M., *and* RENFREW, C. (1971). Obsidian Source identification by fission track analysis. *Nature*, **233**, 242–5.

EDWARDS, I. E. S. (1970). Absolute dating from Egyptian records and comparison with carbon-14 dating. *Phil. Trans. R. Soc. Lond. A.* **269**, 11–18.

EMILIANI, C. (1969). The significance of deep-sea cores. In *Science in Archaeology* (ed. D. Brothwell *and* E. S. Higgs), pp. 109–17. Thames and Hudson.

EVERNDEN, J. F. *and* CURTIS, G. H. (1965). The potassium–argon dating of Late Cenozoic rocks in East Africa and Italy. *Curr. Anthropol.* **6**, 343–85.

FERGUSON, C. W. (1968). Bristlecone pine: science and esthetics. *Science*, **159**, 839–46.

FITCH, F. J. (1972). Selection of suitable material for dating and assessment of geological error in potassium–argon age determination. *Calibration of Hominid Evolution* (ed. W. W. Bishop *and* J. A. Miller), pp. 77–92. Scottish Academic Press, Edinburgh.

FITCH, F. J. *and* MILLER, J. A. (1970). Radioisotope age determinations of Lake Rudolf artefact site. *Nature*, **226**, 226–8.

FLEISCHER, R. L. *and* HART, H. R. (1972). Fission track dating: techniques and problems. *Calibration of Hominid Evolution* (ed. W. W. Bishop *and* J. A. Miller), pp. 135–70. Scottish Academic Press, Edinburgh.

FLEISCHER, R. L. *and* PRICE, P. B. (1964). Glass dating by fission fragment tracks. *J. geophys. Res.* **69**, 331–9.

FLEISCHER, R. L., PRICE, P. B., WALKER, R. M., *and* LEAKEY, L. S. B. (1965). Fission-track dating of Bed I, Olduvai Gorge. *Science*, **148**, 72–4.

FORNACA-RINALDI, G. (1968). $^{230}Th/^{234}Th$ dating of cave concretions. *Earth Planet. Sci. Lett.* **5**, 120–2.

FRITTS, H. C. (1966). Growth-rings of trees: their correlation with climate. *Science*, **154**, 973–9.

FROMM, E. (1970). An estimation of errors in the Swedish varve chronology. *Radiocarbon Variations and Absolute Chronology*, Ed. I. V. Olsson (Almqvist *and* Wiksell, Stockholm). pp. 163–72.

GEER, G. de (1940). Geochronologia Succia principles. *K. Svenska Vetensk-Akad. Handl.* Ser. 3, 18, No. 6.

GENTNER, W. *and* LIPPOLT, H. J. (1969). The potassium–argon dating of Upper Tertiary and Pleistocene deposits. In *Science in Archaeology* (eds. D. Brothwell *and* E. Higgs), pp. 88–100. Thames and Hudson, London.

GRASTY, R. L. *and* MITCHELL, J. G. (1966). Single sample Potassium–argon ages using the Omegatron. *Earth Planet. Sci. Lett.* **1**, 121–2.

HANSEN, R. O. *and* BEGG, E. L. (1970). Age of Quaternary sediments and soils in the Sacromento area, California by uraniumand actinium series dating of vertebrate fossils. *Earth Planet. Sci. Lett.* **8**, 411–9.

HUANG, W. H. *and* WALKER, R. M. (1967). Fossil α particle recoil tracks. *Science*, **155**, 1103–4.

JOHNSON, S. J., DANSGAARD, W., CLAUSEN, H. B., *and* LANGWAY, C. C. (1972). Oxygen isotope profiles through the Antarctic and Greenland ice sheets. *Nature*, **235**, 429.

MERRIHUE, C. M. *and* TURNER, G. (1966). Potassium argon dating by activation with fast neutrons. *J. geophys. Res.* **71**, 2852–7.

MICHELS, J. W. (1973). *Dating Methods in Archaeology*. Seminar Press, New York and London.

MICHELS, J. W. *and* BEBRICH, C. A. (1971). Obsidian hydration dating in *Dating Techniques for the Archaeologist*, pp. 164–221 (ed. H. N. Michael and E. K. Ralph) MIT Press, Cambridge, Massachusetts and London, England.

MILLER, J. A. (1972). Dating Pliocene and Pleistoscene strata using the potassium argon and the argon-40/argon-39 methods. *Calibration of Hominid Evolution* (ed. W. W. Bishop *and* J. A. Miller), pp. 63–76. Scottish Academic Press, Edinburgh.

MITCHELL, J. G. (1968). The argon-40 argon-39 method for potassium–argon age determination. *Geochim. Cosmochim. Acta*, **32**, 781–90.

NEWTON, R. G. (1966). Some problems in the dating of ancient glass by counting the layers in the weathering crust. *Glass Technol.* **7**, 22–5.

NEWTON, R. G. (1969). *Glass Technol.* **10**, 40–2.

NEWTON, R. G. (1971). The enigma of the layered crusts on some weathered glasses, a chronological account of the investigations. *Archaeometry*, **13**, 1–9.

NISHIMURA, S. (1971). Fission track dating of archaeological materials from Japan. *Nature*, **230**, 242–3.

OAKLEY, K. P. (1969). Analytical methods of dating bones. In *Science in Archaeology* (eds. D. Brothwell *and* E. Higgs) pp. 35–45. Thames and Hudson, London.

PRICE, P. B. *and* WALKER, R. M. (1963). Fossil tracks of charged particles in mica and the age of minerals. *J. geophys. Res.* **68**, 4847–62.

RALPH, E. K. (1971). Carbon-14 dating. In *Dating Techniques for the Archaeologist* (ed. H. N. Michael *and* E. K. Ralph), pp. 1–48. MIT Press, Cambridge, Massachusetts.

ROSHOLT, J. N., EMILIANI, C., GEISS, J., KOCZY, F. F., *and* WANGERSKY, P. J. (1961). Absolute dating of deep-sea cores by the $^{231}Pa/^{230}Th$ method. *J. Geol.* **69**, 162–185.

SAVE-SODERBURGH, T. *and* OLSSON, I. V. (1970). C14 dating and Egyptian chronology. *Radiocarbon Variations and Absolute Chronology*, ed. I. V. Olsson (Almqvist *and* Wiksell, Stockholm). pp. 35–55.

SHACKLETON, N. J. (1967). Oxygen isotope analyses and Pleistocene temperatures reassessed. *Nature*, **215**, 15–17.

SHACKLETON, N. J. (1973). Oxygen isotope analysis as a means of determining season of occupation of prehistoric midden sites. *Archaeometry*, **15**, 133–44.

SHAW, G. (1965). Weathered crusts on ancient glass. *New Scientist*, **27**, 290–1.

STORZER, D. *and* WAGNER, G. A. (1969). Correction of thermally lowered fission track ages of tektites. *Earth Planet. Sci. Lett.* **5**, 463–8.

SZABO, B. J., MALDE, H. E., *and* IRWIN-WILLIAMS, C. (1969). Dilemma posed by uranium-series dates of archaeologically significant bones from Valsequillo, Puebla, Mexico. *Earth Planet. Sci. Lett.* **6**, 237–44.

SZABO, B. J. *and* Rosholt, J. N. (1969). Uranium-series dating of Pleistocene molluscan shells from Southern California—an open system model. *J. geophys. Res.* **74**, 3253–60.

TAUBER, H. (1970). The Scandinavian varve chronology and C14 dating. *Radiocarbon Variations and Absolute Chronology*, ed. I. V. Olsson (Almqvist *and* Wiksell, Stockholm). pp. 173–96.

THOM, A. (1967). *Megalithic Sites in Britain*, Clarendon Press, Oxford.

THOM, A. (1969). *Megalithic Lunar Observations*, Clarendon Press, Oxford.

TUREKIAN, K. K. *and* BADA, J. L. (1972). The dating of fossil bones. *Calibration of Hominid Evolution* (ed. W. W. Bishop *and* J. A. Miller), pp. 171–86. Scottish Academic Press, Edinburgh.

TUREKIAN, K. K., KHARKAR, D. P., FUNKHOUSER, J., *and* SCHAEFFER, O. A. (1970). An evaluation of the uranium–helium method of dating of fossil bones. *Earth Planet. Sci. Lett.* **7**, 420–4.

TURKOWSKY, C. (1969). Electron-microscopic observation of artificially produced alpha-recoil tracks in albite. *Earth Planet. Sci. Lett.* **5**, 492–6.

VOLCHOK, H. L. *and* KULP, J. L. (1957). The ionium method of age determination. *Geochim. Cosmochim. Acta*, **11**, 219–46.

WATANABE, N. *and* SUZUKI, M. (1969). Fission track dating of archaeological glass materials from Japan. *Nature*, **222**, 1057–8.

ZEUNER, F. E. (1958). *Dating the Past*, 4th edn. Methuen, London.

2 Radiocarbon Dating

2.1. Introduction

WHEN cosmic rays enter the earth's atmosphere neutrons are produced. These particles, being uncharged, are particularly effective in causing transmutations in the nucleus of any atom with which they collide. Such nuclear reactions have been extensively studied using artificially produced neutrons, and from an appraisal of this data Libby (1946) concluded that nearly all cosmic-ray neutrons would end their lives by converting atmospheric nitrogen into a weakly radioactive isotope of carbon†, *carbon*-14 (or *radiocarbon* as it is called alternatively). Because its chemical behaviour is the same as that of stable carbon, Libby hypothesized that it should form carbon dioxide molecules and mix in with the ordinary carbon dioxide of the atmosphere (present to 0·046% by weight). Plant-life grows by photosynthesis of atmospheric carbon dioxide and in turn animals eat plants; consequently all the living animal and vegetable world (the *biosphere*) should be very weakly radioactive owing to the presence of a minute proportion of carbon-14 (roughly one atom of carbon-14 to a million million atoms of ordinary carbon). Atmospheric carbon dioxide also enters the oceans as dissolved carbonate, so that this too should be weakly radioactive and any shells and deposits formed from it.

The same minute proportion of radiocarbon should also be present in human excreta, and confirmation of Libby's predictions was first

† The stable istopes of carbon are carbon-12 and carbon-13; they are present in natural carbon with abundances of 98·9% and 1·1% respectively. All carbon isotopes have 6 protons in the nucleus and 6 extranuclear electrons; the number of neutrons in the nucleus is 6, 7, and 8 respectively for carbon-12, -13, and -14.

obtained by measurements on samples of the methane given off by City of Baltimore sewage (Anderson, Libby, Weinhouse, Reid, Kirschenbaum, *and* Gross, 1947). Subsequently measurements were made on living wood and there was the same level of radiocarbon activity; on extending the investigation to samples of wood from different continents the level was found to be uniform on a worldwide basis, and so too for samples of recently formed sea shell (Libby, Anderson, *and* Arnold, 1949).

All this was very satisfying confirmation of scientific theory; in addition Libby and his collaborators saw the possibility of age determination and they included in their measurements samples of wood from the tombs of the Egyptian kings Zoser and Sneferu. Radioactive atoms decay at a rate that is characteristic of the isotope and independent of all external conditions; for carbon-14 this rate is 1% per 83 years, equivalent to a *half-life*† of 5730 years. In atmospheric carbon dioxide this loss is made up by continued upper altitude production but once wood molecules are formed such replenishment cannot occur so that after 5730 years the specific radioactivity should be half that of recently grown wood. From historical records it was known that Zoser and Sneferu died within 75 years of 2700 B.C. and 2625 B.C. respectively, and consequently the specific radioactivity was expected to be a little over half the value for living wood today. In fact the value measured experimentally, of 7·04 (±0·2) counts per minute per gram of natural carbon, agreed with the expected value to within the limits of error, giving a powerful illustration of the archaeological potentialities.

Further checks with samples of known age were then carried out (Arnold *and* Libby, 1949). The results were satisfactory (see Fig. 2.1) and confirmed the validity of reversing the process and using the specific radiocarbon activity to obtain the age of undated specimens, at any rate from 3000 B.C. forward. Application to archaeology has had a dramatic impact—'the radiocarbon revolution'—and it now provides the backbone of prehistoric chronology. In general it has shown that civilization developed substantially earlier than had been previously assumed; for instance, the beginning of Jericho (the pre-pottery Neolithic phase) has been put back, by several thousand years, to 8000 B.C. It has been vitally important in paleobotany (see, for

---

† The time in which the number of radioactive atoms decreases to one half of the number present initially.

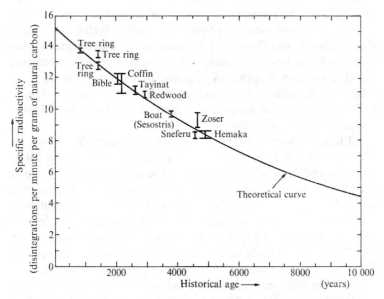

Fig. 2.1. The first comprehensive test using known-age samples (Arnold *and* Libby, 1949). The theoretical curve is based on the 'old' half-life of 5568 years; this was the preferred value at the time.

instance, Godwin 1960) and in all earth sciences concerned with developments during the last 50 000 years.

Systematic errors: calibration

As the accuracy of measurement techniques was improved, it became evident that discrepancies between radiocarbon age and historically known age were not always within the limits of experimental error. Determination of a radiocarbon age is essentially a comparison of the measured activity of the sample today with the activity it is assumed to have had at the time of the event being dated. Libby's initial tests showed that to within 5–10% it was valid to assume that the sample had the same initial activity as material currently growing at the time of measurement. These tests were prior to 1954 when hydrogen bomb explosions commenced and substantial quantities of carbon-14 were released into the atmosphere. However, even prior to 1954 there was man-made disturbance to the carbon-14 level in the atmosphere. The burning of coal and oil since the middle of the nineteenth century has released carbon that is deficient in carbon-14 and caused a drop in the atmospheric concentration by about 3%; this is the *fossil-fuel effect* (Suess, 1955).

These man-made effects can be investigated and quantified and, although they may complicate the method, they do not make it less absolute. On the other hand it is now well-established that there have been natural fluctuations in the atmospheric carbon-14 concentrations, and allowance for these can only be made by empirical calibration using samples dated by other means—unless a precise understanding of their cause is eventually established. Of particular concern is the evidence that prior to 1500 B.C. there was a significant long-term excess in concentration that had lasted for several millennia at least. At times this excess reached almost 10% and uncorrected radiocarbon ages are then too recent by about 800 years; hence some of man's developments are really even earlier than first indicated by the method.

The basis of the calibration is dendrochronology, i.e. the counting back in time of the annual rings formed by trees. For some species (notably the pine, oak, and sequoia) a distinctive pattern of wide and narrow rings is determined by climate, and by successive matching of the pattern of the inner rings of one tree with that of the outer part of an older tree which just overlaps it, it has been possible from trees grown in California to obtain dated wood samples back to 6000 B.C. (Ferguson 1969, 1970, 1972). Radiocarbon measurement of these samples, first done by Suess (1965, 1970), have yielded the *tree-ring calibration*, alternatively called the *bristlecone pine correction*. For millennia earlier than the limit of the tree-ring chronology, an indirect source of calibration going back to 10 000 B.C. is the annual layers of sediment on lake bottoms, notably the glacial varves in Sweden. Before this it is a matter of intercomparison with thermoluminescent dating, or, of prediction from the calculated effect on cosmic-ray intensity of geomagnetic field variation as determined by archaeomagnetic studies. However, although these can give useful information in evaluating long-term trends, it is only tree-ring dating that is precise enough to calibrate short-term errors of the order of a century.

The archaeological implications of the tree-ring calibration—'the second radiocarbon revolution'—have been more serious than a further lengthening of prehistoric time-scales. The revision of dates has accentuated the difficulty, already indicated by uncorrected dates, of accepting the traditional interpretation of archaeological evidence in terms of outward diffusion from the Near East. Back to 3100 B.C. the chronology of the Near East is based on links with astronomically dated Egyptian history and, compared to the corpus of dates that has been built up for regions remote from it, the available radiocarbon dates for the Near East are sparse. Hence any revision of the radiocarbon time-scale creates a chronological 'fault-line' geographically located where dependence on radiocarbon begins. According to the tree-ring calibration the first temples in Malta predate the pyramids by several centuries and the trilithons of Stonehenge (phase III) are earlier than Mycenae (e.g. Renfrew, 1970, 1973). The beginning of settled farming communities in central Europe, the Neolothic age, already put 1500 years earlier by conventional radiocarbon dating than had been assumed, is pushed back a further 700 years to *circa* 5000 B.C. or earlier (Neustupny, 1968, 1969).

These implications are by no means fully accepted (e.g. Milojčić 1967; Hood 1967; Branigan 1972), and being accustomed to regional chronologies archaeologists have questioned whether the indications of trees grown at an altitude of 3 kilometres in California are relevant to low altitude samples on the other side of the world. A conclusive answer is given by the results of measurements made on samples closely linked to the Egyptian chronology: these affirm the general validity of the tree-ring calibration for Old World archaeology, though it is possible to argue that in some periods the correction indicated by the Egyptian samples is about two centuries less. Having regard to the various factors that complicate radiocarbon dating and to the fragmentary nature of some of the evidence on which the Egyptian chronology is based, even if the reality of this small discrepancy is accepted the agreement is a remarkable tribute to scientific technique on the one hand and historical scholarship on the other.

Publication and availability

There are nearly a hundred laboratories throughout the world and the number of samples measured is upwards of 30 000. Results are published in *Radiocarbon*, a supplement of the *American Journal of Science*; they are also available on punched cards and in computer storage. A list of laboratories is given in each volume of *Radiocarbon*. The majority are university-based and engaged primarily on their own research projects but some take additional samples by special arrangement and there are others that measure samples on a commercial basis†—the cost is upwards of £50 per sample. An account of the method and its inception has been given by Libby (1955), who has also reviewed subsequent developments from time to time (for example, Libby 1967, 1970, 1971a, 1972). Every few years there are international conferences at which current research is reported; recent ones have been in Cambridge, England (1962), Pullman, Washington (1965), Monaco (1967), Uppsala (1969), and Lower Hutt City, New Zealand (1972).

2.2. Production of radiocarbon

On entering the atmosphere cosmic-rays produce high-energy neutrons and, after slowing down by collision processes, these are highly effective in transmuting atmospheric nitrogen into carbon-14 according to the reaction:

$$^{14}N + n = {}^{14}C + {}^{1}H. \tag{2.1}$$

The cross-section‡ for this reaction is about 1.7×10^{-24} cm^2. It is the dominant way in which neutrons interact with nitrogen and for oxygen the neutron cross-section is lower by a factor of a thousand. Free neutrons decay into protons, with a half-life of 12 minutes, but the high probability of reaction (2.1) means that the effective fate of each neutron is to produce a carbon-14 atom. It is known from high altitude balloon measurements that the average neutron production rate is about 2 per second per cm^2 of the earth's surface, and this yields a global production of 7.5 kg of carbon-14 per year.

Variation with height. The neutron intensity builds up from zero at the outer limit of the stratosphere to a maximum at a height of around

† For example:

Carbon-14 Measurement Laboratory, Building 10.46, A.E.R.E., Harwell, Didcot, Berks, England, OX11 ORA.

Gakushuin University, Mejiro, Toshima-ku, Tokyo, Japan.

Geochron Laboratories Inc., 24 Blackstone St., Cambridge, Mass. 02139, U.S.A.

Radiocarbon Dating Unit, Scottish Research Reactor Centre, National Engineering Laboratory, East Kilbride, Glasgow, Scotland.

Radiocarbon Ltd., 4 Tice Court, Spring Valley, N.Y. 10977, U.S.A.

Teledyne Isotopes, 50 Van Buren Avenue, Westwood, New Jersey 07675, U.S.A.

‡ The cross-section represents the *effective* target area presented to a beam of neutrons by each nitrogen nucleus; any neutron scoring a hit produces the reaction to which the cross-section refers. It represents the probability of reaction rather than the actual physical size of the nucleus.

15 km; it then falls off again and for the latitude range 50°–90° it reaches 3% of the maximum value at about 3 km and about 0·3% at sea-level.

Variation with latitude. The primary cosmic-ray particles are electrically charged and they are deflected by the magnetic field of the earth unless they are travelling parallel to the lines of force. Consequently the cosmic ray intensity is a maximum at the poles and a minimum around the geomagnetic equator; the corresponding neutron intensities in the stratosphere are in the ratio of about 5 to 1. However, the mixing of carbon-14, in the atmosphere is sufficiently rapid and thorough for these production inhomogeneities in height and latitude to be unimportant when considering the uniformity of carbon-14 concentration (though there may be minor latitudinal variations from other causes). It is presumed that the newly formed carbon-14 atoms combine with oxygen to form 'heavy' carbon dioxide which, except in respect of radioactive decay (and isotopic fractionation effects), is indistinguishable from the ordinary carbon dioxide of the atmosphere; consequently carbon-14 circulates through the biosphere and the oceans in the same pattern as ordinary carbon.

Variation with time. Although latitudinal differences in carbon-14 production may not matter, the dependence of the overall global production on the earth's magnetic field strength is important in view of the archaeomagnetic evidence that substantial changes in field strength have happened in the past. A stronger magnetic field means a greater degree of shielding of the earth from the primary cosmic-ray flux and therefore a lower production of carbon-14. This is discussed further in section 2.8.

It should be noted that although variations in the rate of production are of critical importance, the determination of age does not require quantitative evaluation of this rate. Its initial interest was in predicting the level of carbon-14 activity likely to be found in living matter from the point of view of feasibility of detection; also, since the observed level is a measure of the average production-rate over the past 8000 years (the *mean lifetime* of carbon-14) quantitative agreement with the predicted level (based on the *current* production-rate) was evidence that gross variations in the rate had not occurred.

2.3. Radioactive decay

Radioactive equilibrium

Because it is radioactive the amount of carbon-14 on earth does not increase indefinitely but remains at a constant level (assuming the production-rate to be constant). This is the level at which loss by radioactive decay just balances production. The loss-rate is defined by the 5730-year half-life of carbon-14 and corresponds to 1% decaying within 83 years. Hence if x is the equilibrium amount on earth then

$$x \times \frac{1}{100} \times \frac{1}{83} = \text{production rate} = 7.5 \text{ kg per year}$$

$$\therefore \qquad x = 62 \text{ metric tons.} \qquad (2.2)$$

This is distributed between the atmosphere, the biosphere, and the oceans—known collectively as the carbon exchange reservoir. Since this reservoir contains about 42 million million tons of ordinary carbon the concentration of carbon-14 by weight is $1\frac{1}{2}$ parts per million million.

Specific radioactivity

Such minute concentrations of carbon-14 are only detectable by virtue of the weak β-particles (maximum energy, 160 keV) emitted when the atoms decay:

$$^{14}\text{C} = {}^{14}\text{N} + \beta^-. \qquad (2.3)$$

In 1 gram of natural carbon taken from the exchange reservoir there are 5×10^{22} atoms of carbon-12 and 6.6×10^{10} atoms of carbon-14. Since 1% of the carbon-14 atoms decay in 83 years, there will be 15 decays per minute per gram of natural carbon. This is also the rate of emission of β-particles, and expressed in the usual units for radioactivity it is 6.8 picocuries† per gram of natural carbon.

Decay of radioactivity

For carbon that is no longer 'in exchange' with the reservoir, the content of carbon-14 slowly decreases, and hence also the specific radioactivity. This decay may be expressed by the differential equation

$$-\frac{dN}{dt} = \frac{1}{\tau} \times N \qquad (2.4)$$

† 1 curie (symbol, Ci) is defined as 3.7×10^{10} disintegrations per second.

where N is the number of carbon-14 atoms present at time t, and τ is the mean lifetime (= 8300 years). The solution of (2.4) obtained by integration, is

$$N = N_0 \exp(-t/\tau) \qquad (2.5)$$

where N_0 is the initial number of atoms (at $t = 0$). Eqn (2.5) indicates that the form of the decay is exponential and can be evaluated by reference to mathematical tables. The half-life is defined as the value of t for which $(N/N_0) = \frac{1}{2}$, and it is useful to remember that the half-life $t_\frac{1}{2} = 0\cdot693\tau$. With each succeeding half-life (N/N_0) decreases by a further factor of 2; thus:

after 5730 years $(t_\frac{1}{2})$	$N = \frac{1}{2}N_0$
after 11 460 years $(2t_\frac{1}{2})$	$N = \frac{1}{4}N_0$
after 17 190 years $(3t_\frac{1}{2})$	$N = \frac{1}{8}N_0$
after 22 920 years $(4t_\frac{1}{2})$	$N = \frac{1}{16}N_0$

.

.

.

after 57 300 years $(10t_\frac{1}{2})$ $\qquad N = \dfrac{1}{1024} N_0$

Because the specific radioactivity is proportional to N it will decrease in the same way. Thus the specific activity per gram for a sample that is 57 000 years old is down to 2·2 disintegrations per *day* or 0·007 picocuries, and it is not surprising that this is at the limit of detection.

Statistical fluctuations; standard deviations; use of quartiles

Because radioactive decay is a spontaneous process, the observed rates of disintegration will vary randomly about the average values—a useful analogy to bear in mind is the number of raindrops falling on a penny in a given time of observation. The probability that a particular carbon-14 atom will disintegrate within a minute is 1 in 4×10^9 and clearly the term decay *rate* has no meaning in this context. But in respect of the $6\cdot6 \times 10^{10}$ atoms contained in a gram of 'live' carbon, the combined probabilities give a more or less steady rate.

Statistical considerations show that if n β-particles are counted by the detector within a time t, there is a 68% probability that the true average rate lies between

$$\frac{n - \sqrt{n}}{t} \quad \text{and} \quad \frac{n + \sqrt{n}}{t}.$$

Expressed in percentage these limits of error correspond to

$$\pm \frac{100}{\sqrt{n}}\%$$

so that the longer the measurement time the smaller the percentage uncertainty; to achieve $\pm 1\%$ requires $n = 10\ 000$. Because the decay is exponential an uncertainty in the count-rate of $\pm x\%$ gives rise to an uncertainty in the calculated age of $\pm(83 \times x)$ years. This latter is known as the *standard deviation* (abbreviation: s.d., symbol: σ) in the age and as with the count-rate, there is a 68% probability that the true age lies within $\pm 1\sigma$ of the calculated age. If the limits are extended to 2σ the probability is 95·5%, and for 3σ it is 99·7%. It is now the practice of most laboratories to include only the experimental error in their computation of standard deviation, but in the past some have also included allowance for uncertainty arising from variations in atmospheric carbon-14 concentration.

In comparing two dates having standard deviations σ_1 and σ_2, statistical considerations indicate that if the dates differ by more than $(\sigma_1 + \sigma_2)$ there is a 90% probability the events are not contemporary. However, on the basis of the dictum that 'one date is no date' such comparisons must be treated with reserve.

An alternative approach to the intercomparison of radiocarbon dates which does not involve standard deviations explicitly, and which does not put significance on singletons, has been suggested by Ottaway (1973). All available dates for a culture are arranged in order and numbered serially: $1, 2, 3, \ldots n$. Positioning arrows for the lower and upper quartiles are inserted at $(\frac{1}{4}n + \frac{1}{2})$ and $(\frac{3}{4}n + \frac{1}{2})$, and the inter-quartile range so defined is taken as indication of the duration of the culture. If the inter-quartile ranges of two cultures do not overlap it is considered that the intensity of contact between them will not have been great enough for significant cultural transmission to have occurred. Expressed statistically the probability of non-contemporaneity is 97% if the inter-quartile ranges just fail to overlap and there are nine dates for each culture; if there are more than nine the probability is higher.

'Old' and 'new' half-lives

The half-life of 5730 years (± 30) used earlier in this chapter is the mean of three independent laboratory determinations (see Godwin, 1962; Hughes *and* Mann, 1964), the error limit quoted corresponding to 1 standard deviation. The value is calculated from the observed disintegration rate of a known amount of artificially produced carbon-14; the disintegration rate is determined by means of a beta counter of precisely-known absolute efficiency and the amount of carbon-14 by means of a mass spectrometer.

The value of 5730 years is 3% higher than the value of 5568 which was used by Libby at the inception of the method on the basis of the best determinations then available. However, for the time being, dates published in *Radiocarbon* are on the basis of the 'Libby half-life' so as to avoid confusion and risk of multiple correction. These 'straight' dates are often quoted in 'years b.p.' (meaning 'before present', but for convenience defined as 'before A.D. 1950') and should be regarded as the age in 'radiocarbon years' rather than in calendar years.† The effect of using the revised half-life is to increase the age by 3%, e.g. a date of 1000 b.c. is changed to 1090 and a date of 6000 b.c. to 6240. At any rate during the period 2000–5000 B.C., the change due to the bristlecone-pine calibration is several times larger than the half-life correction alone.

When a corrected radiocarbon date is quoted the corrections that have been applied should be stated, e.g. 'on the new half-life', or 'corrected by bristlecone-pine calibration'. In the latter case it is desirable to state the magnitude of the correction—or to give the uncorrected date as well.

2.4. The carbon exchange reservoir

Atmospheric carbon dioxide is taken into plants by photosynthesis, and since animals live off plants carbon-14 spreads throughout the biosphere. Also, atmospheric carbon dioxide enters the oceans as dissolved carbonate, so this too contains carbon-14. The carbon withdrawn from the atmosphere by plant and animal life is eventually returned to it by decomposition after death—except for the very small proportion that is locked up in well-preserved remains (which are the materials that provide samples for dating). The carbonate in the ocean is formed by an exchange reaction, so that carbon dioxide leaves as well as enters the ocean—again except for a small proportion which is locked up for long periods, this time in shells and other deposits of carbon (these too are materials for dating). Thus the

---

† The convention suggested editorially on p. 265 of *Antiquity*, **46** (1972) is being followed: a.d., b.c., and b.p. are used for straight radiocarbon dates on the old half-life, but A.D., B.C., and B.P. for calendar dates.

atmosphere, biosphere, and ocean form an exchange reservoir throughout which the carbon atoms circulate comparatively rapidly and the residence time in any component (except some parts of the deep ocean), is much shorter than the mean lifetime of a carbon-14 atom. Of the 42×10^{12} tons of ordinary carbon in the reservoir, 93% is in the deep ocean, 2% in the surface (mixed) ocean, 1·6% in the atmosphere, 0·8% in the terrestrial biosphere, and 2·6% in humus.

Concentration variations

The average ratio of carbon-14/carbon-12 in the reservoir is $1·5 \times 10^{-12}$ (weight for weight)—determined by the admixture of the equilibrium 62 tons of carbon-14 into the 42×10^{12} tons of carbon-12. As emphasized earlier, a radiocarbon date is based essentially on the ratio between the observed carbon-14 concentration in the sample today (measured in terms of β-activity) and the value the sample is assumed to have had at the time of its withdrawal from exchange with the reservoir. In later sections we shall be considering the evidence that there have been variations in the initial activity; in the meantime it is useful to list the main determining factors:

(i) *Global equilibrium tonnage of carbon-14.* Since radioactive decay proceeds at an immutable rate, this tonnage depends only on the rate of carbon-14 production. Variation in this rate is currently considered to be the dominant reason for the observed long-term variations in concentration.

(ii) *Overall tonnage of natural carbon in the reservoir.* This is effectively determined by the amount of dissolved carbonate in the oceans and the vast size and inertia of the latter is one constituent reason why the technique is viable. The most obvious cause for change in size is the gradual melting of glaciers following the end of the last Ice Age. Carbon that is locked up in glaciers is not part of the exchange reservoir and so it is 'old' carbon, deficient in carbon-14, and it is estimated that its gradual release would cause an increase of $2\frac{1}{2}$% in ocean volume (see Libby, 1955; also Schell, Fairhall, *and* Harp, 1967). A contrary effect associated with warmer climate is the decrease in carbonate solubility; except for the amount lost by precipitation, this does not cause a change in total reservoir size since the amount lost by the ocean is gained by the atmosphere. However, the carbon-14 concentration in the ocean is a few per cent lower than in the atmosphere (see below) so that release of carbon from the ocean causes a transient decrease in atmospheric concentration.

(iii) *Mixing rates.* Although owing to magnetic deflection of the primary cosmic rays the production rate at the poles is an order of magnitude greater than at the equator, the mixing of carbon dioxide within the atmosphere is sufficiently rapid to remove any long-term latitude dependence of the carbon-14 concentration. However, as explained in the next paragraph there is an effective difference in concentration between atmosphere and ocean, so that when dating a sample such as shell an initial activity value appropriate to ocean carbonate must be used. The atmosphere/ocean difference is determined by the rates of interchange between atmosphere, surface ocean, and deep ocean, and since these rates will be influenced by circulation patterns there is the possibility that in the past there have been variations in the atmosphere/ocean difference due to changes in climatic regime. Because the bulk of the carbon is in the oceans, it is the atmospheric rather than the ocean concentration that would have varied.

Figure 2.2 shows a simplified 'box model' of the carbon exchange reservoir, showing the total carbon in each component part and the annual transfer between parts. Within a compartment the mixing is assumed to be infinitely rapid (though this is hardly true for the deep ocean); the average residence time in a compartment is the reciprocal of the fraction transferred out of it annually.

Carbon atoms spend only a few tens of years in the atmosphere and surface ocean before reaching the deep ocean, but the residence time in the deep ocean is the order of a thousand years. Consequently in the deep ocean there is a measurable deficiency in carbon-14 because there is time for significant loss by radioactive decay. Hence if measured relative to the atmosphere the carbon of the deep ocean has an apparent age; some deep water samples from the Pacific Ocean show apparent ages of up to two thousand years (Bien, Rakestraw, *and* Suess, 1963). The surface ocean is intermediate since the carbon in it is a mixture of 'reinvigorated' carbon from the atmosphere and 'old' carbon from the deep ocean—the apparent age is about 400 years (after correction for isotopic fractionation).

More complex models than the one shown in Fig. 2.2 are necessary in order to get a detailed understanding of the actual situation. For instance, the atmospheric circulation systems of northern and southern

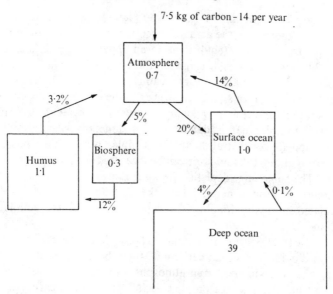

FIG. 2.2. The carbon exchange reservoir. The heavy arrow at the top represents the production of carbon-14 in the atmosphere by cosmic ray induced neutrons. The figure in each compartment is the carbon-12 content in units of 10^{12} tons; the transfer out of a compartment is expressed as the percentage of carbon-12 in that compartment which leaves each year. The surface ocean is the mixed layer which is separated from the deep ocean by the thermocline at about 100 metres.

hemispheres are separate and measurements indicate that the carbon-14 concentration in the southern atmosphere is about 0·5% lower than in the northern hemisphere—corresponding to an apparent age difference of 40 years (Lerman, Mook, *and* Vogel, 1970); the explanation given is based on the 40% greater area of ocean in the southern hemisphere.

Another facet not included in Fig. 2.2 is direct interchange between atmosphere and deep ocean through the upwelling of deep water. Since such water can have an apparent age of one or two thousand years, an increase in the amount of upwelling could cause a significant fall in the atmospheric carbon-14 concentration and climatically controlled changes such as these may account for some of the short-term variations shown in Fig. 2.5; alternatively, during a cold period, the rate of exchange between atmosphere and ocean could be reduced by increased coverage with ice, and this would cause an increase in the atmospheric concentration.

(iv) *Isotopic fractionation.* Although plants obtain their carbon from the atmosphere, the actual concentration of carbon-14 in them is lower by 3 or 4% (equivalent to an apparent age difference of 240–320 years). This is because in the process of photosynthesis carbon-14 is not taken up as readily as carbon-12. There are small variations from species to species in the degree of this isotopic fractionation, and it is now common practice to evaluate the effect for each sample that is dated. This is done by measurement of the carbon-13 concentration in the sample; this stable isotope is present to about 1% and so it can be measured with a mass spectrometer. The percentage depletion for an isotope is proportional to the difference in atomic mass; hence the depletion for carbon-14 is calculated simply by doubling the depletion found in the sample for carbon-13.

Isotopic fractionation also occurs in the exchange reaction between carbon dioxide and ocean carbonate, there being an enrichment of 1·5% when carbon goes from atmosphere to ocean. Hence, relative to plant life there is an isotopic enrichment of ocean carbonate by about 5%. This compensates for the deficiency in ocean carbonate due to the effect of finite mixing rates and the directly-measured carbon-14 concentrations are the same. But when the correction for isotopic fractionation is made, the ocean carbonate shows an apparent age relative to plant-life of around 400 years.

Isotopic fractionation complicates the experimental determination of a date but, unlike mixing-rates, it is not a fundamental source of uncertainty.

Principle of simultaneity

It is now well-established that an age in radiocarbon years may be significantly different to the true calendar age. The question then arises as to whether the radiocarbon time-scale is worldwide, i.e. were the carbon-14 concentration variations simultaneous throughout the exchange reservoir? Other than the 40-year apparent age difference between northern and southern hemispheres already noted, there is no evidence against the principle of simultaneity (except possibly the 11-year variations discussed in section 2.6). Indeed the same precise study on tree-rings from different parts of the world which revealed the 40-year difference (Lerman *et al.*, 1970), also showed that at any rate over the last millennium the concentration variations have been synchronous.

2.5. Measurement

Sample integrity

Some discussion of suitable sample materials has already been given in Chapter 1. The essential requirement is that over the centuries of burial the sample has not acquired any fresh carbon from the exchange reservoir. This must be obeyed stringently, since only a small amount of new carbon makes the apparent age appreciably too recent. Thus in a sample which is 17 000 years old the carbon-14 concentration is one eighth of the reservoir concentration and the addition of only 1% of new carbon will give an age that is too recent by 600 years; for a 34 000-year-old sample the same percentage causes an error of 4000 years, and for a 51 000-year-old sample the error is 15 000 years. For an infinitely old sample, the addition of 1% of new carbon will give an apparent age of 38 000 years. In view of the foregoing figures the question arises as to whether there are in fact any materials having sufficient integrity, and freedom from contamination, to make dating of old samples a practical proposition.

The question is best answered by quoting remarks made by Libby (1967) in recalling early thoughts on sample integrity . . . 'There was hope that this was so because of the unique nature of biochemical processes. It seemed very likely that only living processes can produce the molecules of which living things consist; thus the remains would retain their individuality in death, and contaminants would not imitate them so closely as to be inseparable. The contaminants would be of higher molecular weight in general and chemically distinguishable. Of course, there was the problem of sheer physical contamination, but it seemed possible that this could be solved by careful examination and cleaning. Thus a technique was developed for cleaning samples and authenticating them, which involved mechanical washing followed by chemical treatments to remove contaminants such as the humic acids from soil and calcium carbonate from limestone, etc. The proof of the adequacy of these techniques necessarily lay in finding the same age for a given site with a variety of different materials . . .'

Sample pre-treatment

Humic acids are removed by washing in alkali (e.g. 1% sodium hydroxide), and carbonates by washing in acid (e.g. 5% hydrochloric acid). Notes on a few special points are given below; for further details of procedures and other experimental aspects the reader should refer to Ralph (1971).

Carbonates. The presence of carbonates in an organic sample, e.g. by deposition from ground water in a limestone region represents contamination by 'old' carbon; this is not usually as serious a problem as humic acid since the error in age from a given percentage contamination is much less for old carbon than a new—a 1% addition of old carbon gives an apparent age that is too old by 80 years, irrespective of age. Although deposited carbonate can be removed by acid washing, it should be noted that there is no pre-treatment that can deal with old carbon that has been incorporated by photosynthesis such as may occur with aquatic plants (Deevey, Gross, Hutchinson, *and* Kraybill, 1954; Shotton, 1972).

Shell. This material—composed almost entirely of calcium carbonate—is difficult because of continued exchange after formation, particularly with land shells; a powdery appearance is indication that substantial exchange has occurred. One approach is to subject the material to increasing severity of acid attack and to determine a date after each treatment. Layers in which exchange has occurred are on the outside and more vulnerable, and when these have been removed there is a levelling-off of the dates obtained.

Shells for which the calcium carbonate is in the form of aragonite are safer than those for which it is in the form of calcite. This is because aragonite is metastable and converts to calcite; thus if the shell is free from calcite there is built-in evidence that no exchange has occurred and the presence of calcite, down to 10%, can be detected by X-ray diffraction (Grant-Taylor, 1973). Another possibility with shell is to utilize the organic protein constituent, conchiolin, which is present to one or two per cent in modern shell (Berger, 1964).

Bone. The inorganic calcium phosphate and calcium carbonate which constitute about 60% of dry modern bone present the same exchange risk as calcium carbonate in shell, but if sufficient sample is available this risk can be avoided by extracting collagen, the organic protein constituent of bone. In modern bone there is about 25% collagen but unfortunately it decreases with age (at a rate dependent on burial conditions) so that in old bone it may be present to only a fraction of a percent. Consequently reliable dating of bone, or of shell, may require a kilogram or more of material. Special pre-treatment is necessary to ensure that the collagen is free from humic acids (Haynes, 1967).

Wood. Although this is straightforward material in routine archaeo-logical application, when dated rings are used for calibration purposes it is given special pre-treatment. This is in order to eliminate the lignin and the resin so that only the celluose structure is used for dating. For some trees examined (e.g. Fairhill *and* Young, 1970; Jansen, 1970) the resin fraction shows a higher carbon-14 activity than the cellulose. This is not surprising in species in which there are resin channels running through both heartwood and sapwood; the results obtained by Jansen imply that the resin in an inner ring can contain carbon assimilated from the atmosphere several centuries later than the date of formation of the cellulose.

There is also the possibility that through food storage the carbon in the cellulose may correspond to an earlier year; at worst this would be limited to the extent of the living sapwood which is not usually more than 20 or 30 rings thick, though it amounts to about 100 in bristlecone pine (Berger, 1970). Because of the importance of the latter for calibration purposes extensive tests have been made to check for the presence of non-contemporary carbon in the cellulose structure. Inward movement of carbon can be checked very sensitively by testing pre-1954 rings for the presence of excess carbon-14 activity from hydrogen bomb explosions and so far the evidence is strongly against this (Berger, 1972). Note however this does not check on the reverse possibility of incorporation of carbon assimilated from the atmosphere in earlier years.

Measurement of radioactivity

Accurate measurement is difficult and tedious for several reasons. Because the specific radioactivity is very low, each measurement must continue for a long time (usually at least 24 hours) in order to average out statistical fluctuations, and this requires good stability both in electronics and in background. Even with stringent precautions the background count-rate is of the same order as that due to an old sample. The counting chamber must be constructed from materials that are free from radioactivity and it must be shielded both from environmental gamma radiation and from the small percentage of cosmic rays that do reach the earth's surface; about ten or twenty tons of steel are used, and additionally the chamber is surrounded by anti-coincidence counters. The latter are necessary because the steel shield does not stop the highly-penetrating muon component of cosmic radiation; the electronic circuitry is arranged so that particles entering the chamber from outside are ignored on account of recording simultaneously in the anti-coincidence counters.

Besides being weak in number per minute, the β-particles are weak in terms of penetrating power; they have a maximum energy of 160 keV and their intensity is halved by a 10 micron thickness of aluminium. It is therefore necessary that the sample should be inserted into the sensitive volume of the counting chamber rather than separated from it by a window.

The solid-carbon technique. This was the original technique used by Libby (1955). The sample is converted to carbon dioxide by combustion and then reduced to carbon black by heating with magnesium. The carbon black is then painted onto the inner wall of a modified Geiger counter. One disadvantage is that the painting process entails exposure to the atmosphere of the highly absorptive carbon with consequent risk of radioactive contamination, a risk that became particularly serious subsequent to the beginning of hydrogen-bomb testing in 1954. Another disadvantage is that only a small proportion of the β-particles are detected—due to poor geometry and self-absorption—and about ten grams of actual carbon are required, implying an often unobtainably large archaeological sample. The technique has now been superceded.

The proportional gas counter. This is the technique employed by the majority of laboratories at present. The carbon is converted into carbon dioxide, methane, or acetylene and this is used as the counting gas of a proportional counter. In addition to high efficiency of detection this has the advantage that electronic pulse-height discrimination can be used to reject large pulses arising from α-particle contamination. The volume of the chamber is typically several litres and it is filled to a pressure of one or two atmospheres, so that the amount of carbon measured is 1 or 2 grams; the count-rate for modern carbon is of the order of 10–20 counts per minute and with good shielding the background can be as low as 1 count per minute.

The liquid scintillation technique. For this the carbon is converted into an organic liquid, such as benzene, that can be used as solvent for a liquid scintillator. This is contained in a 20 cc vial and viewed by two photomultipliers (connected in coincidence so as to eliminate photocathode noise pulses); these detect the scintillations produced by the β-particles from the carbon-14 in the solvent. As with the proportional counter, pulse-height discrimination is used.

Because a given amount of carbon is contained in a much smaller volume than for measurement as a gas, shielding against cosmic rays is easier and the anti-coincidence counters can be dispensed with altogether. Another important advantage is the ease with which measurement of sample, standard, and background can be alternated (automatically), thus eliminating drifts in detection sensitivity or background; also, liquid samples occupy very much less storage space than gas samples. The technique deals with large samples more easily than does the gas counter; it is straightforward to use a sample containing about 10 grams of carbon and this gives a counting rate for modern material somewhat over 100 counts per minute—to be compared with a background typically in the range 5–10 counts per minute. On the other hand the chemistry is more complex, the background is less predictable, and it is not such a convenient system for handling small samples (of less than 1 gram of carbon). The technique has been described by Polach (1969).

Nuclear-track emulsions. Jeffreys, Larson, *and* French (1972) have reported the detection of β-particles from natural carbon by means of the tracks they produce in photographic emulsion; 0·2 gram of solid carbon was used, spread over an area of 9 cm². With experience β-particle tracks can be distinguished from a background of tracks from other particles, and the authors claim that with patience and diligence the technique can be used for dating. A ten-week exposure to modern carbon gives 160 tracks per cm² with a background level of 20 tracks per cm².

Thermoluminescent dosimetry. The radiation dose-rate within a sample of modern carbon is about 6 millirads per year. Although there are thermoluminescent dosimeter materials (e.g. rare-earth activated calcium sulphate) that are sufficiently sensitive to measure such rates with an exposure of a few months, the problems of background suppression appear to be insuperable. The cosmic ray dose-rate inside a typical radiocarbon counter shield is of the order of 10 millirads per year and, because this is due to the penetrating high-energy component, it would be necessary to go to great depths to make this small compared to even the modern carbon dose-rate; unlike the counting techniques or the emulsion technique, there is no way of discriminating against contaminating radioactivities. An experimental appraisal has been made by Winter (1972).

Isotopic fractionation

The level of counter background sets a limiting age of about 50 000 years for an installation designed specially for old samples. To attempt measurement of older samples it is necessary to enrich the carbon-14 concentration by isotopic fractionation in a thermal diffusion column. This was in fact the procedure used in the initial detection of carbon-14 when only high background counters were available, but used in conjunction with a low background counter it made it possible to detect the β-activity corresponding to a 70 000-year-old sample (Haring, de Vries, *and* de Vries, 1958). However, problems of sample contamination and sample integrity then become formidable and in practice the limit remains at about 50 000 years.

It is important that isotopic enrichment does not occur unintentionally in the course of routine sample preparation. Since isotopic fractionation is inherent in some chemical processes it is desirable to secure 100% conversion of the sample's carbon into gas or liquid in order to avoid risks that enrichment has occurred.

Radiocarbon activity standards

In order to avoid the effects of fossil-fuel combustion and nuclear-weapon tests, the value used for the activity of recently grown material is obtained by measuring wood grown in the nineteenth century and making allowance for radioactive decay. For archaeological comparisons based on dates determined by different laboratories to be valid, it is essential that precise inter-relation is made of the mid-nineteenth century wood used by each. This is done by means of an international reference standard of oxalic acid (available from the National Bureau of Standards, Washington, D.C.) and 95% of the A.D. 1958 activity of this, after allowance for isotopic fractionation effects, is agreed as the present-day value for wood grown in A.D. 1890 (Broecker *and* Olsson, 1959). The 95% figure arises because the oxalic acid was prepared subsequent to the beginning of nuclear weapons testing.

Oxalic acid can give erroneous results because of non-uniformity problems associated with isotopic fractionation during conversion to carbon dioxide, particularly if wet combustion is used (Grey, Damon, Haynes, *and* Long, 1969; Polach, 1972). A limited quantity of wood spanning A.D. 1846–55 has now been prepared as an alternative intercomparison standard (Bannister *and* Damon, 1972) and related to the oxalic acid standard (Polach, Krueger, Bannister, Damon, *and* Rafter, 1972); sucrose is under preparation at the Australian National University as an international secondary standard (Polach *and* Krueger, 1972).

2.6. Recent fluctuations in radiocarbon concentration

The fossil-fuel effect

The combustion of coal and oil releases into the atmosphere large quantities of carbon dioxide in which the carbon-14 has long since decayed, because coal and oil were removed from the exchange reservoir millions of years ago. This 'old' carbon significantly dilutes the carbon-14 concentration in the atmosphere and the activity of wood samples grown in A.D. 1950 (prior to hydrogen-bomb testing) is in fact lower than samples grown in A.D. 1850 (prior to the industrial revolution) despite the decay that has occurred in the latter. The effect was first observed by Suess (1955) using samples of recent wood and further work by Houtermans, Suess, *and* Munk (1967) has indicated that the variation observed is unlikely to be one of the natural fluctuations discussed in section 2.7. Also, it has been found that the atmospheric carbon-14 concentration is lower in the neighbourhood of large cities than elsewhere.

The carbon-14 activity of samples grown around 1950 is about 3% lower that what would be expected from measurements on wood grown before 1850, after making allowances for decay. This is more than ten times the effect expected on the basis that the estimated amount of 'old' carbon released from 1860 to 1950 amounts to only 0·2% of the total carbon in the exchange reservoir (Baxter *and* Walton, 1970). The observed effect is much stronger because of the so-called 'hold up' in the atmosphere; the finite mixing rate between atmosphere and sea means that the fossil carbon has not had time to mix uniformly throughout the reservoir. The observed degree of hold up can be used to estimate the average lifetime of a carbon dioxide molecule in the atmosphere before it dissolves in the sea (e.g. Revelle *and* Suess, 1957).

Effect of nuclear weapons testing

It has been estimated that up to 1962 the neutrons released by fission and fusion explosions will have caused the formation of about 2 tons of carbon-14 (Walton, Baxter, Callow, *and* Baker, 1967). Distributed uniformly throughout the reservoir this would increase the carbon-14 concentration by about 3%. However, as with the fossil-fuel effect there is hold up in the atmosphere and the actual rise is much stronger; at present the atmospheric carbon-14 concentration (as determined from measurements on recently grown plants, or on recently made whisky—see Walton *et al.*) is approximately double the level in the pre-nuclear era. As the extra carbon-14 gradually reaches the deep ocean the level will fall to the 3% excess representing uniform distribution—assuming hopefully that there are no further substantial explosions.

The sharp injection of carbon-14 into the atmosphere in this way allows useful study of mixing rates between different parts of the exchange reservoir (see, e.g., Nydal, 1967, Munich, *and* Roether, 1967; Fairhill, Young, *and* Bradford, 1972; Rafter *and* O'Brien, 1972; Vogel 1972; Gulliken *and* Nydal, 1972; Linick *and* Suess, 1972). In particular the 1961–2 explosions at high altitudes introduced carbon-14 into the same regions as are most important in natural carbon-14 production and so the route revealed as the artificial excess moves through the various components of the reservoir is also that for natural carbon-14.

Another use of these sharp rises in carbon-14 concentration is in confirming the integrity of sample materials. Measurements on a bristlecone pine and an oak (Berger 1972) showed that wood formed immediately before the sharp rise in atmospheric concentration did not contain any excess carbon-14; this was also true for a red cedar examined by Fairhill *and* Young (1970) as long as the cellulose structure was used, but the resin extract showed a sharp rise in carbon-14 activity for rings formed up to a dozen years earlier than the occurrence of the atmospheric excess.

The Tunguska meteor

In 1908 a meteor fell in Siberia and, to explain the absence of a crater, and other peculiar circumstances, the suggestion was made (Cowan, Atluri, *and* Libby, 1965) that annihilation of anti-matter in the atmosphere might be involved and that if so the neutrons generated would have produced an increase of 7% in the atmospheric carbon-14 concentration. Although initial tree-ring measurements suggested the possibility of a 1% increase for 1909, subsequent measurements by Lerman, Mook, *and* Vogel (1967) on a poplar that had grown in Norway excluded the possibility of any increase in excess of 0·3%.

Response time of the reservoir

With the effects due to fossil fuel and nuclear weapons the change in atmospheric concentration is accentuated because of the time taken for carbon atoms to reach the deep ocean after release into the atmosphere. On the other hand in considering changes in production rate, such as the sunspot activity effects considered in the next section, we shall find that the percentage variation in concentration is much smaller than the percentage variation in rate.

It is helpful at this stage to consider a simple electrical analogy. In Fig. 2.3, C_1 represents the atmosphere, biosphere, and surface ocean,

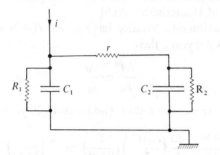

FIG. 2.3. Electrical analogy of simplified two-compartment model of the carbon exchange reservoir. The current i represents production of carbon-14 in the atmosphere, C_1 represents the atmosphere, biosphere, and surface ocean and C_2 the deep ocean. The resistor r simulates interchange between the two compartments; R_1 and R_2 simulate radioactive decay.

and C_2 the deep ocean. The resistors R_1 and R_2 have values such that $(R_1 C_1) = (R_2 C_2) = 8300$ years, and simulate radioactive decay. The resistor r simulates interchange between the two compartments. Numerically $C_2 \approx 30C_1$, so that $R_2 \approx 1/30 R_1$; if we take 20 years as the residence time before reaching the deep ocean then $(rC_1) = 20$, so that $R_1 = 415r$ and $R_2 = 11r$.

The nuclear-weapons effect corresponds to the dumping onto C_1 of a fixed amount of charge. The instantaneous change in voltage is (q/C_1), but this decays (with a 25-year time constant) to a final level of $q/(C_1 + C_2)$, i.e. the immediate effect is 31 times the permanent effect.

The effect of periodic production rate changes can be simulated by feeding C_1 with a current $i = i_0 + \Delta i \sin \omega t$. If the resultant voltage

on C_1 (analogous to the atmospheric carbon-14 concentration) is
written in the form

$$V_1 = V_0 + \Delta V \sin(\omega t + \delta) \tag{2.6}$$

then $\qquad\qquad V_0 \simeq (r + R_2)i_0 \tag{2.7}$

and,

$$\frac{\Delta V}{V_0} \simeq \frac{\Delta i}{i_0} \sqrt{\frac{1 + \left(\dfrac{C_2}{C_1} 25\omega\right)^2}{(1 + 8300^2\omega^2)(1 + 25^2\omega^2)}}. \tag{2.8}$$

The exact expression and an evaluation of the phase angle, δ, will be
found on p. 5 of Houtermans (1966).

If the production rate variation has a period $T(=2\pi/\omega)$ that is long
compared to 8300 years, then

$$\frac{\Delta V}{V_0} \simeq \frac{\Delta i}{i_0}. \tag{2.9}$$

At the other extreme, for T short compared to 20 years,

$$\frac{\Delta V}{V_0} \simeq \frac{\Delta i}{i_0}\left(\frac{C_2/C_1}{2\pi}\right)\left(\frac{T}{8300}\right) \simeq \frac{\Delta i}{i_0}\left(\frac{T}{2600}\right) \tag{2.10}$$

The ratio of compartment sizes (C_2/C_1), which we have taken as 30,
represents accentuation due to delay in reaching the deep ocean but
this is overwhelmed by the attenuation $(T/8300)$ resulting from the
slow response of the system. Evaluation of (2.8) for periods between
the two extremes has been given by Houtermans (1966):

$$\left.\begin{array}{l} \text{for } T \sim \quad 10 \text{ years,} \dfrac{\Delta V}{V_0} \simeq \dfrac{1}{180}\dfrac{\Delta i}{i_0} \\[3mm] \text{for } T \sim \quad 100 \text{ years,} \dfrac{\Delta V}{V_0} \simeq \dfrac{1}{22}\dfrac{\Delta i}{i_0} \\[3mm] \text{for } T \sim 1000 \text{ years } \dfrac{\Delta V}{V_0} \simeq \dfrac{1}{14}\dfrac{\Delta i}{i_0} \end{array}\right\} \tag{2.11}$$

and

Houtermans also considers the effects of modulation of residence
time and of reservoir size. The analysis has been extended to the more
complex case of a three-compartment model by Houtermans, Suess,
and Oeschger (1973); the characteristics are essentially the same.

Sunspot activity: heliomagnetic modulation

Cosmic-ray data taken over the past few 11-year solar cycles indicate that when sunspot activity is high the cosmic ray intensity is depressed. It is presumed that with high sunspot activity there is an associated intensification of the weak interplanetary magnetic field carried by the solar wind, and that this deflects cosmic rays away from the earth's vicinity, particularly the lower energy component responsible for carbon-14 production. Corresponding diminutions in high altitude neutron flux have been observed. From an analysis of these data Lingenfelter (1963) has put forward the following empirical relation for the effect on production of carbon-14:

$$Q = 2\cdot 64 - \frac{S}{337} \qquad (2.12)$$

where Q is the carbon-14 production (expressed as atoms per second per cm^2 of the earth's surface) and S is the annual sunspot number. Over the last six solar cycles S has varied between near zero at sunspot minimum to around 100 at sunspot maximum and so, according to Lingenfelter's relation, an overall variation of 10% in the carbon-14 production-rate is to be expected. More detailed calculations for a specific fairly strong cycle give a variation of 20% (Lingenfelter *and* Ramaty, 1970).

If the atmospheric carbon-14 concentration varied by the same percentage then radiocarbon dating would hardly be a practical proposition—the percentages quoted correspond to age shifts of 800 and 1600 years respectively. However, as discussed above, because of the slow response time of the reservoir a production-rate variation with a period of around 10 years will be severely attenuated and the resultant concentration variations should be less than 0·1%—corresponding to an age shift less than 8 years.

Records of sunspot activity have been kept at Zurich since A.D. 1700 and estimates based on such phenomena as aurora borealis and solar flares have been made back to A.D. 300 (Shove 1955), extending to 600 B.C. with lessening reliability. These data indicate that the intensity of the maximum of the 11-year cycle has varied between 50 and 150 and that the activity has been greater in even centuries than in odd ones—suggesting a 200-year periodicity in the amplitude of the cycle. For such longer periodicities the attenuation due to the response time of the reservoir is less severe and variations in atmospheric concentration of the order of 1% are to be expected. The observed deviations of radiocarbon age from calendar age indicated by measurements on dated tree-rings give evidence that such an effect does occur (Stuiver 1961). For instance the sixteenth century was a period of high sunspot activity and this agrees well with the gradual decrease in atmospheric concentration occurring during that century. Detailed studies over the past 1000 years have confirmed correlation on a

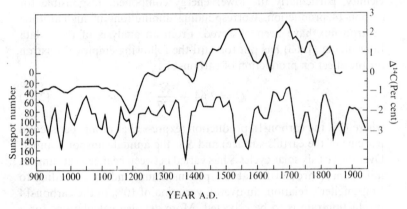

YEAR A.D.

FIG. 2.4. Comparison of atmospheric carbon-14 concentration variations (upper curve) with solar activity (lower curve). The concentration variations are from tree-ring measurements. The solar activity is represented by the estimated sunspot number at the maximum of the 11-year cycle. The scale is inverted so as to illustrate that a sustained period of low sunspot activity tends to be followed by a period of high concentration, and vice versa (after Houtermans, Suess, *and* Munk, 1967.)

statistical basis (Houtermans, Suess, *and* Munk, 1967), and there is good agreement between the observed variations and the variations predicted by a model that allows for the attenuation and lag introduced by the slow response of the reservoir (Grey 1969).

In view of this it is reasonable to presume that heliomagnetic modulation is the cause of similar short-term variations revealed by tree-ring measurements for earlier millennia. Support for this is given by the observation (see Figs. 2.5 and 2.8) that the short-term variations are less pronounced during periods when the geomagnetic moment is high; the heliomagnetic affects the lower energy cosmic rays and when the geomagnetic moment is high these are deflected away from the earth anyway.

Another effect associated with high solar activity is the occurrence of solar flares; the associated particles will produce carbon-14 and hence there could be a tendency to obscure the heliomagnetic modulation effect. Lingenfelter *and* Ramaty (1970) estimate that the increase in atmospheric carbon-14 concentration due to a single event could be of the order of 1% and that solar flares may be responsible for some of the sudden short-term increases implied in Fig. 2.5. These authors also consider possible increases in carbon-14 production that might arise from a supernovae explosion.

Evidence for 11-year variations. Although the amplitude predicted for concentration variations associated with the 11-year cycle is below detectable limits, a detailed study back to A.D. 1890 by Baxter *and* Walton (1971) gives evidence for concentration variations which do show correlation with this cycle. The materials used were samples of whisky, wine, seeds, cereal, and wool for which the year of plant growth was known. The overall magnitude of the variation sometimes reaches 3%—corresponding to an age shift of 240 years; the authors propose an explanation of this anomalously large amplitude in terms of hold up of carbon-14 in the stratosphere before release into the lower atmosphere from which plants draw their carbon dioxide. It is suggested that transfer from the stratosphere is affected by solar activity through the influence which incident ultraviolet and corpuscular radiation have on relevant temperature gradients.

A further study by Farmer *and* Baxter (1972), of single rings for the years A.D. 1829 to 1865 from an oak grown in Britain also shows variations; the overall amplitude is between 1 and 2% and there is significant correlation with the 11-year cycle. On the other hand the same authors found no such correlation for the rings of a New Zealand pine spanning A.D. 1910 to 1950. Like the oak tree, the plant materials showing the 3% variations were from Britain (or its vicinity) and the authors suggest that the effect may be latitude dependent—possibly it is attenuated in the southern hemisphere because the much larger oceanic surface there allows a more rapid interchange between atmosphere and ocean. Also, strong spatial variations have been observed in the descent of carbon-14 from high altitude nuclear explosions. The authors comment that the mechanism may vary with time; this is in respect of the observation that in the plant-derived material (whisky, wine, etc.) the maximum carbon-14 concentration lagged the sunspot minimum by about 10 years whereas in the oak the lag was 5 years.

Damon, Long, *and* Wallick (1973) have examined the A.D. 1940 to

1954 rings of a Douglas fir grown at high altitude in Arizona and although the variations show some correlation with the 11-year cycle, the overall amplitude is fairly small. These authors review other evidence from single-ring measurements and find no support for the existence of larger variations. The arguments for the alternative viewpoint have been summarized by Baxter *and* Farmer (1973) and Baxter, Farmer, *and* Walton (1973); further comment has been made by Damon, Long, *and* Wallick (1973a).

In assessing these conflicting points of view another possibility to be borne in mind is that in some species of tree the 11-year variations could be smeared out through interchange of carbon within the sapwood layer. As mentioned earlier (section 2.5), although there is strong evidence against the inclusion, in the cellulose structure, of carbon that was assimilated by the tree in a year later than that in which the ring was formed, the tests employed would not show up the incorporation of carbon assimilated in an earlier year.

Irrespective of what is the correct explanation, the conclusion for archaeological dating seems to be that samples spanning only a year's growth are liable to an error of ± 120 years (assuming the effect to have had a similar magnitude during earlier millennia). Thus if short growth period materials are used there is risk of this error, while if a decade's worth of wood growth is used in order to average it out there is the uncertainty as to how many years elapsed between formation and the archaeological event being dated.

2.7. Concentration variations during past millennia: evidence

Dated tree rings

For the tree-ring studies just discussed the date of a ring is established simply by counting inwards from the outermost ring. However, as explained in section 1.4, by careful application of dendrochronological techniques to sequoia and bristlecone pine that died in antiquity it has been possible to obtain dated wood samples back to 6000 B.C. Evidence that there have been fluctuations in atmospheric carbon-14 concentration was first obtained by de Vries (1958) using European and American trees—hence the term *de Vries effect*. This type of measurement was extended back a further 800 years by Willis, Tauber, *and* Munnich (1960) and subsequently to earlier periods by a number of others. The bristlecone pines which grow at 3000 metres in the White Mountains of California are of unique importance in this context because these sometimes grow to ages of more than 4000 years and are well preserved after death. Intensive study at the Tree-Ring Research Laboratory of the University of Arizona has resulted in the establishment of a 8200-year chronology with expectation of extension back to 9000 years (Fergusson, 1969, 1970, 1972).

Measurements on rings from this sequence (in 10 year bundles, thereby avoiding any possible 11-year cycle effects) have been made by the radiocarbon laboratories of the Universities of Arizona, California (La Jolla), and Pennsylvania. The first results available were those from the La Jolla laboratory, and the age error indicated by the now-classic 'Suess curve' drawn through them freehand (Suess 1970) is shown in Fig. 2.5. The results were based on measurement of about three hundred samples, and as each was counted successively in each of two counters to a statistical accuracy of better than $\frac{1}{2}\%$, the experimental effort was formidable. As the figure shows, there have been short-term fluctuations with periodicities of the order of a hundred years throughout most millenia; these are superimposed on a long-term trend which during the fourth and fifth millennia B.C. was equivalent to an excess concentration approaching 10%. As will be seen later this long-term excess is confirmed by checks using Egyptian material of known date, and by comparison with varve-dating; also, it agrees well with prediction based on the geomagnetic field determined by archaeomagnetic studies.

The short-term 'kinks and wriggles' of the Suess curve have some alarming implications for archaeological dating. At some times the decrease in carbon-14 concentration is so rapid that in principle an older sample may give a more recent radiocarbon age than a younger one. In practice such reversals tend to be obscured by the standard deviation of measurement and the effective consequence is that in such periods a given radiocarbon age may correspond to a range of calendar dates that is several times wider than the span indicated by the standard deviation. To take one extreme example, close inspection of Fig. 2.5 will show that over the calendar date range 2900 B.C. to 2550 B.C. the expected radiocarbon date remains within 50 years of 2150 b.c.

The reality of the Suess wriggles has been the subject of much discussion. Certainly the two peaks occurring around A.D. 1500 and A.D. 1700 are well-established and have been found in trees from different latitudes in both northern and southern hemisphere,

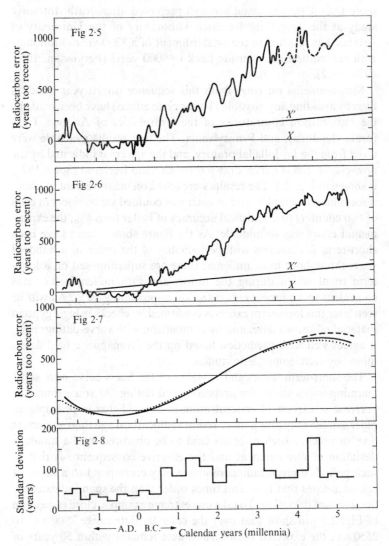

FIGS. 2.5–2.8

For captions see facing page

indicating not only reality but also worldwide simultaneity (Lerman, Mook, *and* Vogel, 1970); a valuable source of material for such studies is Medieval constructional timber (e.g. Berger 1970a, Fletcher 1970). There is no reason why similar fluctuations should be absent during earlier millennia. Whether all the fluctuations are exactly as drawn, and are on a worldwide basis, must await the availability of tree-ring dated wood from other parts of the world—such as the sequences from Irish bog oaks in preparation by Smith *et al.* (1972) at Belfast.

It is not practical to count each sample for any longer than is necessary to achieve a better statistical accuracy than $\pm\frac{1}{2}\%$; this corresponds to ±40 years and so in drawing a curve through the points there is a degree of subjectiveness in judging which irregularities are genuine and which are random error. To avoid this Ralph, Michael, *and* Han (1973) have employed a 9-sample averaging procedure in presenting their own results from the University of Pennsylvania, together with the Suess results and the results from the University of Arizona, 630 in all. By this averaging, the standard deviation for each point is reduced to about ±13 years which is small compared to the amplitude of the irregularities. The relationship between radiocarbon age and dendrochronological age so obtained is shown in Figs. 2.12–2.17; each point is the floating average of 9 adjacent

---

FIG. 2.5. Age error indicated by measurements on dated tree rings (derived from Suess, 1970). The value obtained by measuring upwards from the conventional horizontal axis X indicates the error when the radiocarbon age is calculated on the basis of the Libby half-life of 5568 years. Measuring from the inclined axis X' gives the error on the basis of the revised half-life of 5730 years. The figure also indicates the excess concentration of carbon-14 in the atmosphere above the nineteenth century level: an age error of $+83$ years on the revised half-life corresponds to an excess of 1 per cent.

FIG. 2.6. Age error according to 9-sample averaging of tree-ring measurements (derived from the data of Ralph *et al.* shown in Figs. 2.12–2.17).

FIG. 2.7. Age error trends indicated by tree-ring measurements, on the basis of the 5730-year half-life. Ralph *et al.*—full curve; Damon *et al.*—dotted curve; Wendland and Donley—dashed curve. The horizontal line at 310 years indicates the average over the period and corresponds to an excess atmospheric concentration of approximately 4 per cent above the nineteenth-century level.

FIG. 2.8. Standard deviation of 25-year averages from trend shown in Fig. 2.7 (Damon *et al.*).

samples, appropriately weighted. A plot of the difference between radiocarbon age and dendrochronological age is shown in Fig. 2.6; this substantiates the majority of the Suess kinks and wriggles, though as is to be expected on account of the averaging the amplitude of the short duration ones has been attenuated.

Another analysis of the bulk of this data, plus some additional results from the laboratory at Yale University, has been made by Damon, Wallick, *and* Long (1972). After calculation of averages for 25-year intervals the trend determined by 250-year running averages has been tabulated, together with the standard deviation from the trend, of the 25-year averages in each successive 250-year period. The standard deviations are shown in Fig. 2.8 and the age error evaluated from the tabulated 250-year trend values are shown in Fig. 2.7. Also shown in the latter is the polynomial derived by Ralph *et al.* as a best fit to their 9-sample date, and an earlier polynomial derived by Wenland *and* Donley (1971) by multiple regression analysis of 500 tree-ring data from various laboratories including that of Suess.

The polynomial of Ralph *et al.* is

$$T_{C-14} = -44 + 0.918 \times T_D + 7.17 \times 10^{-5} \times T_D^2 +$$
$$+1.18 \times 10^{-8} \times T_D^3, \qquad (2.13)$$

where T_D and T_{C-14} are the dendrochronological and 5730-yr radiocarbon dates, positive for A.D. and negative for B.C. This polynomial is shown as a dashed line in Figs. 2.12–2.17 and it will be seen that the deviations from it of the 9-sample averages do not exceed 100 years except around 2200 B.C., when the deviation is 140 years.

The polynomial of Wendland *and* Donley is

$$A = 112 + 0.690\,R + 0.152 \times 10^{-3}\,R^2 - 0.138 \times 10^{-7}\,R^3, \quad (2.14)$$

where A is the dendrochronological age and R is the 5730-year radiocarbon age. Back to 4000 B.C. the age errors indicated by any of the three trend representations agree to within a span of 40 years. The form of variation is sinusoidal with a period of about 10 000 years; the expression

$$(A - R) = 310 - 370 \sin 2\pi \left(\frac{t + 1000}{10\ 000}\right) \qquad (2.15)$$

fits the curves of Ralph *et al.* and Damon *et al.* to within 40 years.

In situ production. Since bristlecone pines grow at an altitude of 3 km, the cosmic-ray neutron flux they experience is an order of magnitude greater than at sea level and is about 3% of the maximum flux reached in the stratosphere at 15 km. There is the possibility that the long-term excess concentration indicated by bristlecone pines may be due to *in situ* production of carbon-14 from the nitrogen-14 which is present in the wood†. There could also be an effect from the neutrons generated in lightning (Libby *and* Lukens 1973), particularly on account of the vulnerability to lightning of high altitude trees on exposed ridges. However, carbon-14 produced *in situ* is not necessarily incorporated into the molecules forming the cellulose structure of the tree and it may be removed in the course of the chemical pre-treatment employed before measurement; artificial irradiation of wood by Harkness *and* Burleigh (1974) with a dosage of neutrons equivalent to that generated during 9000 years by the cosmic-ray flux at 3 km did not produce any detectable amount of carbon-14.

Egyptian chronology

Although tree-ring samples can be dated precisely they are not representative of archaeological samples. First, they have grown at high altitude as just noted. Secondly, the material used for dating, instead of being buried, has been encased in younger material, and for perhaps one or two thousand years while the tree was still alive it has been permeated with younger sapwood; although only the cellulose fractions were used for dating and tests based on hydrogen-bomb produced carbon-14 have shown this to be immune to incorporation of later carbon there remains the possibility that in a tree of great antiquity some slight incorporation does take place. Thus there are good reasons to lay emphasis on tests with historically dated samples, quite apart from the archaeologist's instinct that, before accepting the serious implications of the bristlecone pine calibration for the radio-carbon-based chronologies in their relationship to the Egyptian calendar-based chronology of the Near East, there should be comparison of 'like with like'.

The basis of the Egyptian chronology has been outlined in section 1.5; the beginning of the First Dynasty is dated to 3100 B.C. with an uncertainty that is estimated to be no worse than ±100 years, and as

† Reported values for the amount of nitrogen present in bristlecone pine vary widely: Harkness *and* Burleigh (1974) quote 8·5%, Libby *and* Lukens (1973) quote 0·2%, and Damon *et al.* (1973a) quote 0·05%.

2000 B.C. is approached the uncertainty lessens, being better than ±20 years thereafter. There is liable to be a greater uncertainty in linking the sample to the historical chronology but by using samples from royal tombs this can be limited. Figure 2.9 shows results obtained from some of the samples specially selected for reliability of linking in a joint measurement programme by the laboratories of the British Museum and the University of California (Los Angeles). Many of the samples are reed that had been used as bonding between courses of mud-brick walling; in considering the results emphasis is to be placed on such short-growth samples rather than on the wood samples, because of the risk that the date of formation of the latter was appreciably earlier than the date of the historical context.

Also shown in Fig. 2.9 is the 9-sample-average version of the tree-ring calibration (Ralph *et al.*) The comparison illustrates that at any rate during the third millenium the Egyptian samples show much the same error as the tree-ring samples—as has been discussed by Edwards (1970), by Berger (1970), and by Clark *and* Renfrew (1973). The same conclusion was reached by Säve-Söderburgh *and* Olsson (1970), and by Michael *and* Ralph (1970), from measurements on an earlier collection of samples.

On closer inspection of the figure (or reference to column 6 of Table 2.1) it will be seen that of the 23 samples earlier than 1200 B.C., 8 show age errors that are less than the tree-ring indication by more than one standard deviation, but only 2 show age errors in excess of the tree-ring indication; if the wood samples are excluded the figures are 6 and 0 respectively, out of a total of 12. This bias was mentioned by Berger (loc cit.) and has been strongly emphasized by McKerrell (1972). Reinforcing the evidence with archaeological samples from Greece, the latter concludes that over the period 1200 to 2200 B.C. the bias amounts to one or two hundred years, and proposes the use of a correction based on historical samples for this period. Although the bias is small, it is critical in considering the extent to which contact with Mycenae influenced the Wessex culture of southern England, and whether in the trilithons of Stonehenge we do in fact have a dramatic manifestation of imported technology as has usually been supposed.

Questions such as the preceding are concerned with whether or not there is a *difference* between the accepted Egyptian chronology and the tree-ring chronology. In absolute terms there is a degree of uncertainty in the former and this has been ignored in Fig. 2.9; if the samples at *circa* 2600 B.C. and *circa* 3000 B.C. are placed one century earlier,

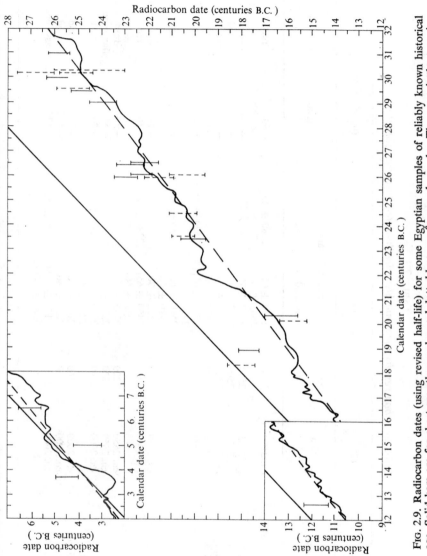

Fig. 2.9. Radiocarbon dates (using revised half-life) for some Egyptian samples of reliably known historical age. Solid bars are for short-growth samples and dotted bars are for wood samples. The curve is the tree-ring calibration of Ralph *et al.* and the dotted line its best-fit polynomial.

TABLE 2.1

Radiocarbon results for some historically-dated Egyptian samples

(1) dynasty	(2) historical date B.C.	(3) expected radiocarbon date	(4) measured radiocarbon date individual	(5) average	(6) (4) or (5) minus (3)	(7) material	(8) sample code no.
I (Hor Aha)	ca. 3100	2500	2480 ± 65 / 2685 ± 60	2580 ± 45	+80	reed	228 / 1200
I (Wadji)	ca. 3025	2500	2402 ± 70		−100	wood	319
I (Wadji)	ca. 3025	2500	2382 ± 80		−120	wood	320
I (Wadji)	ca. 3025	2500	2680 ± 80		−180	wood	321
I (Wadji)	ca. 3025	2500	2529 ± 70		+30	wood	322
I (early)	ca. 3000	2470	2710 ± 65 / 2470 ± 60	2590 ± 45	+120	reed	229 / 1201
I (mid)	ca. 2950	2380	2560 ± 65 / 2410 ± 60	2485 ± 45	+105	reed	230 / 1202
I (mid)	ca. 2950	2380	2522 ± 70		+140	wood	323
I (late)	ca. 2900	2330	2450 ± 65 / 2315 ± 60	2380 ± 45	+50	reed	231 / 1203
III	ca. 2650	2220	2215 ± 60		−5	reed	507
III	ca. 2650	2220	2275 ± 60		+55	flax rope	508
III–IV	ca. 2600	2160	2240 ± 65 / 2220 ± 60	2230 ± 45	+70	reed	235 / 1207
IV (Sneferu)	ca. 2600	2160	2143 ± 70		−15	wood	324
IV (Sneferu)	ca. 2600	2160	2033 ± 80		−125	wood	325
IV (Cheops)	ca. 2600	2160	2150 ± 105 / 2385 ± 60	2295 ± 50	+135	grass rope	332 / 1389

Table 2.1 continued

(1)	(2)	(3)	(4)	(5)	(6)	(7)	(8)
			measured radiocarbon date				
dynasty	historical date B.C.	expected radiocarbon date	individual	average	(4) or (5) minus (3)	material	sample code no.
V	ca. 2450	2040	2056 ± 64		+15	wood	401
VI (Teti)	ca. 2350	2020	1930 ± 85 2120 ± 60	2050 ± 50	+30	wood	331 1388
VI (early)	ca. 2350	2020	1930 ± 115 2030 ± 60	2005 ± 55	−15	reed	330 1387
XI	ca. 2030	1660	1630 ± 70		−30	skin	1696
XI (Mentuhotep II)	ca. 2010	1640	1586 ± 65		−55	wood	317
XII (Sesostris II)	1897–1877	1580	1740 ± 65 1800 ± 60	1770 ± 45	+190	reed	238 1212
XII (Sesostris III)	1830	1570	1800 ± 60		+230	wood	900
XIX (Ramesses II)	1290–1224	1090	1070 ± 100 1220 ± 60	1180 ± 50	+90	reed	333 1390
XXV–XXVI	690–610	540	570 ± 70 655 ± 60	610 ± 45	+70	reed	334 1391
XXVII	510	530	361 ± 60		−170	cloth	509
XXX	380–363	260	430 ± 80 455 ± 60	445 ± 50	+185	reed	340 1397

The data of this table are drawn from the publications of Barker, Burleigh, *and* Meeks (1969, 1971), Berger (1970, 1972), *and* Edwards (1970); samples for which the published information indicates an element of possible uncertainty in linking the sample to the historical chronology have been omitted.

Column (1): Inclusion of a king's name indicates direct association of the sample with a royal tomb.

Column (2): The basis of the historical dating used by the authors is the *Cambridge Ancient history*, vol. I (3rd ed. 1970).

Columns (3)–(6): All radiocarbon dates are on the basis of the 5730-year half-life.

Column (3): This date is obtained from the historical date (using the mid date in the case of a span) by means of the calibration curve published by Ralph *et al.*

Column (4): The first date quoted for each sample is the result from the British Museum Laboratory (BM) and the second date is from the University of California (Los Angeles) Laboratory (UCLA). All single dates are BM except for sample nos. 900 and 1696 which are UCLA.

Column (5): In calculating the average the individual dates have been weighted in proportion to the reciprocal of the square of the individual standard deviations.

then the samples straddle the tree-ring line without appreciable bias. A possible reason for *random* deviation of rapid-growth samples is the 11-year variation discussed in section 2.6. The wood samples might be expected to show evidence of delay between formation and utilization; there is no sign of this on average but such delay may be showing itself in some individual cases. For instance the sample at 1830 B.C. is a deckboard from the funerary ship of Sesostris III and since this is securely dated by the recording of a heliacal rising of Sothis during that king's reign, a likely explanation of the deviation is that the board was cut from the inner part of an old tree.

Varve chronologies

It has been explained in section 1.4 that the Swedish glacial varve chronology can be related to the changing spectrum of pollen found in nearby peat bogs and hence to radiocarbon dates obtained for the peat. The results obtained by Tauber (1970) are included in Fig. 2.10; the data point at 4300 B.C. gives corroboration of the long-term concentration excess at that time but earlier data suggests that before 6500 B.C. there was a deficiency of about 3% (corresponding to a negative age error of about 250 years on the basis of the 5730-year half-life). The greatest uncertainty in the varve chronology is the starting date of the river varve series which crosslinks to the zero glacial varve around 7000 B.C. and the corrected varve scale used by Tauber places this 200 years earlier than on the conventional scale. The five most recent of Tauber's radiocarbon dates are associated with the river varves and the agreement of the latest of these with the bristlecone pine calibration suggests that the starting date for the river varve sequence is correct.

The long-term excess indicated by the bristlecone pine measurements is also corroborated by direct measurements made on organic matter in a long core from the Lake of Clouds, Minnesota (Stuiver, 1970); this core contains 9500 thin laminations which are reasonably assumed to be annual layers. On the other hand (see Fig. 2.10), these results indicate there was a carbon-14 excess of about 10% back to 8000 B.C., in strong disagreement with the Scandinavian results.

Further evidence concerning the trend before 6000 B.C. has been provided by the varved marine sediments of Saanich Inlet, British Columbia (Yang *and* Fairhill, 1972). These layers arise through the alternation of marine biological deposit during spring with river sediment deposit during the rest of year. Present-day measurements on

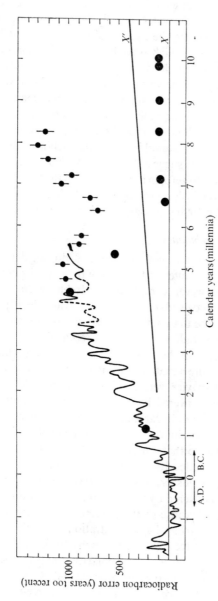

Fig. 2.10. Age error over the past 12 000 years: varve results superimposed on the tree-ring data of Fig. 2.5. The large full circles are the Scandinavian measurements of Tauber (1970) and the dots with vertical lines are the American measurements of Stuiver (1970). There is as yet no explanation of the discordance, before 5000 B.C., between the two sets of varve measurements. There are American measurements more recent than 4500 B.C. (which are not shown in order to avoid confusion) and these are in good agreement with the tree-ring data.

The meaning of the ages X and X' are explained in the caption to Fig. 2.5.

sediments in the water of Saanich Inlet show an apparent radiocarbon age of 1000 years—because the water is partly derived from upwelling of deep Pacific Ocean. Hence the marine biological deposit in the varves give radiocarbon ages which are older than terrigenous organic material (such as twigs, wood chips, and bits of charcoal) which are also contained in the layers. The varves extend back only to 7000 B.C. and within that period the results for the terrigenous material are consistent with the bristlecone-pine calibration and its extension according to the Lake of Clouds varves. Because the marine deposit lags behind the terrigeneous material it reflects the carbon-14 situation pertaining earlier; the results suggest that prior to 7000 B.C. the excess in concentration was near to zero, in agreement with the Scandinavian varves. However this conclusion presumes that the lag of the marine material has always been 1000 years, and this is not necessarily so.

Comparison with other techniques

Since the other techniques outlined in Chapter 1 do not depend on cosmic ray intensity it is of interest to see how their results compare with radiocarbon's. However except for dendrochronology, varve dating, and the Egyptian calendar, the accuracy available at present is not sufficient to do more than make comparisons on a ten per cent basis. The time range of radiocarbon is too recent for potassium–argon dating to give results of the same accuracy that it can achieve in older periods, and it is more a matter of using radiocarbon as a check of potassium–argon than vice versa. With uranium series dating, although the time ranges covered by ionium and protactinium have a much better overlap with radiocarbon, various geochemical uncertainties make the situation similar, though the results of Kulp *and* Volchok (1953) do indicate that variations in the radiocarbon production rate have not exceeded 10–20% over the past 25 000 years.

Thermoluminescence holds prospect of carrying the comparison back beyond the period covered by varve chronology and this would be of particular interest because of the possibility of more marked long-term variations in carbon-14 concentration through climatic changes associated with the Ice Ages and through cosmic-ray intensity changes associated with recent magnetic polarity events (see section 4.7). Preliminary results for the 30 000-year-old Czechoslovak figurine site of Dolni Věstonice are in reasonable agreement with radiocarbon, though possibly the thermoluminescent age is less recent by about 10% (Zimmerman *and* Huxtable, 1971).

2.8. Concentration variations: causes

Geomagnetic field intensity

There is good archaeomagnetic evidence (see section 4.8) that substantial variations have occurred in the overall geomagnetic field intensity and hence in the magnetic moment M. The resulting variation in carbon-14 production, Q, was first considered by Elsasser, Ney, *and* Winckler (1956), who concluded that

$$Q \propto \frac{1}{M^{0.52}}. \tag{2.16}$$

The value of M determines, for a given latitude, the minimum momentum of cosmic ray particle that can reach the atmosphere, and consequently (2.16) is based on the observed spectrum of cosmic rays. The effect has been considered subsequently by others, including Ramaty (1967) and Lingenfelter *and* Ramaty (1970), who are in agreement with (2.16) as a good approximation.

According to the archaeomagnetic data the variation of magnetic moment over the last 9000 years is approximately sinusoidal and the concentration variation predicted from this agrees with the long-term concentration variation implied by the bristlecone-pine calibration. The basis of comparison is along the following lines. By plotting the magnetic data in the form shown in Fig. 2.11 the best sinusoidal representation for the predicted production rate ,Q, is obtained. This is close to

$$Q(t) = Q_0 \left(1 - \frac{1}{3} \sin 2\pi \frac{t}{8000}\right), \tag{2.17}$$

where Q_0 is the average production rate and t is the time before present. It is assumed that the variation has persisted for several cycles. Because the variation is slow the resultant carbon-14 concentration variations are not attenuated to the severe extent that is the case for the heliomagnetic modulation—in fact the magnetic period is close to the mean lifetime of carbon-14 which defines the response time of the reservoir as a whole. Eqn (2.8) indicates an attenuation factor of one-seventh and the phase lag derived from the appropriate equation in Houtermans (1966) is equivalent to about 700 years; hence the prediction for the concentration variation is approximately

$$C(t) = C_0 \left(1 - \frac{1}{20} \sin 2\pi \frac{t + 700}{8000}\right). \tag{2.18}$$

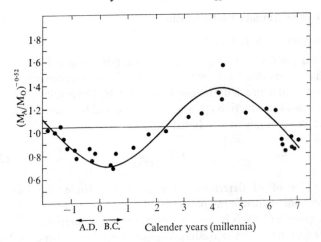

Fɪɢ. 2.11. (Redrawn from Suess, 1970). Production rate variation implied by the geomagnetic moment values evaluated by Bucha (1970); the minimum value of M occurs *circa* 4500 B.C. in this figure instead of 3500 B.C. as in Fig. 4.14 because the radiocarbon dates have been corrected. The production rate is proportional to $(M_A/M_0)^{-0.52}$ where M_A/M_0 is the ratio of the ancient moment to the present day moment.

Remembering that a 1% change in concentration causes an age error of 83 years we see that this equation predicts an age error amplitude of about 400 years. In view of the paucity of the magnetic data this is in remarkable agreement with the age error variation actually observed—see Fig. 2.7 or eqn (2.15). However, it would be rash to assume that there are no other important influences. More comprehensive magnetic data is required, as well as extension of both types of measurement to earlier times.

Geomagnetic reversals. There is now evidence (see section 4.9) that during the period of applicability of radiocarbon dating—the last 50 000 years—there were two geomagnetic polarity excursions. These were not permanent or complete transitions of polarity and their duration was probably only a few thousand years. The most recent of these (the Laschamp–Gothenburg excursion) is the less well documented; it may have been in progress only 12 400 years ago and if so the geomagnetic intensity and carbon-14 concentration variations discussed above may represent transient recovery from the event rather than part of a continuous sinusoidal oscillation. Magnetic evidence from geological times indicates that an abnormally low intensity—less than

20 % of the present value—is usually to be expected during a polarity transition.

The earlier event—recorded in Australian aboriginal fire-places at Lake Mungo—has been dated by radiocarbon as occurring from 31 000 b.p. to 25 000 b.p.; the magnetic measurements indicate that during the later stage of the event the geomagnetic intensity may have been about half of the present value for one or two thousand years, but that for a short period during the earlier stage the intensity reached *six times* the present value. A preliminary estimate of the effect of the low field value is that the subsequent atmospheric carbon-14 concentration may have been in excess by between 33% and 100% (Barbetti, 1972). However, this assumes that these brief excursions are worldwide effects and it is not yet certain that this is so.

Solar activity

It has already been mentioned (section 2.6) that the short-term variations having periodicities of the order of a hundred years are probably due to heliomagnetic modulation. Besides the good agreement between observation and prediction for the two centuries for which reliable sunspot records are available (see Fig. 2.4), there is the circumstantial evidence that the short-term variations—as indicated in Fig. 2.5, or, by the standard deviations shown in Fig. 2.8—are less during periods when the geomagnetic field is high; thus between, A.D. 1000 and 1500 B.C. when the field is high, the standard deviations exceed ±50 years in only three 250-year intervals, whereas between 3000 B.C. and 5500 B.C. when the field is low, the standard deviations do not fall below ±70 years.

Effect of climate

The atmospheric carbon-14 concentration is dependent both on reservoir size and on exchange rates between compartments (see section 2.4). It would be remarkable if climatic regime did not have an effect and this has been considered by a number of authors (e.g. Damon, 1968, Suess 1968, Libby 1973). It was early remarked by de Vries (1958) that the peak concentration occurring around A.D. 1700 followed a general worsening of the climate as evidenced by glacier advance. This peak also followed a period of low sunspot activity, in agreement with other evidence that there is correlation between sunspot activity and climate. The question then arises as to whether solar activity affects the carbon-14 concentration directly, through heliomagnetic modulation, or indirectly via its effect on the climate; the influence of solar activity on climate has been discussed by King (1973).

It has been suggested that climate is affected also by geomagnetic intensity; measurements on deep-sea sediment cores spanning the past half million years (Wollin, Ericson, Foster, *and* Ryan, 1971) show a tendency for colder climate during periods of higher intensity. Thus it is possible that the geomagnetic effect on carbon-14 concentration is via the climate also. However in both cases the quantitative agreement of prediction with observation (Figs. 2.4 and 2.11) suggests that the effects are due to direct modulation of cosmic-ray intensity. This does not rule out the possibility that in respect of the 11-year solar cycle the effect *is* via the climate (see section 2.6).

Effect of lightning. The suggestion by Libby *and* Lukens (1973) that the neutrons generated in lightning bolts could have produced significant amounts of carbon-14 in the bristlecone pines used for calibration, has already been mentioned (section 2.7). Such an effect would falsify the bristlecone pine record. However, there is also the possibility that lightning-generated neutrons contribute to atmospheric carbon-14 production; the same authors suggest that this could amount to 1% of the production by cosmic-ray neutrons and that variations in the frequency of lightning storms over the centuries may be partly responsible for the observed short-term carbon-14 concentration fluctuations.

Indications from other radioisotopes

Data about the constancy of the cosmic-ray flux are available from studies of other radioisotopes produced by cosmic rays, though in practice the precision at present attainable is barely sufficient to make the results relevant to radiocarbon dating. Two such isotopes are argon-39 and krypton-81, with half-lives of 270 years and 210,000 years respectively. Their present concentrations in the atmosphere (when compared with the expected concentration ratios as deduced from data on production cross sections) reflect the cosmic-ray intensity averaged over time periods of the order of their half-lives. Thus the ratio of argon-39 to krypton-81 is a measure of the cosmic intensity over the last few hundred years relative to its average value over the past few hundred thousand. This type of evidence can be extended further back in time by using ice from deep bore holes in Greenland and Antarctica. This has been deposited over 10^5 to 10^6 years, and the argon/krypton ratio in it is representative of atmospheric concentrations at the time of deposition (appropriate allowance being made for radioactive decay).

The concentrations of these rare-gas isotopes will not be affected by climatic changes in the same way as radiocarbon may be, since only small percentages dissolve in the ocean. Hence, when precise measurements become available, if the pattern of fluctuation matches that shown by the carbon-14 variations, this would be evidence that the cause of the variations lies in cosmic-ray changes. There will still be the question of confirming that the long-term concentration variation is a geomagnetic effect rather than due to some extra-terrestrial agency. Evidence about this can be obtained from radio-isotope ratio measurements on meteoritic and lunar materials since the cosmic-ray flux reaching them is not affected by the geomagnetic field. For example, the chlorine-36 (half-life 308 000 years) and argon-39 concentrations in a number of recently fallen meteorites indicate that the average cosmic ray intensity over the past half million years was the same to within 10%, as the value during the past five hundred (Schaeffer, Davis, Stoenner, *and* Heymann, 1963). For further discussion the reader may refer to Oeschger, Houtermans, Loosli, *and* Wahlen (1970), and to Oeschger *et al.* (1972).

2.9. Conversion of radiocarbon dates to calendar dates

The extensive investigations of atmosphere concentration variations have been stimulated jointly by geochemical research interest and the archaeologist's need to obtain dates in calendar years. Although the known deviations of the radiocarbon time-scale are not large in absolute terms, the need becomes crucial when comparison is made with other chronologies; also, when rapidity of development is being considered it is confusing to use a unit of time which does not represent the same number of calendar years in all periods—between 3000 B.C. and the beginning of the A.D. era, 75 radiocarbon years are equivalent to 100 calendar years, whereas in other periods they are more nearly the same.

Conversion is made complex by the existence of the short-term concentration fluctuations—the 'kinks and wriggles' of the Suess curve. These mean that in some periods a given radiocarbon date may correspond to a calendar date range that is appreciably wider than the range indicated by the experimental error limits of the result; this aspect has been discussed recently by Renfrew *and* Clark (1974). Because these short-term fluctuations are an effect in nature, these periods of poorer accuracy are a drawback of the method which no amount of further research can remove.

There are currently three versions of the bristlecone-pine calibration, which have already been discussed in section 2.7 and illustrated in Figs. 2.5–2.8. These are:

(i) the unsmoothed curve of Suess (1970),

(ii) the 9-sample average curve of Ralph *et al.* (1973),

and (iii) the 250-year trend curve of Damon *et al.* (1972).

There is as yet no general agreement as to which should be regarded as definitive. Curve (ii) is shown here in Figs. 2.12 to 2.17; the authors also publish a table of conversions and the two together are described as *the MASCA correction factors*. Three categories of conversion are defined: a *crossing*—in which only one calendar date corresponds to the radiocarbon date; a *span*—in which the portion of the curve corresponding to the radiocarbon date is horizontal; and a *range*— in which several calendar dates correspond to the radiocarbon date. An example of the latter is the radiocarbon date (on the revised half-life) of A.D. 1680 which corresponds to calendar dates of A.D. 1610 and A.D. 1530; hence the range tabulated for this radiocarbon date is A.D. 1610–1530. The authors use the terminology 'dendro-date' and this is useful in indicating the basis of the calibration by which the calendar date was obtained. Figs. 2.12–2.17 are in terms of the revised half-life and for convenience Table 2.2 is included here for conversion of dates quoted on the Libby half-life—which is to be assumed in the absence of indication to the contrary.

The approach of Damon *et al.* differs from that of Suess *and* Ralph *et al.* in treating the short-term variations as an additional source of random error. Conversion is by means of the smooth trend values (see Fig. 2.7) and the effect of short-term variations is introduced by means of the standard deviation, σ_0, for the period (see Fig. 2.8). Thus, the standard deviation for the corrected date is $\sqrt{\sigma_0{}^2 + \sigma_1{}^2}$, where σ_1 is the measurement standard deviation of the radiocarbon laboratory result. This procedure has the advantage that a concise and statistically manageable answer is obtained, though when the date is critical it may be difficult to ignore the additional indications available from (i) and (ii).

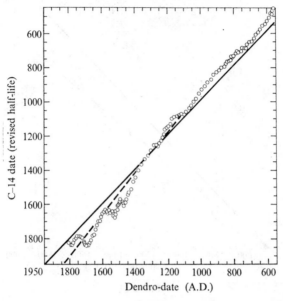

FIG. 2.12

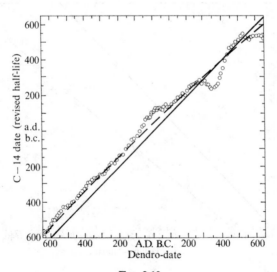

FIG. 2.13

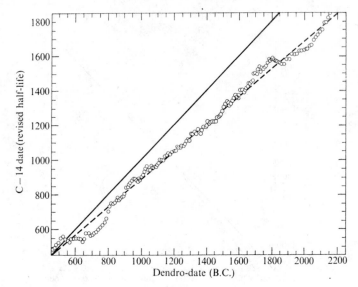

FIG. 2.14

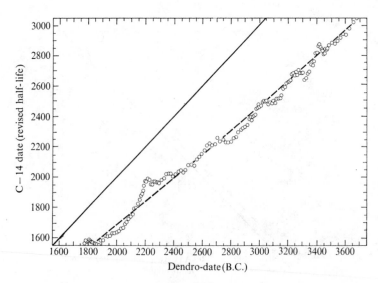

FIG. 2.15

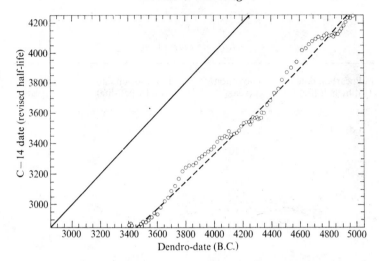

FIG. 2.16

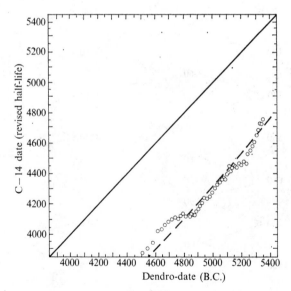

FIG. 2.17

FIGS. 2.12–2.17. Radiocarbon dates, using the revised half-life, *versus* dendrochronological dates (from Ralph *et al.*, by kind permission of the authors). Circles represent 9-sample weighted averages, the dashed line is the best-fit polynomial.

TABLE 2.2
Half-life correction

radiocarbon date (Libby half-life)	correction (years)	radiocarbon date (Libby half-life)	correction (years)
a.d. 1780		b.c. 1880	
	10		120
1450		2220	
	20		130
1120		2550	
	30		140
780		2880	
	40		150
450		3220	
	50		160
120		3550	
	60		170
b.c. 220		3880	
	70		180
550		4220	
	80		190
880		4550	
	90		200
1220		4880	
	100		210
1550		5220	
	110		220
1880		5550	

Note: The correction shown is applicable over the date range indicated. It should be added to b.c. dates but subtracted from a.d. dates.

TABLE 2.3

Examples of date conversion

(1)	(2)	(3)	(4)	(5)
radiocarbon date			standard deviation of conversion, σ_0 (for t)	corrected date
Libby half-life	revised half-life	limits (for n)		
a.d. 1000 ± 40	970 ± 40	—	±40	(t) 1020 ± 60
		920–1020	—	(n) 1020 ± 50
570 ± 40 b.c.	650 ± 40	—	±100	(t) 700 ± 110
		600–700	—	(n) 780 ± 50
1900 ± 40 b.c.	2020 ± 40	—	±110	(t) 2430 ± 120
		1970–2070	—	(n) 2200–2480

(t)—using trend curve; (n)—using 9-sample averages.

Table 2.3 shows examples of converting dates using both the trend curve (t) and the 9-sample averages (n). With the latter, the uncertainty in the conversion is introduced by adding 10 years to the measurement standard deviation; if the date limits in column (3) do encompass only single crossings, as in the first two examples, then the corrected date can be quoted in the usual form but if, as in the last example, multiple crossings (spans and ranges) are encompassed, then the corrected date has to be quoted in the form shown. The last two examples have been chosen to illustrate extreme cases and fortunately these are not the general rule.

The preferred method of conversion depends on the particular application. If the two methods give answers that are significantly different having regard to the problem concerned, then it should be accepted that too high an accuracy is being demanded of the method. Obviously this is more likely to be the case in a 'wriggly' period. Besides the uncertainty associated with conversion there are a number of other complicating effects relevant to the archaeological interpretation of radiocarbon dates that have been mentioned in the course of the chapter. Some of the more important points are reiterated here:

(i) the ± error quoted usually corresponds to a 68% probability that the true date lies within the date limits given by that error. For 95% probability the ± error should be doubled;

(ii) if the sample is of wood there is the possibility that the date of formation, which is the event dated by radiocarbon, is appreciably earlier than the archaeological context with which the sample is associated;

(iii) if the sample is of short-growth material there may be an error due to the possible 11-year concentration variations (section 2.6). This error may amount to $\pm$ 120 years but confirmatory research is in progress. This source of error can be removed by averaging a sufficient number of samples;

(iv) because of differing contamination risks, because of the possibility of out-of-context samples, and also because of (iii), it is desirable to base the dating of a cultural phase on as many different types of sample from as many different types of site as possible. 'One date is no date'.

The danger of too rigid an interpretation of single dates can be seen from Table 2.1 and Fig. 2.9; one could deduce for instance that Sesostris II and III of the 12th Dynasty preceeded Mentuhotep II of the 11th Dynasty by a couple of centuries. Consideration of the various complicating effects, and of the Egyptian results, suggests that ± 150 years is a realistic assessment of the level of accuracy that the method can achieve in practice.

Dating of floating tree-ring sequences

In special circumstances the short-term fluctuations can be utilized to give a more precise date than just quoted. This is when a large beam of wood provides a tree-ring sequence of a hundred years or more; the technique is to match the carbon-14 concentration fluctuations in this floating sequence with the pattern in the bristlecone pine sequence. In this way the Neolithic site of Auvernier has been dated to an accuracy of ± 50 years (Suess *and* Strahm, 1970); relevant statistical considerations have been discussed by Clark *and* Renfrew (1972), and by Clark *and* Sowray (1973). Besides use for dating, such measurements are valuable in establishing the worldwide reality of the short-term fluctuations (e.g. Mook, Munaut, *and* Waterbolk, 1972).

REFERENCES

ARNOLD, J. R. *and* LIBBY, W. F. (1949). Age determinations by radiocarbon content. Checks with samples of known age. *Science*, **110**, 678–80.

ANDERSON, E. C., LIBBY, W. F., WEINHOUSE, S., REID, A. F., KIRSCHENBAUM, A. D., *and* GROSSE, A. V. (1947). Radiocarbon from cosmic radiation. *Science*, **105**, 576.

BANNISTER, B. *and* DAMON, P. E. (1972). A dendrochronologically-derived primary standard for radiocarbon dating. *Proc. 8th Int. Conf. on Radiocarbon Dating* (eds. T. A. Rafter *and* T. Grant-Taylor). Published by Roy. Soc. New Zealand. pp. 676–85.

BARBETTI, M. (1972). Geomagnetic field behaviour between 25 000 and 35 000 years B.P. and its effect on atmospheric radiocarbon concentration. *Proc. 8th Int. Conf. on Radiocarbon Dating* (eds. T. A. Rafter and T. Grant-Taylor). Published by Roy. Soc. New Zealand. pp. 98–107.

BARKER, H., BURLEIGH, R., *and* MEEKS, N. (1969). British Museum natural radiocarbon measurements VI. *Radiocarbon*, **11**, 278–94.

BARKER, H., BURLEIGH, R., and MEEKS, N. (1971). British Museum natural radiocarbon measurements VII. *Radiocarbon*, **13**, 159–66.

BAXTER, M. S. *and* FARMER, J. G. (1973). Radiocarbon: Short-term variations. *Earth Planet. Sci. Lett.* **20**, 295–9.

BAXTER, M. S., FARMER, J. G., *and* WALTON, A. (1973). Comments on 'On the magnitude of the 11-year radiocarbon cycle by P. E. Damon, A. Long, and E. I. Wallick'. *Earth Planet. Sci. Lett.* **20**, 307–10.

BAXTER, M. S. *and* WALTON, A. (1970). A theoretical approach to the Suess effect. *Proc. R. Soc. Lond. A.* **318**, 213–30.

BAXTER, M. S. *and* WALTON, A. (1971). Fluctuations of atmospheric carbon-14 concentrations during the past century. *Proc. R. Soc. Lond. A.* **321**, 105–27.

BERGER, R. (1970). Ancient Egyptian radiocarbon chronology. *Phil. Trans. R. Soc. Lond. A.* **269**, 23–36.

BERGER, R. (1970a). Radiocarbon dating in the Middle Ages. In *Scientific Methods in Medieval Archaeology* (ed. R. Berger); pp. 89–140. University of California Press.

BERGER, R. (1972). Tree ring calibration of radiocarbon dates. *Proc. 8th Int. Conf. on Radiocarbon Dating* (eds. T. A. Rafter *and* T. Grant-Taylor). Published by Roy. Soc. New Zealand. pp. 91–7.

BERGER, R., HORNEY, A. G., *and* LIBBY, W. F. (1964). Radiocarbon dating of bone and shell from their organic components. *Science*, **144**, 999–1001.

BIEN, G. S., RAKESTRAW, N. W., *and* SUESS, H. E. (1963). Radiocarbon dating of the deep water of the Pacific and Indian Oceans. *Radioactive Dating*, pp. 105–18, I.A.E.A., Vienna.

BIEN, G. *and* SUESS, H. E. (1967). Transfer and exchange of ^{14}C between the atmosphere and the surface water of the Pacific Ocean. *Radioactive Dating and Methods of Low-level Counting*, pp. 105–14, I.A.E.A., Vienna.

BRANIGAN, K. (1972). Wessex and the Common Market. *Studi micenei ed egeo-anatolici*, **15**, 147–55.

BROECKER, W. S. *and* OLSSON, E. A. (1959). Lamont radiocarbon measurements. VI. *Radiocarbon*, **1**, 111–32.

CLARK, R. M. *and* RENFREW, C. (1972). A statistical approach to the calibration of floating tree-ring chronologies using radiocarbon dates. *Archaeometry*, **14**, 5–19.

CLARK, R. M. *and* RENFREW, C. (1973). Tree-ring calibration of radiocarbon dates and the chronology of ancient Egypt. *Nature*, **243**, 266–70.

CLARK, R. M. *and* SOWRAY, A. (1973). Further statistical methods for the calibration of floating tree-ring chronologies. *Archaeometry*, **15**, 255–66.

COWAN, C., ATLURI, C. R., *and* LIBBY, W. F. (1965). Possible anti-matter content of the Tunguska meteor of 1908. *Nature*, **206**, 861–65.

DAMON, P. E. (1968). Radiocarbon and climate. *Meteorological Monigraphs*, **8**, 151–4.

DAMON, P. E., LONG, A., *and* Wallick, E. I. (1972). Dendrochronology calibration of the carbon-14 time scale. *Proc. 8th Int. Conf. on Radiocarbon Dating* (eds. T. A. Rafter *and* T. Grant-Taylor), pp. 44–59. Published by Roy. Soc., New Zealand.

DAMON, P. E., LONG, A., *and* WALLICK, E. I. (1973). The magnitude of the 11 year radiocarbon cycle. *Earth Planet. Sci. Lett.* **20**, 300–6.

DAMON, P. E., LONG, A., *and* WALLICK, E. I. (1973a). Comments on "Radiocarbon- short-term variations" by M. S. Baxter and J. G. Farmer. *Earth Planet. Sci. Lett.* **20**, 311–14.

DEEVEY, E. S., GROSS, M. S., HUTCHINSON, G. E., *and* KRAYBILL, H. L. (1954). The natural C^{14} contents of materials from hard-water lakes. *Proc. nat. Acad. Sci., Washington*, **40**, 285–8.

ELSASSER, W., NEY, E. P., *and* WINCKLER, J. R. (1956). Cosmic ray intensity and geomagnetism. *Nature*, **178**, 1226–7.

FAIRHALL, A. W. *and* YOUNG, J. A. (1970). Radiocarbon in the environment. *Advances in Chemistry*, **93**, 401–18.

FAIRHILL, A. W., YOUNG, A. W., *and* BRADFORD, P. A. (1972). Radiocarbon in the sea. *Proc. 8th Int. Conf. on Radiocarbon Dating* (eds. T. A. Rafter *and* T. Grant-Taylor), pp. 226–40. Published by Roy. Soc., New Zealand.

FARMER, J. G. *and* BAXTER, M. S. (1972). Short term trends in natural radiocarbon. *Proc. 8th Int. Conf. on Radiocarbon Dating* (eds. T. A. Rafter *and* T. Grant-Taylor), pp. 74–85. Published by Roy. Soc., New Zealand.

FERGUSON, C. W. (1969). A 7104-year annual-tree-ring chronology for bristlecone pine, *Pinus aristata*, from the White Mountains, California. *Tree-Ring Bulletin*, **29**, 3–29.

FERGUSON, C. W. (1970). Dendrochronology of bristlecone pine, *Pinus aristata*. Establishment of a 7484-year chronology in the White Mountains of eastern-central California, U.S.A. *Radiocarbon Variations and Absolute Chronology*, ed. I. V. Olsson. (Almqvist and Wiksell, Stockholm). pp. 237–61.

FERGUSON, C. W. (1972). Dendrochronology of bristlecone pine prior to 4000 B.C. *Proc. 8th Int. Conf. on Radiocarbon dating* (edit. T. A. Rafter and T. Grant-Taylor), pp. 17–26. Published by Roy. Soc., New Zealand.

FLETCHER, J. M. (1970). Radiocarbon dating of Medieval timber-framed cruck cottages. In *Scientific Methods in Medieval Archaeology* (ed. R. Berger), pp. 141–158. Univ. of California Press.

GODWIN, H. (1960). Radiocarbon dating and Quarternary history in Britain. *Proc. R. Soc. Lond. B.* **153**, 287–320.

GRANT-TAYLOR, T. L. (1972). Conditions for the use of calcium carbonate as a dating material. *Proc. 8th Int. Conf. on Radiocarbon Dating* (edit. T. A. Rafter *and* T. Grant-Taylor), pp. 592–6. Published by Roy. Soc., New Zealand.

GREY, D. C. (1969). Geophysical mechanisms for C^{14} variations. *J. Geophys. Res.* **74**, 6333–40.

GREY, D. C., DAMON, P. E., HAYNES, C. V., *and* LONG, A. (1969). Carbon-isotope fractionation during wet oxidation of oxalic acid. *Radiocarbon*, **11**, 1–2.

GULLIKSEN, S. *and* NYDAL, R. (1972). Further calculations on the C-14 exchange between the ocean and the atmosphere. *Proc. 8th Internat. Conf. on Radiocarbon Dating* (eds. T. A. Rafter and T. Grant-Taylor), pp. 286–96. Published by Roy. Soc., New Zealand.

HARING, A., DE VRIES, A. E., *and* DE VRIES, H. (1958). Radiocarbon dating up to 70 000 years by isotopic enrichment. *Science*, **128**, 472–3.

HARKNESS, D. D. *and* BURLEIGH, R. (1974). Possible carbon-14 enrichment in high altitude wood. *Archaeometry*, **16**, 121–8.

HAYNES, C. V. (1967). Bone organic matter and radiocarbon dating. *Radioactive Dating and Methods of Low-level Counting*, pp. 163–68. I.A.E.A., Vienna.

HOOD, M. S. F. (1967). The Tartaria tablets. *Antiquity*, **41**, 99–113.

HOUTERMANS, J. (1966). On the quantitative relationships between geophysical parameters and the natural C^{14} inventory. *Zeitschrift für Physik*, **193**, 1–12.

HOUTERMANS, J., SUESS, H. E., and MUNK, W. (1967). Effect of industrial fuel combustion on the carbon-14 level of atmospheric CO_2. *Radioactive Dating and Methods of Low-level Counting*, pp. 37–68. I.A.E.A., Vienna.

HOUTERMANS, J. C., SUESS, H. E., and Oeschger, H. (1973). Reservoir models and production rate variations of natural radiocarbon. *J. geophys. Res.* **78**, 1897–908.

HUGHES, E. E. and MANN, W. B. (1964). The half-life of carbon-14: comments on the mass-spectrometric method. *Intern. J. Appl. Radiation Isotopes*, **15**, 97–100.

JANSEN, H. S. (1970). Secular variations of radiocarbon in New Zealand and Australian trees. *Radiocarbon Variations and Absolute Chronology* (ed. I. V. Olsson, pp. 261–74. Almqvist and Wiksell, Stockholm.

JEFFREYS, D., LARSON, D., and FRENCH, J. D. (1972). C^{14} dating with nuclear track emulsions, *Am. J. Phys.* **40**, 1400–3.

KING, J. W. (1973). Solar radiation changes and the weather. *Nature*, **245**, 443–6.

KULP, J. L. and VOLCHOK, H. L. (1953). Constancy of cosmic ray flux over the past 30 000 years. *Phys. Rev.* **90**, 713–14.

LERMAN, J. C., MOOK, W. G., and VOGEL, J. C. (1967). Effect of the Tunguska meteor and sunspots on radiocarbon in tree rings. *Nature*, **216**, 990–1.

LERMAN, J. C., MOOK, W. G., and VOGEL, J. C. (1970). C-14 in tree rings from different localities. *Radiocarbon Variations and Absolute Chronology* (ed. I. V. Olsson), pp. 275–302. Almqvist and Wiksell, Stockholm.

LIBBY, W. F. (1946). Atmospheric helium three and radiocarbon from cosmic radiation. *Phys. Rev.* **69**, 671–2.

LIBBY, W. F. (1955). *Radiocarbon Dating*, 2nd ed. University of Chicago Press, Chicago.

LIBBY, W. F. (1967). History of radiocarbon dating. *Radioactive Dating and Methods of Low-level Counting*, pp. 3–27. I.A.E.A, Vienna.

LIBBY, W. F. (1970). Ruminations on radiocarbon dating. *Radiocarbon Variations and Absolute Chronology* (ed. I. V. Olsson), pp. 629–41. Almqvist and Wiksell, Stockholm.

LIBBY, W. F. (1970a). Radiocarbon dating. *Phil. Trans. R. Soc. Lond. A.* **269**, 1–10.

LIBBY, W. F. (1972). Radiocarbon dating memories and hopes. *Proc. 8th Int. Conf. on Radiocarbon Dating* (eds. T. A. Rafter *and* T. Grant-Taylor), pp. xxvii–xliii. Published by Roy. Soc., New Zealand.

LIBBY, L. M. (1973). Globally stored organic carbon and radiocarbon dates. *J. geophys. Res.* **78**, 7667–70.

LIBBY, W. F., ANDERSON, E. C., *and* ARNOLD, J. R. (1949). Age determination by radiocarbon content: World-wide assay of natural radiocarbon. *Science*, **109**, 227–8.

LIBBY, L. M. *and* LUKENS, H. R. (1973). Radiocarbon dating: effect of lightning. *J. geophys. Res.* **78**, 5902–3.

LINGENFELTER, R. E. (1963). Production of carbon 14 by comic-ray neutrons. *Rev. Geophys.* **1**, 35–55.

LINGENFELTER, R. E. and RAMATY, R. (1970). Astrophysical and geophysical variations in C14 production. *Radiocarbon Variations and Absolute Chronology* (ed. I. V. Olsson), pp. 513–38. Almqvist and Wiksell, Stockholm.

LINICK, T. W. *and* SUESS, H. E. (1972). Bomb produced radiocarbon in the surface water of the Pacific ocean. *Proc. 8th Int. Conf. on Radiocarbon Dating* (eds. T. A. Rafter *and* T. Grant-Taylor), pp. 304–10. Published by Roy. Soc., New Zealand.

McKERRELL, H. (1972). On the origins of British faience beads and some aspects of the Wessex-Mycenae relationship. _Proc. prehist. Soc._ **38**, 286–301.

MICHAEL, H. N. _and_ RALPH, E. K. (1970). Correction factors applied to Egyptian radiocarbon dates from the era before Christ. _Radiocarbon Variations and Absolute Chronology_ (ed. I. V. Olsson), pp. 109–28. Almqvist and Wiksell, Stockholm.

MILOJČIĆ, V. (1957). Zur Anwendbarkeit der C14-Datierung in der Vorgeschichsforschung. _Germania_, **35**, 102–110.

MILOJČIĆ, V. (1958). Zur Anwendbarkeit der C14-Datierung in der Vorgeschichsforschung. _Germania_, **36**, 409–417.

MILOJČIĆ, V. (1961). Zur Anwendbarkeit der C14-Datierung in der Vorgeschichsforschung. _Germania_, **39**, 434–53.

MILOJČIĆ, V. (1967). 'Die absolute Chronologie der Jungsteinzeit in Südosteuropa und die Ergebnisse der Radiocarbon', published in _Jahrbuch des Romisch-Germanischen Zentralmuseums Mainz_, **14**, 9–37.

MOOK, W. G., MUNAUT, A. V., _and_ WATERBOLK, H. T. (1972). Determination of age and duration of stratified prehistoric bog settlements. _Proc. 8th Int. Conf. on Radiocarbon Dating_ (eds. T. A. Rafter _and_ T. Grant-Taylor), pp. 491–503. Published by Roy. Soc., New Zealand.

MUNNICH, K. O. _and_ ROETHER, W. (1967). Transfer of bomb ^{14}C and tritium from the atmosphere to the ocean. _Radioactive Dating and Methods of Low-level Counting_, pp. 93–104. I.A.E.A., Vienna.

NEUSTUPNY, E. (1968). Absolute chronology of the Neolithic and Aeneolithic periods in central and south-eastern Europe. _Slovenka Archeologia_, **16**, 19–56.

NEUSTUPNY, E. (1969). Absolute chronology of the Neolithic and Aeneolithic periods in central and south-east Europe. _Archeologicke Rozhledy_, **21**, 783–810.

NYDAL, R. (1967). On the transfer of radiocarbon in nature. _Radioactive Dating and Methods of Low-level Counting_, pp. 119–28. I.A.E.A., Vienna.

OESCHGER, H., HOUTERMANS, J., LOOSLI, H., _and_ WAHLEN, M. (1970). _Radiocarbon Variations and Absolute Chronology_ (ed. I. V. Olsson), pp. 471–500. Almqvist and Wiksell, Stockholm.

OESCHGER, H., STAUFFER, B., BUCHER, P., FROMMER, H., MOLL, M., LANGWAY, C. C., HANSEN, B. L., _and_ CLAUSEN, H. (1972). C-14 and other isotope studies on natural ice. _Proc. 8th Int. Conf. on Radiocarbon Dating_ (eds. T. A. Rafter _and_ T. Grant-Taylor), pp. 381–9. Published by Roy. Soc., New Zealand.

OTTOWAY, B. (1973). Dispersion diagrams: A new approach to the display of carbon-14 dates. _Archaeometry_, **15**, 1–5.

POLACH, H. A. (1969). Optimization of liquid scintillation radiocarbon age determinations and reporting of ages. _Atomic Energy in Australia_, **12**, 21–8.

POLACH, H. A. (1972). Cross checking of NBS oxalic acid and secondary laboratory radiocarbon dating standard. _Proc. 8th Int. Conf. on Radiacarbon Dating_ (eds. T. A. Rafter _and_ T. Grant-Taylor), pp. 688–717. Published by Roy. Soc., New Zealand.

POLACH, H. A., KRUEGER, H. A., BANNISTER, B., DAMON, P. E., _and_ RAFTER, T. A. (1972). Correlation of C14 activity of NBS oxalic with Arizona-1850 wood and ANU-sucrose radiocarbon dating standards. _Proc. 8th Int. Conf. on Radiocarbon Dating_ (eds. T. A. Rafter _and_ T. Grant-Taylor), pp. 686–7. Published by Roy. Soc., New Zealand.

RAFTER, T. A. _and_ O'BRIEN, B. J. (1972). Recalculation of the exchange rates between the atmosphere and the ocean. _Proc. 8th Int. Conf. on Radiocarbon Dating_ (eds. T. A. Rafter _and_ T. Grant-Taylor), pp. 251–66. Published by Roy. Soc., New Zealand.

RALPH, E. K. (1971). Carbon-14 dating. In *Dating Techniques for the Archaeologist* (eds. H. N. Michael *and* E. K. Ralph), pp. 1–48. MIT Press, Cambridge, Massachusetts.

RALPH, E. K., MICHAEL, H. N., *and* HAN, M. C. (1973). Radiocarbon dates and reality. *MASCA Newsletter*, **9**, 1–18.

RAMATY, R. (1967). The influence of geomagnetic shielding on C14 production and content. In *Magnetism and the Cosmos* (ed. S. K. Runcorn), pp. 66–78. Oliver and Boyd, Edinburgh.

RENFREW, C. (1968). Wessex without Mycenae. *Ann. Br. Schl. Archaeol., Athens*, **63**, 277–85.

RENFREW, C. (1969). The autonomy of the south-east European Copper Age. *Proc. prehist. Soc.* **35**, 12–47.

RENFREW, C. (1970). New configurations in Old World archaeology. *Wld. Archaeol.* **2**, 199–211.

RENFREW, C. (1971). Sitagroi, radiocarbon and the prehistory of south-east Europe. *Antiquity*, **45**, 275–282.

RENFREW, A. C. (1973). *Before Civilization: the Radiocarbon Revolution and Prehistoric Europe.* Jonathan Cape, London.

RENFREW, A. C. *and* CLARK, R. M. (1974). Problems of the radiocarbon calendar and its calibration. *Archaeometry*, **16**, 5–18.

REVELLE, R. *and* SUESS, H. E. (1957). Carbon-dioxide exchange between atmosphere and ocean, and the question of an increase of atmospheric CO_2 during the past decades. *Tellus*, **9**, 18–27.

SAVE-SODERBURGH, T. *and* OLSSON, I. V. (1970). C14 dating and Egyptian chronology. *Radiocarbon Variations and Absolute Chronology* (ed. I. V. Olsson), pp. 35–55. Almqvist and Wiksell, Stockholm).

SCHELL, W. R., FAIRHALL, A. W., *and* HARP, G. D. (1967). An analytical model of carbon-14 in the atmosphere. *Radioactive Dating and Methods of Low-level Counting*, pp. 79–91. I.A.E.A., Vienna.

Schove, D. J. (1955). The sunspot cycle 649 B.C. to A.D. 2000. *J. geophys. Res.* **60**, 127–45.

SCHAEFFER, O. A., DAVIS, R., STOENNER, R. W., and HEYMANN, D. (1963). The temporal and spatial variation in cosmic rays. *Proc. Int. Conf. Cosmic Rays, Jaipur, India*, **3**, 480–9.

SHOTTON, F. W. (1972). An example of hard-water error in radiocarbon dating of vegetable matter. *Nature*, **240**, 460–1.

SMITH, A. G., BAILLIE, M. G. L., HILLAM, J., PILCHER, J. R., *and* PEARSON, G. W. (1972). Dendrochronological work in progress in Belfast. *Proc. 8th Int. Conf. on Radiocarbon Dating* (eds. T. A. Rafter *and* T. Grant-Taylor), pp. 104–8.

STUIVER, M. (1961). Variations in Radiocarbon concentration and sunspot activity. *J. geophys. Res.* **66**, 273–6.

STUIVER, M. (1970). Long-term C14 variations. *Radiocarbon variations and Absolute Chronology* (ed. I. V. Olsson), pp. 197–214. Almqvist and Wiksell, Stockholm.

SUESS, H. E. (1955). Radiocarbon concentration in modern wood. *Science*, **122**, 415–17.

SUESS, H. E. (1965). Secular variations of the cosmic-ray-produced carbon-14 in the atmosphere. *J. geophys. Res.* **70**, 5937–52.

SUESS, H. E. (1968). Climatic changes, solar activity, and the cosmic-ray production rate of the natural radiocarbon. *Meteorological Monographs*, **8**, 146–50.

SUESS, H. E. (1970). Bristlecone pine calibration of the radiocarbon time-scale 5200 B.C. to the present. *Radiocarbon Variations and Absolute Chronology* (ed. I. V. Olsson), pp. 303–13. Almqvist and Wiksell, Stockholm.

SUESS, H. E. and STRAHM, C. (1970). The neolithic of Auvernier, Switzerland. *Antiquity*, **44**, 91–9.

SWITZUR, V. R. (1973). The radiocarbon calendar recalibrated. *Antiquity*, **47**, 131–7.

TAUBER, H. (1970). The Scandinavian varve chronology and C14 dating. *Radiocarbon Variations and Absolute Chronology* (ed. I. V. Olsson), pp. 173–96. Almqvist and Wiksell, Stockholm.

VOGEL, J. C. (1972). Radiocarbon in the surface waters of the Atlantic Ocean. *Proc. 8th Int. Conf. on Radiocarbon Dating* (eds. T. A. Rafter and T. Grant-Taylor), pp. 267–79. Published by Roy Soc., New Zealand.

VRIES, H. DE (1958). Variation in concentration of radiocarbon with time and location on earth. *Koninkl. Nederlandse Akad. Wetensch. Proc. ser B*. **61**, 1–9.

WALTON, A., BAXTER, M. S., CALLOW, W. J., and BAKER, M. J. (1967). *Radioactive Dating and Methods of Low-level Counting*, pp. 49–55. I.A.E.A., Vienna.

WENDLAND, W. M. and DONLEY, D. L. (1971). Radiocarbon-Calendar Age relationship. *Earth Planet. Sci. Lett.* **11**, 135–9.

WHIPP, D. and HOOD, M. S. F. (1972). The Tartaria tablets. *Antiquity*, **43**, 147–9.

WILLIS, E. H., TAUBER, H., and MUNNICH, K. O. (1960). Variations in the atmospheric radiocarbon concentration over the past 1300 years. *Radiocarbon*, **2**, 1–4.

WINTER, J. (1972). Radiocarbon dating by thermoluminescent dosimetry. *Archaeometry*, **14**, 281–6.

WOLLIN, G., ERICSON, D. B., RYAN, W. B. F., and FOSTER, J. H. (1971). Magnetism of the earth and climatic changes. *Earth Planet. Sci. Lett.* **12**, 175–83.

YANG, A. E. C. and FAIRHALL, A. W. (1972). Variations of natural radiocarbon during the last 11 millennia and geophysical mechanisms for producing them. *Proc. 8th Int. Conf. on Radiocarbon Dating* (eds. T. A. Rafter and T. Grant-Taylor), pp. 60–73. Published by Roy. Soc., New Zealand.

ZIMMERMAN, D. W. and HUXTABLE, J. (1971). Thermoluminescent dating of Upper Paleolithic fired clay from Dolni Vestonice. *Archaeometry*, **13**, 53–8.

3 Thermoluminescent dating

3.1. Introduction

CONTRARY to the situation with radiocarbon, the thermoluminescent (TL) signal increases with age of sample, as is illustrated in Fig. 3.1. Other important differences are that the relevant radioisotopes are long-lived natural impurities in clay and soil, and that any effect due to variation of cosmic-ray intensity is insignificant.

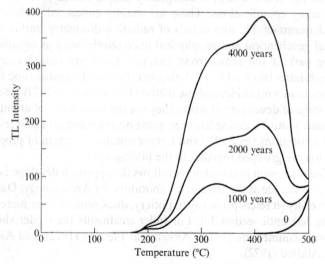

FIG. 3.1. Growth of TL with age: glow curves that would have been observed with a sample taken from a pottery fragment at various lengths of time after firing by ancient man from raw clay. Existing TL in the raw clay is removed by this firing, so that at $t = 0$ only red-hot glow would have been observed.

It is convenient to discuss the method in terms of the *age relation* which in its simplest form is

$$\text{age} = \frac{\text{natural TL}}{(\text{TL per unit dose}) \times (\text{dose per year})} \qquad (3.1)$$

Natural TL refers to the first glow curve measured from the sample and for the present 'TL' is to be taken as referring to the level at a glow-curve temperature of around 400°C.

TL per unit dose is the sensitivity (or susceptibility) of the sample for acquiring TL; it is measured by exposing the sample to a known dose of nuclear radiation from an artificial radioisotope source and then noting the level of TL in the resultant glow curve, referred to as the 'artificial TL'.

Dose per year is evaluated from radioactive and chemical analysis of the uranium, thorium, and potassium contents of the sample and its surrounding soil; the *dose*† is the amount of energy absorbed from the nuclear radiation per unit weight of sample.

The age relation (3.1) is deceptively simple and in practice there are many complications. These are mainly concerned with actual mechanisms of TL, and details of radiation dosimetry, rather than wider geochemical and geophysical uncertainties such as occupied a large part of the radiocarbon chapter. There are indeed external uncertainties involved in TL dating but these are immediate and local rather than worldwide, and the method has not yet (in 1973) reached the stage of development where they are the main focus of attention. Research into TL dating has been going on at a number of universities and institutions since 1960 and a representative selection of progress reports are grouped together in the bibliography.

The discussion in this chapter follows the approach developed over the past decade at the Research Laboratory for Archaeology, Oxford University; it refers primarily to pottery, discussion of other materials being left until section 3.9. For fuller treatments the reader should consult Zimmerman (1971), Aitken *and* Fleming (1972), and Aitken *and* Alldred (1972).

---

† The unit of measurement is the rad (Radiation Absorbed Dose) which is defined as the absorption of 100 ergs per gram; the more familiar *roentgen* is the unit of radiation exposure. In air exposed to 1 *roentgen* of X-rays the absorbed dose is approximately 0·87 rad.

3.2. Thermoluminescence

There are three constituent processes:

(i) *The absorption of energy from nuclear radiation.* This occurs because in passing through matter nuclear radiation gives rise to ionization—the detachment of electrons from their parent atoms. The amount of ionization depends both on the chemical constitution of the sample and on the type of radiation: the ionization produced by an alpha particle per unit length of track is about 100 times that for a beta particle and 10 000 times that for a gamma ray.

(ii) *The storage of some of the absorbed energy.* Most of the ionized electrons recombine with parent atoms, but a small proportion are

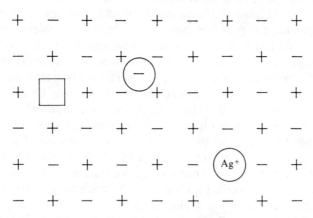

FIG. 3.2. Simple types of defect in lattice structure of ionic crystal. From left to right: negative-ion vacancy, negative-ion interstitial, substitutional impurity centre.

trapped at defects in the crystal lattice structure. An electron in a 'trap' is in a higher energy state than when recombined and consequently such trapping represents storage of energy. There are many types of defect which can act as traps, of which the simplest to understand is a negative-ion vacancy—the local deficit of negative charge attracts and traps an ionized electron if it diffuses into the vicinity. There are several causes for the presence of defects in the lattice—e.g. impurity atoms, rapid cooling from the molten state, and damage caused by nuclear radiation.

(iii) *The release of the stored energy, some of it as light*. If the temperature of the sample is raised, the amplitude of vibration of the crystal lattice increases and this allows escape of electrons from traps. Some of these reach luminescent centres and in the process of combining into the atom or ion forming the centre, photons of visible light are emitted. Luminescent centres are a particular type of defect and are usually due to impurities—Ag^+ or Mn^{++} for instance. The colour spectrum of the emitted photons is characteristic of the impurity— blue/violet for silver, and green for manganese. The spectrum is broad, 1000–2000 Å in width.

The types of trap and centre responsible for the TL in an archaeological sample are rarely known, and even with pure substances containing known impurities identification is difficult. Consequently the energy-level representation used in Fig. 3.3 is of great utility in discussing TL. The trap is characterized by the energy E, which the electron must acquire from the lattice vibrations in order to escape, and the frequency factor s, which can be regarded as the number of times per second the electron attempts to escape. Implicit in the diagram is the concept of the 'hole'; an atom from which an electron has been detached can be said to be charged with a hole. By gaining an electron from a neighbouring atom the hole can be passed on, and it is convenient to regard it as a carrier of positive charge. Ionization can be thought of as the formation of electrons and holes, and luminescence as the recombination of electrons and holes at a luminescent centre; if the recombination occurs at a non-luminescent centre (sometimes called a 'killer' centre) there is no emission of light and the excess energy is dissipated as heat. Holes can be trapped in a similar manner to electrons and rôles are then reversed; however for most discussions it is simpler to presume that electrons are the carriers.

The processes described above are possible in solids which are insulators or semi-conductors, but not in metals. Despite the absence of a lattice-structure, glass can carry TL.

Non-radiation-induced TL

Trapped electrons can be produced by agencies other than nuclear radiation, e.g. by pressure (*piezo*-TL), friction (*tribo*-TL), by light (*photo*-TL). In the context of archaeological dating it is convenient to regard radiation-induced TL as 'true TL', and other types as 'spurious TL'. Although the mechanisms responsible are not at all

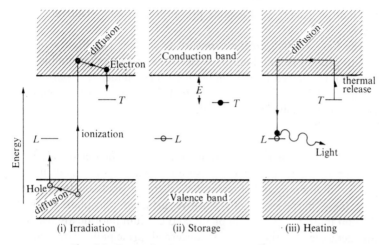

FIG. 3.3. Energy-level representation of TL process.

(i) The effect of ionizing radiation is to detach an electron from its parent atom or ion so that it is free to diffuse about the crystal (i.e. it is in the conduction band) until trapped at a defect T. The 'hole' left in the valence band diffuses similarly until it is trapped at the centre L.

(ii) The lifetime of the electron in the trap depends on the depth E below the conduction band. There is usually a range of different trap depths and for dating purposes we are interested in those deep enough ($\sim 1\frac{1}{2}$ electronvolts or more) for the lifetime to be of the order of a million years.

(iii) If the sample is heated there is a certain temperature at which thermal vibration of the crystal lattice is sufficient to allow the electron to escape from the trap. After diffusing about in the conduction band it may be attracted to the luminescent centre L and if so visible light is emitted in the process of combining into that centre (and thereby annihilating with the hole); the wavelength of the light is determined by the atom or ion forming the centre, not by the depth of L below the conduction band. Alternatively the electron may recombine at a non-luminescent centre (a 'killer' centre) or be captured by a deeper trap.

well understood, techniques have been developed for adequate suppression of spurious TL and this is an extremely important requirement in measurement (Aitken, Fleming, Reid, *and* Tite, 1968; Fleming 1968; Göksu *and* Fremlin, 1972).

Trapped electrons can be released by other means than heat. Release by light is referred to as *photo*luminescence, and before measurement of TL it is important to avoid too much exposure to light because of risk of 'bleaching' (or alternatively of photo-TL); blue and violet light is more effective than red, and having discarded the surface layer of a pottery fragment sample preparation in subdued red light is usually an adequate precaution (Aitken, Tite, *and* Reid, 1963).

The light emitted during exposure to nuclear radiation, which is due to prompt recombination of electrons and holes (at luminescent centres), is referred to as *radio*luminescence. Similarly *chemi*luminescence and *bio*luminescence refer to light emitted in the course of chemical and biological processes.

TL dosimetry

The most widespread utilization of the phenomenon of TL is in measuring the accumulated exposure to radiation of patients undergoing radiotherapy and of research workers subject to nuclear hazard. For these purposes, highly-sensitive artificial phosphors such as lithium fluoride, calcium sulphate, and calcium fluoride are used. In archaeological dating we are concerned principally with natural minerals but as we shall see in section 3.4 the techniques of TL dosimetry are a convenient adjunct for measuring the dose-rate experienced by samples.

3.3. Measurement

Although the TL exhibited by some geological specimens can be seen with the naked eye, the level of the TL emitted by ancient pottery is very faint. Not only is a highly sensitive photomultipler† required in order to detect it, but it is important also to discriminate against thermal radiation (i.e. 'red-hot glow' or incandescence) from the sample by means of carefully-selected colour filters, and to suppress any spurious TL. In the early development of TL dating the radiation-induced TL from a sample was sometimes completely swamped by spurious TL that had been induced in the process of grinding up the sample for measurement, and the technique might well have been abandoned had it not been for the fortunate discovery that this spurious TL could be suppressed by making the measurement in an atmosphere of oxygen-free nitrogen. Other inert gases, such as argon and carbon dioxide, are equally efficacious—as long as the oxygen and moisture contents are below a few parts per million.

A block diagram of suitable apparatus for measurement is given in Fig. 3.4. The sample, directly in powder form or deposited on a thin aluminium disc, is placed on a nichrome strip that can be heated

† e.g. Type 9635 from E.M.I. Hayes, Middlesex, England.

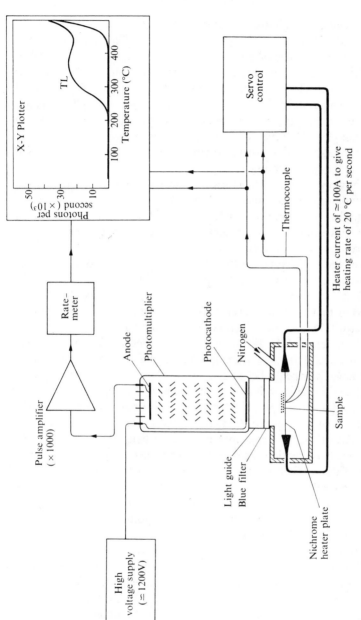

Fig. 3.4. Apparatus for TL dating measurements.

electrically. The photons emitted as the temperature is raised are detected with a photomultiplier. The output of the photomultiplier is fed to the Y-axis of a co-ordinate plotter, the X-axis of which is driven by a thermocouple that measures the temperature of the nichrome strip. Hence the plotter draws out a glow-curve of light emitted *versus* temperature. The light emitted consists not only of TL but also, as the temperature approaches 500°C, an appreciable component of red-hot glow. However, on a second heating of the same sample there is only red-hot glow because the trapped electrons were all released during the first heating.

The glow curve shown in Figs. 3.1 and 3.4 are typical of the TL from a sample taken from ancient pottery. For traps of a given type and depth the glow curve is a single peak of width about 50°C. (The peak is narrow because once the temperature becomes sufficient to cause appreciable release of electrons, a further slight increase in temperature causes the rate of release to become very rapid indeed; the slower the heating the narrower is the peak.) Since the glow curve shown is evidently composed of a number of overlapping peaks, it is to be inferred that there are several types of trap present in the sample, either within the same mineral or in several different minerals.

The absence of TL below about 250°C does not necessarily imply the absence of traps which empty in that temperature region; traps that have their peaks below 250° are shallow, and consequently they will have suffered serious loss of electrons during the centuries of burial. For dating purposes it is only traps that have accumulated electrons without leakage that are of interest; this usually means traps that have their TL peaks at a glow-curve temperature of 350°C or more, and as mentioned earlier it is to be taken for granted in discussion of dating that it is this 'stable' region of the glow curve that is being considered.

The foregoing remarks are illustrated in Fig. 3.5. This shows typical natural and artificial glow-curves, together with a plot of the ratio of natural TL to artificial TL as a function of glow-curve temperature. This ratio rises from zero below 200°C, to a plateau beginning around 350°C as the traps become deep enough for negligible leakage during centuries of burial, i.e. the plateau identifies the stable region of the glow curve that is to be used for dating. The actual value of the ratio in this region leads to a convenient way of expressing the level of the natural TL; for example if the ratio is 0·7 and the artificial dose 1000 rads, then the *Equivalent Dose* (*ED*) is

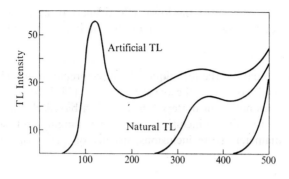

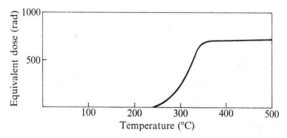

Temperature (°C)

FIG. 3.5. The plateau test. The upper part shows the glow-curves corresponding to the natural TL and to the artificial TL following 1000 rads of beta irradiation. The lower part shows the *Equivalent Dose*, which here is taken to be equal to $\left(\dfrac{\text{Natural TL}}{\text{Artificial TL}} \times 1000 \text{ rads}\right)$, as a function of temperature. The onset of the plateau is indicative that a sufficiently high glow-curve temperature has been reached for the TL to be associated with traps that are deep enough to retain their electrons with negligible leakage during archaeological times. The onset of the plateau is usually around 350°C.

700 rads. For the moment let us assume that this is the same as the *Archaeological Dose* (*AD*) so that

$$AD = ED = \frac{\text{natural TL}}{\text{TL per rad}}. \tag{3.2}$$

In this terminology eqn (3.1) may be rewritten as

$$\text{Age} = \frac{AD}{\text{rads per year}}. \tag{3.3}$$

In practice *AD* is different to *ED* because of the *supralinearity* and *pre-dose* effects discussed in section 3.7; another complication in evaluating TL per rad is the lower effectiveness of alpha particles, relative to beta particles and gamma radiation in inducing TL.

Sample preparation

For accurate dating, the technique of sample preparation is intrinsic to the principles on which the age is calculated. This is because of the heterogeneous nature of pottery fabric—it is a baked clay matrix in which there are mineral inclusions, sometimes ranging up to a milli-metre in diameter; these inclusions, usually of quartz or feldspar,

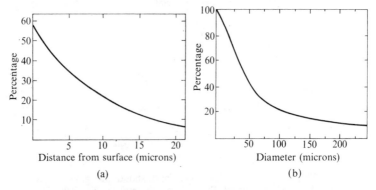

(a)   (b)

Fig. 3.6. (a) Alpha dose in interior of 100-micron diameter quartz grain embedded in clay matrix having equal uranium and thorium activities (from Fleming 1969). The dose is expressed as a percentage of that which would be experienced by a grain small enough for attenuation effects to be negligible (i.e. of diameter less than a few microns). (b) Average alpha dose versus diameter for quartz grains embedded in matrix as above (from Fleming 1969).

were either present in the raw clay or were added by the potter in order to improve refractory qualities. The TL sensitivity of these inclusions is much higher than that of the clay matrix but in general the radioactive impurities are carried in the latter. The average range of the alpha particles from uranium and thorium, which provide a substantial part of the total radiation dosage, is only about 25 microns and as a consequence the dose at a point in the interior of an inclusion falls off rapidly with distance from the surface; (see Fig. 3.6(a)); thus the average dose received by the whole inclusion decreases with size once the diameter exceeds a few microns (see Fig. 3.6(b)). Since the grain-size distribution varies between fragments of different pottery, for accurate results it is necessary to separate out grains of a given size range and to use these for measurement of TL both natural and artificial.

In the *fine-grain technique*, the material extracted consists of matrix and inclusion grains that are small enough for the attenuation of the alpha dosage to be negligible. In the *quartz inclusion technique*, the grains selected are large enough for there to be severe attenuation of the alpha dosage, though not so large that there is significant attenuation of the beta dosage; by etching these grains in hydrofluoric acid the outer skin that has received alpha dosage is removed and in evaluating the rads per year for insertion in eq. (3.3) only the contribution from beta and gamma radiation is included. The preferred technique in a given case depends on the characteristics of the pottery, both with respect to TL and to radioactivity. Ideally both techniques are used on each pottery specimen and since there is a differing degree of dependence on various factors (potassium content, abnormal fading, environmental dose-rate) agreement of the calculated ages gives added confidence in reliability; there is also the possibility of subtraction dating in which dependence on environmental dose-rate is eliminated (see section 3.4). These two techniques were developed from consideration of the radiation microdosimetry of the situation with the expectation that the dates obtained would be correct on an absolute basis, without adjustment by any calibrating factor determined using pottery of known age; this expectation has been largely substantiated by tests with known-age pottery (see Table 3.7). Notes on these two techniques are given below, and also on several other preparation techniques. In general these latter do not give absolute dates and require calibration by means of known age pottery.

The fine-grain technique (Zimmerman, 1971). The pottery fragment is crushed by slowly squeezing in a vice; grains in the size range 1 to 8 microns are separated by suspending in acetone and utilizing the fact that the settling time is determined by the diameter. After separation, the selected grains are re-suspended in acetone and deposited on aluminium discs (usually 10 mm diameter and 0·5 mm thick) in a thin layer of a few microns thick. About a dozen such discs are prepared; each carries a few milligrams of sample and has a TL reproducibility of about ±5%. Such discs are a convenient way of handling the sample for measurement (the disc as a whole being placed on the heater plate) and are remarkably robust—although the powder can be removed by wiping, there is not usually any loss on dropping. The alpha particle attenuation considerations mentioned above make it important to avoid breaking down larger grains into fine ones when crushing the fragment in the vice. It may be noted incidentally that before crushing, the outer one or two millimetres of the fragment are removed with a diamond-wheel saw, and that subsequent to this all operations are carried out in subdued red light to avoid the risks of 'bleaching' of the natural TL and acquisition of light-induced TL (photo-TL).

The quartz inclusion technique (Fleming, 1970). Large crystalline inclusions are obtained from the crushed fragment by sieving and by the mineralogical technique of magnetic separation. Weighed amounts of these (typically 5 to 10 mg) then form the samples on which the TL measurements are made, these being placed directly on the heater plate. It is desirable to restrict the grain size of the inclusions utilized to the range 90 to 105 microns and this is possible as long as they are abundant (which may not be the case in fine pottery). After separation from the matrix the inclusions are treated with hydrofluoric acid thereby removing minerals other than quartz—mainly feldspar—and at the same time etching away the surface of the quartz grains. This not only removes the alpha-irradiated skin but also improves the TL characteristics—the outer layer contributes a glow-curve that is more complex than that due to pure quartz, possibly because of diffusion in of impurities from the clay matrix.

The feldspar inclusion technique (Mejdahl, 1969, 1972, 1972a). In this the grains used are in the size range 0·3–0·5 mm and they are separated from the clay matrix by sifting. After washing with dilute hydrochloric acid and dilute hydrofluoric acid, magnetic grains are removed with a magnet. If necessary the samples are suspended in a mixture of bromoform and acetone adjusted so that grains with a density lower than that of quartz and feldspar can be removed. The grains are large enough for the alpha particle contribution to the TL to be negligible and etching away of the surface layer is not necessary. It is to be expected that there will be significant attenuation of the beta dose, particularly in the larger grains—unless the beta dose is predominantly from impurities within the grains themselves, as is the case for potassium feldspars. Although quartz is present in the grains measured, because its TL sensitivity is an order of magnitude lower than feldspar the light observed is predominantly from the latter.

Radioactive inclusion dating (Zimmerman, 1971a). Grains of uranium-rich minerals such as zircon and apatite are separated by using heavy liquids (e.g. bromoform and acetone, as above). The TL from these grains is predominantly due to alpha particles and by careful evaluation of the microdosimetry absolute ages can be obtained. Because the alpha dosage is so high the gamma dose makes a negligible contribution and consequently there is immunity from environmental influences.

The 'whole-grain' technique. This is a convenient way of describing a preliminary measurement in which the pottery fragment is crushed in an agate mortar and a sample of this powder transferred to the glow-plate without separation of minerals or grain sizes. The equivalent dose (ED) determined with such a sample is not usually less than half that obtained using the fine-grain technique.

The silk-screen silicone oil technique (Ralph *and* Han, 1969). The pottery fragment is ground to less than 75 microns in a ball mill and after mixing with silicone oil it is applied to a carrier of aluminium foil by means of a silk screen. The use of silicone oil has the incidental advantage of helping to suppress spurious TL. The method is calibrated by means of known-age pottery and relies on similarity of inclusion grain-size distributions to avoid error due to varying degrees of alpha dose attenuation.

Sampling by drilling (Fleming, 1971). This is the routine method used in authenticity testing of works of art. A small hole is made with a $\frac{1}{16}$ inch tungsten carbide drill and the resultant 20 or 30 milligrams of powder collected. This is then either put directly on the glow-plate or deposited on aluminium discs from acetone suspension as in the fine-grain method. Because the drill tends to avoid breaking up inclusions the latter procedure is preferred since the equivalent dose obtained is then not much less than if the fine grains are obtained by the standard vicing technique.

The slice technique (Göksu *and* Fremlin, 1972). This was developed primarily for flint but is applicable also to other hard materials. The initial slice is cut to a thickness of about 0·7 mm with a diamond wheel; it is then ground down to about 0·3 mm using fine aluminia powder and water on plate glass and finally polished with diamond dust. Because the surface area for a given weight of sample is very much less than if it is ground up, the spurious TL is minimized and also the 'regenerative' TL that has been observed to occur with flint—the slow growth with time of spurious TL in a stored sample.

Washing. Some samples exhibit spurious TL even though the inert gas used as atmosphere during measurement is pure. This may be particularly marked with samples from some limestone regions and it is sometimes advantageous to wash the crushed sample in dilute acid in addition to routine soaking of the fragment in distilled water prior to crushing. In other cases washing in hydrogen peroxide or in domestic water-softener (e.g. 'calgon'—sodium hexametaphosphate) may help. The presence of spurious TL in the natural glow-curve shows itself by destroying the plateau (see Fig. 3.5); with some types it appears in the second glow curve (the 're-run') of an already-glowed sample.

3.4. Sample radioactivity

The preceding section was concerned with evaluation of the TL carried by the sample. We now turn to the *rads per year*, *D*, responsible for inducing the TL. In Table 3.1 some details are given of the radioactive decay of the radioelements concerned—thorium-232, uranium-238, and potassium-40 (present to 0·012% in natural potassium); in addition there is also a small contribution from uranium-235 (present to 0·72% in natural uranium). Only the features of the decay chains that will come up in later discussion have been included in Table 3.1 a dashed arrow indicates the omission of intervening decay products, the number of alpha and beta particles emitted being given alongside.

Alpha activity

The typical levels of uranium and thorium in pottery are 3 and 12 ppm respectively, giving an alpha activity of about 2 picocuries per gram. This can be measured with the following simple technique (Turner, Radley, *and* Mayneord, 1958; Cherry 1964). A layer of powdered sample a few millimetres thick is spread in direct contact with a 42 mm diameter scintillation screen formed by sprinkling zinc sulphide† onto Sellotape; this screen is placed on top of a photomultiplier which detects the scintillations that the alpha particles produce in the zinc sulphide. Typical pottery gives a count rate of about 1000 per day whereas the background is only about 10 per day.

---

† E.g. nickel-killed silver-activated ZnS such as G345 from Levy West, Bush Fair, Harlow, Essex, England.

TABLE 3.1

Radioactive decay schemes of thorium, uranium, and potassium
(Abbreviations: yr—year, d—day, m—minute, s—second)

Thorium series		Uranium/radium series		Uranium/actinium series (natural abundance 0·72%)		Potassium-40 (natural abundance 0·012%)
Nuclide	Half-life	Nuclide	Half-life	Nuclide	Half-life	
thorium-232	14·1 × 10⁹ yr	uranium-238	4·51 × 10⁹ yr	uranium-235	0·713 × 10⁹ yr	potassium-40 (half-life: 1·3 × 10⁹ yr)

Thorium series:

thorium-232 (14·1 × 10⁹ yr) $\xrightarrow{2\alpha,\ 2\beta}$ radium-224 (3·64 d) $\xrightarrow{1\alpha}$ radon-220 (*thoron*) (55s) $\xrightarrow{1\alpha}$ polonium-216 (0·16 s) $\xrightarrow{2\alpha,\ 2\beta}$ lead-208 (stable)

Uranium/radium series:

uranium-238 (4·51 × 10⁹ yr) $\xrightarrow{1\alpha,\ 2\beta}$ uranium-234 (250 × 10³ yr) $\xrightarrow{1\alpha}$ thorium-230 (*ionium*) (75·2 × 10³ yr) $\xrightarrow{1\alpha}$ radium-226 (1620 yr) $\xrightarrow{1\alpha}$ radon-222 (3·83 d) $\xrightarrow{3\alpha,\ 2\beta}$ lead-210 (22 yr) $\xrightarrow{2\beta}$ polonium-210 (138 d) $\xrightarrow{1\alpha}$ lead-206 (stable)

Uranium/actinium series (natural abundance 0·72%):

uranium-235 (0·713 × 10⁹ yr) $\xrightarrow{1\alpha,\ 1\beta}$ protactinium-231 (32·4 × 10³ yr) $\xrightarrow{2\alpha,\ 1\beta}$ radium-223 (11·1 d) $\xrightarrow{1\alpha}$ radon-219 (*actinon*) (3·9 s) $\xrightarrow{1\alpha}$ polonium-215 (1·8 × 10⁻³ s) $\xrightarrow{2\alpha,\ 2\beta}$ lead-207 (stable)

Potassium-40 (natural abundance 0·012%):

potassium-40 (half-life: 1·3 × 10⁹ yr)
- 11% γ(1·46 MeV) → argon-40 (stable)
- 89% β(1·36 MeV) → calcium-40 (stable)

Such a low level of background is possible because the associated electronic circuitry is arranged so that only the large scintillation pulses due to alpha particles are counted; no shielding against alpha particles is required because of their short range and the background is due only to radioactive impurities in the zinc sulphide and the Sellotape.

Knowing the energy release per particle from nuclear data tables (e.g. Lederer, Hollander, *and* Perlman, 1967), the dose-rates corresponding to a given count rate can be calculated. These are given in Table 3.2. It will be noted that for a given count rate the beta and gamma dose rates are markedly different between uranium and thorium. Fortunately, except for mineralogically abnormal samples, it is valid to assume that half of the alpha particles counted are from uranium and half from thorium and to use the average values shown in the Table.

The 'pairs' technique. This can be used to check that the uranium/thorium ratio in a sample is sufficient close to normal for the above assumption to be valid. Although the average time interval between alpha counts from the uranium chain is determined by the count rate, for the thorium chain about 3% of the counts occur in pairs—that is, within about 0·2 seconds of each other. This is because the alpha emitter polonium-216 has a half-life of only 0·16 seconds and it follows immediately from another alpha emitter. The number of pairs occurring with a spacing of less than 0·2 seconds is recorded by an electronic coincidence circuit, and the 'pairs rate' derived is a measure of the thorium activity: the pairs rate actually observed includes also pairs due to chance coincidences (equal to 0·2 second × count-rate) and the pairs rate due to polonium-216 is obtained by subtraction.

The only other half-life between two alpha emitters that is short enough to contribute pairs is the 0·002 second half-life of polonium-215 in the uranium-235 series, but since the abundance of the latter in natural uranium is low (0·72%), these make only a small contribution (about 9% for the normal uranium/thorium ratio).

Effective alpha dose-rate. Quite apart from the grain-size effect discussed in section 3.3, a given dosage from alpha particles is less effective in inducing TL than the same dosage from beta particles or gamma radiation. The degree of ineffectiveness varies from sample to sample and is expressed as the *k-value* (see section 3.7). The effective

TABLE 3.2

Component dose-rate† for typical pottery and soil

	α	β	γ	Total	Effective‡ total
Thorium-232 series:				783	193
Radioisotopes before thoron	295⎫ 695	8·5⎫ 23	26·2⎫ 65·5		
Thoron and later products	400⎭	14·5⎭	39·3⎭		
Uranium-238 series:				812	178
Radioisotopes before radon	320⎫ 745	14·5⎫ 34	0·7⎫ 32·5		
Radon and later products	425⎭	19·5⎭	31·8⎭		
Potassium-40	0	143	43·2	186	186
Totals	1440	200	141	1781	—
Effective‡ dose-rates	216 (39%)	200 (36%)	141 (25%)	—	557

† Dose-rates are given in millrads per year and correspond to pottery and soil having 2·8 ppm of uranium, 10 ppm of thorium, and 2% potassium (measured as K_2O). The corresponding alpha count-rate would be 10 per kilosecond for a thick sample of area 13·8 cm² and a counting efficiency of 85%; the uranium and thorium contributions to the count-rate would be approximately equal.
‡ Assuming $k = 0.15$.

alpha dose-rate is equal to k times the actual dose-rate, and since k is typically in the range 0·1 to 0·2 the typical alpha contribution to the TL (see Table 3.2) is about 40% of the whole, whereas in terms of actual dose-rates the alpha contribution is 80%.

Chemical analysis. An alternative to alpha counting is to determine the uranium and thorium contents by analysis, e.g. neutron activation. The drawback to this approach is that it could lead to gross errors if the decay chains were not in equilibrium; for instance if the geological origin of the uranium impurity is such that chemical separation occurred within the last half million years the chain will be missing from uranium-234 onwards and the actual dose-rate corresponding to a given concentration of uranium will be approximately one-eighth of what is assumed. There is also the likelihood of some disequilibrium due to emanation of radon (see below), and the more remote possibility of an effect due to leaching of radium by ground water.

Beta dose-rate

The contribution from uranium and thorium is derived from the alpha count using Table 3.2. The contribution from potassium-40 is determined from chemical analysis of total potassium content either by flame photometry or by X-ray fluorescent spectrometry; using the values given in Table 3.1 for branching ratio, half-life, beta energy, and natural abundance, the dose-rate corresponding to a K_2O content of 1% is 72 millirads per year.

An alternative is to make a direct measurement of the beta dose-rate by means of TL dosimetry itself (Mejdahl, 1969, 1972a). High-sensitivity TL phosphors (e.g. natural fluorite, and rare-earth activated $CaSO_4$) are available with which one can measure a dose of as little as 1 millirad. By exposing a tray of such phosphor to the sample material in a standard geometry the beta dose-rate can be determined after a week or two of storage; a plastic foil is interposed to eliminate the dose from alpha particles.

Since the beta particles have an effective range of about 2 mm the beta dose at the surface of a buried pottery fragment is contributed partly by the pottery and partly by the soil. However the error that might arise due to the soil having a different level of radioactivity to the pottery is avoided by sawing off and discarding the outer 2 mm of the fragment as a preliminary to sample preparation for measurement of TL.

Gamma dose-rate

Because gamma rays are highly penetrating, the gamma dose is effectively determined by the radioactivity of the soil; 50% of the dose comes from soil within a sphere of radius 8 cm and 90% from within a radius of 30 cm. The soil radioactivity can be determined in the same way as for the pottery fragment but because of the radon emanation and soil moisture effects discussed below the preferred method is certainly TL dosimetry (Aitken 1969; Mejdahl 1970, 1972a). A small capsule of sensitive TL phosphor is buried in as similar a context as possible to that from which the pottery was removed. Because of seasonal effects it is desirable to leave the capsule for a year before retrieval.

Cosmic radiation. At ground level the dose-rate is about 30 millirads per year and falls to a steady level of about 15 millirads per year by a depth of 0·6 metres (Aitken 1969). Thus the cosmic ray contribution is only a minor part of the overall dose-rate and it is usual to allow for it by adding a standard 15 millirads per year to the gamma dose-rate.

Radon emanation

Midway through the decay chain of uranium (see Table 3.1) is the gas radon (Rn-222). This is chemically inert and so quite mobile through pores and air gaps in pottery and soil. This movement ceases with decay of the gas into immobile polonium-218 and in dry soil the 3·8 day half-life of radon allows an average diffusion distance of about a metre (Tanner 1964). Diffusion can be inhibited in wet situations but as far as the soil is concerned there may be bulk transportation by ground-water movement.

Laboratory experiments on pottery and soil indicate an escape of 10% of the radon to be quite common and much higher percentages are not unknown. When a given amount of radon escapes the decrease in alpha count and dose-rate is not only that corresponding to the loss of radon, but also that corresponding to the loss of the same percentage of the members following radon in the chain. Because 98% of the gamma dose-rate of the uranium chain is from members of the chain *beyond* radon, the reduction in gamma dosage is particularly serious—hence the desirability of direct *in situ* measurement by means of a TL phosphor capsule. Fortunately the uranium chain supplies only about a quarter of the total gamma dosage from typical soil.

For the alpha and beta dose-rates the loss due to radon escape is much less serious, the details being given in Table 3.2. The magnitude of the effect for each sample can be evaluated by using a sealed sample and comparing the alpha count-rate obtained immediately after sealing with that obtained a couple of weeks later when the radon has had time to build up to equilibrium. If the effect is strong then subsidiary experiments are necessary to estimate where between these two extremes lay the actual situation when the pottery was in the ground (Desai *and* Aitken, 1974).

Because the corresponding gaseous member of the thorium chain—thoron (Rn-220)—has a half-life of only 55 seconds, its travel before decay is small and the associated effects are of minor importance.

Moisture content

Laboratory evaluation of radioactive content is made on a sample after it has been dried in the course of preparation. Except in arid regions a buried pottery fragment carries a significant amount of water as is also the case for soil. This has the effect of 'diluting' the radioactivity in the sense that the energy release per gram is less. Consequently the energy absorption per gram is less too and the dose-rate as evaluated from measurements on a dry sample is an overestimate of the dose-rate actually experienced. The saturation water content of most types of pottery is between 10 and 20 %; this can be measured for each sample, and for the wet climates of north western Europe it is fairly safe to assume that the fragment has been permanently saturated. Where the climate is intermediate or where there is uncertainty about past climate the limits of accuracy of the date obtained may be worsened significantly, though the saturation content does at least indicate the upper limit of the appropriate correction.

For soil the saturation content is often much higher than 20% and this is another argument in favour of field measurement of the gamma dose-rate by means of TL phosphor. By prolonging this measurement over a year seasonal variations are averaged out but of course this does not alleviate uncertainty due to the climate having been different in earlier times.

Although the assumption that energy absorption per gram equals energy release per gram is a satisfactory one for the constituents of dry pottery and soil, it needs modification when water is present. This is because the energy absorbed per gram of water from a given flux of radiation is greater than the energy absorption per gram of pottery or soil. In water the energy absorption per gram is higher by 50% for α-particles, by 25% for β-particles, and by 14% for gamma radiation. Consequently a given percentage of water content gives rise to a somewhat greater percentage reduction in dose-rate.

Another cause of uncertainty with wet sites is the possibility that there has been movement of radioactivity in and out of the pottery due to deposition and leaching by ground-water. If this has happened to any extent there is the possibility that the radioactive content as measured today is significantly different to the average content during burial.

The archaeological context

Because the gamma dosage is provided by the surrounding 30 cm of soil the contexts from which TL samples are obtained need careful vetting. In general the stones and rocks on a site have a different level of radioactivity to the soil—limestone and chalk are weak whereas granite and shales are strong (see Table 3.3). Thus the proximity of the sample to stone or rock may mean that the gamma dose-rate is significantly different to that evaluated from measurements on a soil sample. Measurement of the radioactivity of the intrusive material gives an indication of how serious the error might be but the geometry of the situation is usually too complex to allow correction for it. The alternative technique of evaluation by means of a TL phosphor capsule does not avoid the difficulty since it is impossible to place the capsule in exactly similar circumstance to that which the sample occupied.

The level of radioactivity may also vary between types of soil; clay usually has a much higher radioactivity than sand for instance and there is also the possibility of downward leaching, particularly of uranium. When the context consists of well-defined layers it is feasible to attempt an estimate of the gamma dose-rate at the find spot of the pottery despite differing radioactivity between layers. Also, in such a context it is possible by means of an auger hole, to place a capsule in a truly representative position—as long as the exact find spot has been noted.

A quick and convenient way of judging which contexts have a sufficiently uniform gamma flux to warrant collection of TL samples is to make on-site measurements with a gamma scintillation counter. A difficulty is that the gamma flux is disturbed by excavation; this can be avoided by positioning the detector 30 cm into the undug section

TABLE 3.3.

Radioactive content of common rock type (from Clark, 1966)

	Uranium (parts per million)		Thorium (parts per million)		Potassium (per cent)	D_γ† (millirads per year)			
	range	mean	range	mean	mean	uranium	thorium	potassium	total
granites	1–6	3·9	1–25	16	4·3	45	87	92	224
common shales	1–13	3·9	2–47	11·5	2·7	45	63	58	166
black shales	14–80	—	3–28	—	—	—	—	—	—
limestone	0·1–9	2·2	0·1–7	2·0	0·27	25	11	6	42
gabbro-basalt	0·2–4·0	0·5	0·5–10	1·6	1·0	6	8·5	22	36
sandstone	0·2–0·6	0·4	0·7–2·0	1·7	0·9	4·6	9·3	20	34

† D_γ is the dose-rate corresponding to the mean concentration indicated, at a point surrounded by rock to a distance of several feet.

of the context by means of a horizontal 2-inch diameter auger hole. The scintillation counter can also be used for an immediate measure of the dose-rate but the capsule technique is preferable because it averages over a year.

A particularly acute case of inhomogeneity in environmental dose-rate is proximity of the TL sample to the ground surface; a substantial part of the soil surround may then be absent altogether. It must also be kept in mind that although the present ground surface is well above the TL sample this may not have been always true for the ancient ground surface. It is necessary to give careful consideration to the archaeological indications of how quickly the sample became buried; as a general rule the sample should have been buried to a depth exceeding 30 cm for at least two-thirds of the burial time, but in a given case some relaxation of this may be allowed depending on the relative levels of radioactivity between soil and pottery.

Subtraction dating

In general the need to have an accurate evaluation of the gamma dose-rate rules out samples from already excavated sites. However when the alpha contribution to the TL is a substantial fraction of the whole a reliable date can be obtained even though a soil sample is not available or the context is known to be unsuitable because of the heterogeneity of the materials that might have been in the proximity of the samples. This is done by using the fine-grain technique and the quartz inclusion technique in subtraction mode (Fleming *and* Stoneham, 1973).

Writing eqn (3.2) and (3.3) in more detail for the fine-grain technique we have

$$(\text{TL})_{\text{FG}} = \text{Age} \times \{\chi_\alpha D_\alpha + \chi_{\beta,\gamma}(D_\beta + D_\gamma + D_c)\} \qquad (3.4)$$

where χ_α and $\chi_{\beta,\gamma}$ represent (TL per rad), $(\text{TL})_{\text{FG}}$ represents (natural TL) and D_α, D_β, D_γ, and D_c represent (Rads per year), D_c being the cosmic-ray contribution.
Hence

$$(\text{AD})_{\text{FG}} = \text{Age} \times \{kD_\alpha + (D_\beta + D_\gamma + D_c)\} \qquad (3.5)$$

where
$$(\text{AD})_{\text{FG}} = (\text{TL})_{\text{FG}}/\chi_\beta \qquad (3.6)$$

and
$$k = \chi_\alpha/\chi_\beta \qquad (3.7)$$

For the inclusion technique $D_\alpha = 0$, and making the 5% allowance for attenuation of the beta dosage that is appropriate to 100 micron grains, we have

$$(\text{AD})_\text{I} = \text{Age} \times (0\cdot95D_\beta + D_\gamma + D_\text{c}) \tag{3.8}$$

where

$$(\text{AD})_\text{I} = (\text{TL})_\text{I}/(\chi_{\beta,\gamma})_\text{I} \tag{3.9}$$

Hence,

$$\text{Age} = \frac{(\text{AD})_\text{FG} - (\text{AD})_\text{I}}{kD_\alpha + 0\cdot05D_\beta} \tag{3.10}$$

which is independent of D_γ and D_c and only weakly dependent on D_β.

3.5. Archaeological application

We have now outlined the method and covered the environmental complications pertinent to sample collection. The remaining technical sections are concerned mainly with topics internal to the laboratory and so it seems an appropriate juncture to introduce some discussion of application.

With the exception of the 'abnormal fading' discussed in section 3.10 none of the effects that upset the simplicity of eqn (3.1) are severe enough to invalidate the method. However, these effects do mean first, that the expense and effort involved in a TL date is of the same order as for a radiocarbon date, secondly that there are severe restrictions on the archaeological contexts and types of pottery which are suitable, and thirdly, that as with radiocarbon the stored information is not perfectly accurate, making a limitation that is irrespective of the precision of the actual measurements. The causes of inaccuracy are quite different to those for radiocarbon and so there is no question of any systematic error correlation between the two methods. At the time of writing (1973) archaeological application is in an early stage and the main emphasis so far has been on comparisons with radiocarbon and other dating evidence. References to publications are listed in a section of the bibliography at the end of the chapter.

For good accuracy there must be stringent selection of contexts (from the point of view of environmental radiation) and of material (from the points of view of good TL characteristics, low water content, and a low degree of radon escape). The latter can only be dealt with in the laboratory but for the former it is important that the archaeologist and his site assistants are fully cognizant of the method's requirements —such as given in Table 3.4. If possible there should be a visit to the

TABLE 3.4

COLLECTION OF POTTERY SAMPLES FOR
THERMOLUMINESCENT DATING:

Notes issued (1973) by the Oxford Research Laboratory for Archaeology.

THE SHERDS

1. *Number:* A set of between 3 and 12 sherds, for each context.
2. *Size:* At least 5 mm thick, at least 25 mm across. Bigger sherds are preferred.
3. *Type:* A variety of fabric types, if available. Surface decoration or glaze does not matter.
4. *Context:* (i) Only sherds that have been buried to a depth of 30 cm (1 foot) or more for at least two-thirds of their burial time are acceptable. This means that pits and ditches that have been filled up fairly quickly (either by silting or by ancient man) are ideal sources.

   (ii) The sherds should be at least 30 cm from any boundary (*e.g.* edge of pit, change of soil-type, wall, floor, rock surface).

   (iii) The best situation is one of sparsely-occurring sherds in a uniform soil which is relatively free of other materials (*e.g.* rock, building debris, shell or bone). A small scatter of stone does not matter as long as none of the sherds selected were close-up against a stone; the bigger the stone the more serious will be the effect.

TREATMENT

5. Avoid unnecessary exposure to direct sunlight.
6. Avoid excessive heating of the sherds. Their temperature should not exceed the boiling point of water (100° Centigrade, 212° Fahrenheit).
7. Avoid exposure to ultra violet, infra-red, X-rays, beta rays or gamma rays.
8(a) For sites where there is little doubt about the moisture content (*e.g.* typical lowland sites in NW Europe, where it can be assumed that both sherds and soil are saturated) no other precautions are necessary except that detergents or other additives should not be in the water used for washing; shade the sherds from brilliant sunlight when drying them.

   (b) For sites where there is doubt about the degree of saturation (*e.g.* high, well-drained sites, and sites in regions of intermediate rainfall) the sherds should not be washed but put directly in a plastic bag (plus any lumps of earth attached) within a few minutes of removal from the soil and tied up tightly. This bag should be put inside a second outer bag, which should also be tied tightly. This will allow measurement of the water content of the sherds as found in the ground.

   (c) If washing is necessary to confirm the identity of the sherds then this consideration should take priority.

TABLE 3.4—*continued*

BURIAL SOIL

9. A small handful of soil that is typical of that in which the sherds are buried is required. For sites as in 8(a) there is no special procedure to be followed, but for sites as in 8(b) the soil should be tightly double-bagged as for the sherds.

    If adhering lumps of soil have been bagged up with the sherds, then there is no need for additional soil. The preferred soil is such adhering lumps in any case (or soil very close to the sherd) and for option 8(a) it is desirable to collect any adhering lumps before washing and use these as the soil sample, labelling individually (one sample per sherd). An egg-cup full is enough.

10. Exposure of the soil to sunlight, ultraviolet etc., does NOT matter.

11. A sample of each type of material occurring in large proportions within 30 cm of the sherd is also required. In the case of a scatter of small stones in the soil these should be included in the soil-sample in correct proportion.

GENERAL

12. Please, above all, avoid sherds whose inclusion in a set is in any way doubtful. The method gives the date at which the pot was made; consequently residual pottery from earlier periods must be avoided. A sherd which has been burnt at some later period is of no use because the date obtained may be intermediate between the firing and the burning.

13. Information about burial conditions is essential; this should include a sketch section of the context (and, if possible, photographs) showing very roughly the points from which the sherds were taken and the deposits for at least 30 cm around.

14. In the case of sites under 8(b) please try and give a rough estimate of how the average water content of the soil relates to that of the sample supplied. It is also useful to know how the water content of the soil varies between contexts and with respect to surface conditions (*e.g.* 'though bone dry at the surface in these hot climatic conditions, by a depth of 2 metres the soil was pretty well saturated'). Obviously it is also important to know if the water table is (or has been) anywhere near to the contexts concerned. If there is any seasonal or long-term information about variations in rainfall we would like to know it.

15. The sherds are destroyed in the course of measurement.

ACCEPTANCE OF SAMPLES

16. The present policy is to undertake a limited number of specific projects rather than to accept samples on a piecemeal basis.

Primary considerations are:

    (i) whether the present accuracy (between $\pm 5\%$ and $\pm 10\%$ of the age) is good enough for the problem concerned,

    (ii) suitability of site and material for the technique,

    (iii) archaeological importance, and

    (iv) lack of, or ambiguity in, other dating evidence.

site by a member of the laboratory staff for discussion, as well as for scintillation-counter measurements and insertion of TL phosphor capsules.

Assessment of error limits

Whereas some of the effects that cause error are general to a site, others vary from fragment to fragment and it is advantageous to utilize half-a-dozen or more sherds from each context being dated so as to average out such errors. However it is important to realize that systematic errors are not reduced in this way and that in assessing the likely error in the age derived for a context random errors must be distinguished from systematic errors. In the system used at present (Aitken *and* Alldred, 1972), two error limits are quoted with each context date (both at the 68% level of confidence). The error limit *a* is the calculated overall error derived from all known sources of individual error, both systematic and random. The error limit *p* is defined by

$$p = \frac{\sum\limits_{i=1}^{i=N} (A_i - \bar{A})^2}{N(N - 1)} \qquad (3.11)$$

where $A_1, A_2, \ldots A_i \ldots$ are the individual TL ages for the context, $\bar{A}$ is the average TL age, and N is the number of samples. Hence $(pN^{\frac{1}{2}})$ is the observed standard deviation of individual ages from the average age, and p is an experimental estimate of the standard error of the average age, ignoring the possibility of systematic errors. Thus p is more akin to the standard deviation quoted for a radiocarbon date than is *a*. The value of p should be considered as the minimum standard error and useful when comparing different contexts in the same site or locality whereas *a* is more realistic in comparison of TL dates with radiocarbon or other chronology.

As an illustration of the system we may consider the TL dates obtained for baked clay balls found on sites of the Poverty Point culture in Mississippi and Arkansas (Huxtable, Aitken, *and* Weber, 1972). Table 3.5 shows the individual dates obtained for seven balls from one particular site—Teoc Creek—together with the estimated errors. The latter varies from ball to ball because of differing characteristics, e.g. low intensity of TL would increase measurement error, high saturation water content would increase the uncertainty in dose-rate.

TABLE 3.5

TL dates for individual balls from Teoc Creek

Date	Random error	Systematic error
641 B.C.	±200	±160
964 B.C.	±680	±180
967 B.C.	±250	±190
1034 B.C.	±260	±180
1247 B.C.	±290	±200
1280 B.C.	±310	±200
1419 B.C.	±320	±210

The observed standard deviation of the individual dates, calculated as $(pN^{\frac{1}{2}})$ is 260 years which agrees reasonably with the estimated random errors. The value of p is 98 years. From the individual random errors, the random error in the average date is calculated to be $106 = \sigma_r$, and from the individual systematic errors, the systematic error in the average is calculated to be $188 = \sigma_s$. Hence the estimated overall error in the average $\sigma = \sqrt{(\sigma_s^2 + \sigma_r^2)} = 216$. The average date, which is calculated from the individual dates weighted according to their associated random and systematic errors, is 1068 B.C. The form of citation of the date for this site, which is context e in project *143* of the Oxford TL laboratory is

$$1070 \text{ B.C. } (\pm 100, \pm 220, \text{ OxTL 143e}).$$

Table 3.6 shows the average dates for the five main Poverty Point sites from which samples were available. We see that even to within the smaller limit of error quoted for each (the first one, p—appropriate to intercomparisons between similar sites) there is no significant age difference between the sites. The average date is 1000 B.C. with an

TABLE 3.6

TL dates for five sites of the Poverty Point culture

Terral Lewis:	1090 B.C. (±130, ±230)
Poverty Point:	750 B.C. (±200, ±200)
Jaketown:	1080 B.C. (±110, ±250)
Teoc Creek:	1070 B.C. (±100, ±220)
Shoe Bayou:	1000 B.C. (±170, ±220)

error limit of ± 200 years in absolute terms, i.e. calculated from the individual site values for a. The error limit is not much less than the individual values of a because the main contributory error is systematic.

In percentage terms the value of p for Teoc Creek is 3% of the age and the value of a is about 7%. These values are not untypical though for a 'good' site the value of p may be a little less. Except for recent sites in which the natural TL intensity is too low for accurate measurement, the percentage errors are not dependent on age; hence taking 3% and 7% as typical, around A.D. 1000 we expect $p = 30$ years and $a = 70$ years, but at 5000 B.C. for instance we must expect $p = 200$ years and $a = 500$ years.

In radiocarbon dating, because of the exponential form of the decay, a 1% uncertainty in activity corresponds to an 80-year uncertainty in date irrespective of age, so that for the $\frac{1}{2}$% accuracy obtained in a typical measurement the corresponding uncertainty is 40 years. However, as discussed in section 2.9, a more realistic general estimate of the absolute accuracy obtainable is ± 150 years. Thus in the A.D. era TL dating can be expected to provide a comparable or better accuracy, while in earlier times this is not so until the limit of the bristlecone-pine calibration is reached. In general radiocarbon should be regarded as the primary technique on which to place reliance because it is well established and TL dating should be reserved for sites on which there is no material for radiocarbon or on which there is ambiguity in the radiocarbon results.

Tests with known-age pottery

Although the fine-grain and quartz inclusion techniques do not need calibration, in the course of their development tests have been made from time to time in order to check the correctness of the approach. These are summarized in Table 3.7; this also includes a test of the pre-dose technique (see section 3.8). Most of the material for these tests was from Medieval and Roman sites in Britain which were well-dated historically (usually by archaeological links to documentary or numismatic evidence). It is to be noted that the standard deviations quoted are for single samples; for a context from which there are 9 samples the standard error (p) on the average would be one-third of the standard deviation. For further discussion of these tests, and of error estimation, the reader should refer to Aitken *and* Alldred (op cit.), who emphasize that the accuracy

TABLE 3.7

Summary of test programmes (based on Aitken and Alldred, 1972)

Reference	Technique[1]	No. of samples	[4]Standard deviation (%)	[5]Average systematic error (%)
Aitken, Zimmerman and Fleming 1968	f	50	15	−2
Zimmerman 1970	f, w. r, γ	62	15	−1
Thompson 1970	f, w, r, s, γ	17[2]	9(17)	+2(−13)
Fleming 1970	i, w, r. s, β, γ	21	6	<1
Zimmerman 1971	f, w, r, s	14[3]	12	+4
Fleming 1973	p, w, r	30	7	−1

1. Technique: f—fine-grain, i—inclusion, p—pre-dose, w—correction made for water content, r—correction made for radon escape, s—correction made for supralinearity, β—beta dose-rate determined by TLD, γ—gamma dose-rate determined by TLD.
2. These samples were specifically chosen as exhibiting supralinearity. The values in parenthesis correspond to the results obtained if the supralinearity correction is not made.
3. Seven sherds were from Britain, seven from Greece. In all other cases the majority were from Britain.
4. The standard deviation has been calculated as the square root of

$$\frac{(\delta_1{}^2 + \delta_2{}^2 + \ldots)}{N}$$

where $\delta_1, \delta_2 \ldots$ are the percentage deviations of the individual TL ages from the corresponding archaeologic ages and N is the number of samples.
5. The average systematic error has been calculated as

$$\frac{(\delta_1 + \delta_2 \ldots)}{N},$$

a positive value corresponding to TL giving too old a date.

obtainable on sites and contexts specially selected for suitability does not necessarily represent the accuracy obtainable elsewhere; hence the need for a system which predicts the accuracy in a given set of circumstances.

3.6. Authenticity testing of ceramic art objects

It is in this field that thermoluminescence has had a revolutionary impact comparable with that of radiocarbon in archaeology. It is usually a question of deciding between an age of less than a hundred years and one of upwards of a thousand. Uncertainty about gamma dose-rate is then unimportant and it does not matter that the 'burial circumstances' are unknown. The answer obtained is usually clear-cut and the technique provides museum curators with a very powerful independent judgment of what on their shelves is genuine and what imitative. The result of a TL test may alter the value of an object from an astronomical figure to a negligible amount; consequently although high accuracy may not be important, reliability is vital and tests need to be conducted with meticulous care. Reputable art dealers have doubtful pieces tested as a matter of routine, the usual fee for such a service being £50–£100.

There are some styles of ceramic ware for which art historians have had doubts about the group as a whole. Application of TL in such cases has led to reassessment of the visual criteria on which authenticity judgements are based; it has also had academic impact in the sense that previously the art historian may have been studying the forger's view of man's cultural and artistic development rather than actuality. An example of this is the so-called Hacilar ware, anthropomorphic vessels and figurines said to be 7000 years old and to have come from the renowned site of that name in south-west Turkey. Because their supposed origin was from a cultural phase following soon after the first appearance of pottery in that part of the world, the fineness of technique and beauty of form attracted particular interest. The TL finding that out of the seven most important pieces tested—the magnificent double-spouted vessels, each spout being in the form of a head with obsidian eyes—only one was genuine, confirmed the doubts of some scholars but astounded others. Out of a total of 66 pieces tested there were 48 modern forgeries. However although the forger had altered details in the style and added innovations, the genuine pieces (some of them from recorded excavation) do testify to the advanced state of ceramic technology at the time concerned. On the other hand in another application—to Chinese Hui Hsien ware— there have been no genuine examples among the pieces so far available for testing. Publication references to these and other authenticity applications will be found at the end of the chapter.

The re-heating hypothesis. When a substantial number of objects of the same type are indicated by TL to be forgeries, careful considera- tion needs to be given to the possibility that for some special reason the test is giving an incorrect answer—despite its well-established validity in general. An obvious possibility is that the objects have been re-heated in recent times. This question was considered exhaustively in respect of the Hacilar ware since the suggestion was made that the absence of TL was due to re-firing of the pieces by peasants in order to dry them out after retrieval from marshy ground. Laboratory tests indicated that a day or two at 300°C would be necessary to erase the TL, and there are two practical arguments against this having happened. First, risk of damage would dictate that the temperature used for drying out would be no higher than necessary to drive off the water. Secondly, it is unlikely that the available ovens—domestic bread ovens—would reach a temperature in excess of 200°C. In addition to this circumstantial reasoning, conclusive direct evidence against re-heating was obtained by means of the pre-dose dating for those objects—a substantial proportion—having TL characteristics suitable for this technique. As explained in section 3.8 pre-dose dating can be used to derive an upper limit for the age irrespective of whether or not the object has been re-heated (as long as the heating did not exceed 700°C).

The arguments for rejecting the re-heating hypothesis in other cases follow similar lines to those given above. If the decoration is sophisticated then the practical argument is stronger still—additionally one can ask, *why* should the owner have wished to re-heat?

Abnormal fading

Another reason that might be suggested for the absence of TL in a genuine object is that the constituent minerals happen to exhibit the same abnormal fading characteristics that are often typical of minerals in volcanic lava (see section 3.10), i.e. there is no 'stable' region in the TL glow curve and the TL age obtained is only a fraction of the true age. A general argument against this possibility is that not one of the thousands of archaeological pottery fragments that have been measured has shown such behaviour. Certainly there are occasional fragments for which up to about 20% of the TL shows abnormal fading but this is barely significant in the context of authenticity work.

In a specific case when the possibility of abnormal fading is being considered—for instance when the glow-curve shape corresponds to that of a mineral known to exhibit the effect—then the short-term tests developed in connection with volcanic lava can be carried out.

As in the case of re-heating, a still more vigorous exclusion of the possibility can be obtained by using pre-dose dating—as long as there is sufficient quartz in the sample for this technique to be applicable. Because pre-dose dating is specific to one mineral (of proven good behaviour) the possible presence in the sample of 'abnormal' minerals is irrelevant.

Spurious TL

We now turn to the converse question—can a modern forgery exhibit sufficient TL for it to be mistaken for a genuine object? One has only to take a sample from a modern coffee cup and measure its TL without switching on the nitrogen supply to demonstrate that slip shod work could lead to this error. Substantial spurious TL will also arise from the use of poor quality nitrogen and in some samples it may still be there with high purity nitrogen or even argon.

Hence the observation of substantial TL is not in itself a guarantee of authenticity. In addition one must check that the shape of the glow curve agrees with the shape for radiation-induced TL—by means of the plateau test—and that the level of TL is correct having regard to the presumed age of the object, the TL sensitivity, and the dose per year estimated from radioactive analysis. The presence of spurious TL may also be indicated by the emission of light as the sample cools down, and also during its re-heat to measure the level of red-hot glow. Such signs will be noticed by a well-trained and experienced operator; this aspect illustrates the importance of the operator's rôle—however good the equipment a substantial proportion of wrong answers are liable to be obtained by inexperienced hands.

As with the two preceding effects pre-dose dating is immune to upset in this way.

Clandestine irradiation

Can a modern forgery be irradiated so that it will exhibit TL appropriate to a genuine object? An inexperienced operator could be misled by even a clumsy attempt and this possibility again stresses the need for experience and the maintenance of meticulous standards. To make a good attempt at this would require the services of a competent physicist with appropriate experimental facilities, but it is not my intention to indicate the direction in which his difficulties might lie or to advise him on appropriate lines of research.

3.7. TL per rad

We return now to further consideration of the age relation in the form it was developed in eqn (3.4) when discussing subtraction dating. Measurement of χ_β is more straightforward experimentally than measurement of χ_α and for this reason it is usual to express the equivalent dose in terms of χ_β and allow for the difference between the two by converting the actual alpha dose-rate to an effective dose-rate by means of the k-value—see eqn (3.5) and Table 3.2.

The most convenient way of measuring χ_β is by exposure to a known dose from a calibrated beta-emitting radioisotope source† such as strontium-90 which through its short-lived daughter yttrium-90 provides a beta spectrum of maximum energy 2·3 MeV. Alternatively a cobalt-60 gamma source can be used. In either case careful quantitative dosimetry evaluation is necessary, particularly in regard to scattering, as well as due attention to radiation hazard. For measurement of χ_α a radioisotope such as polonium-210, americium-241, curium-242, or curium-244 is used.‡ A source strength of several millicuries is required and stringent precautions must be taken against radioactive contamination; because alpha particles have such a short range the covering window in front of the source has to be very thin and there is risk of leakage. The sample irradiated must be thin too— a few microns—and this is achieved by the fine-grain deposition on disc method described in section 3.3.

k-value

As indicated in eqn (3.7), this is the ratio of the effectiveness of alpha particles in inducing TL to that of beta particles or gamma radiation, for the same amount of deposited energy (i.e. for the same dose, measured in rads). The ratio can be as low as 0·02 (for some types of quartz) and as high as 0·4 (for artificial CaF_2:Mn) but for pottery samples it is usually in the range 0·1 to 0·3. The reason for the lower effectiveness of alpha particles is that the high ionization density in their tracks is more than enough to saturate all the TL traps, and the

† Obtainable from the Radiochemicals Centre, Amersham, Bucks, England. A strontium-90 source type S1P 13 of strength 40 millicurie provides a dose-rate of the order of 100 rads per minute at a distance of 0·6 inches, and ten times that at 0·1 inches.

‡ Satisfactory sources having a thin nickel window (0·6 mg/cm²) are obtainable from: Actinide Orders, Chemistry Division, Building 220, A.E.R.E. Harwell, Berks, England.

excess is wasted. A further consideration, in view of the fact that the spectrum of alpha particles in pottery extends from 0 to 8·9 MeV, is that with decrease in particle energy the ionization density increases and so there is fall off of k-value. However the fall off of k-value is partially compensated by the increased energy deposition, and in terms of TL induced per unit length of track the energy dependence is mild, the difference between 2 MeV and 7 MeV being less than 30% for most minerals. Fortunately the difference in energy dependence from mineral to mineral is not sufficient to make it necessary to measure the energy dependence for each sample dated; it is adequate to measure the k-value for one standard energy—usually 4 MeV.

The detailed way in which the k-value is incorporated into calculation of date and a discussion of its physical implications have been given by Zimmerman (1971, 1972).

Supralinearity; pre-dose effect

Because of their short range and narrow diameter there is negligible overlap of the individual alpha tracks for the dose levels relevant to archaeological dating. Each additional alpha track is a microscopic TL-saturated channel within a macroscopic volume that is mainly virgin; hence the TL induced is strictly proportional to the dose. With beta and gamma radiation the ionization density is many orders of magnitude lower and the TL builds up gradually throughout the whole macroscopic volume of the sample. Hence there is the possibility that the TL induced is not strictly proportional to the dose— because the TL-sensitivity may be influenced by the dose previously received.

Figure 3.7 shows a typical TL growth curve for pottery samples: the sensitivity increases during the first one or two hundred rads and then becomes constant—the initial growth is said to be *supralinear*. At higher doses than are shown in the figure, upwards of ten thousand rads, saturation sets in and the growth becomes sublinear. It is not difficult to suggest mechanisms that might give rise to supralinearity— though far from easy to establish which is operative in any particular mineral. The simplest explanation proposed is that additional traps are being created in the early stages of the irradiation, thereby increasing the sensitivity. An alternative is the 'competition model' in which it is assumed that there is a second set of traps (which do not give rise to TL) competing for electrons. These are assumed to saturate earlier than the TL traps and so as the competing traps gradually approach saturation the competition is suppressed and more electrons are available for the TL traps. Another explanation is in terms of an enhancement in the probability that an electron freed from a trap will produce luminescence—such enhancement could arise because of an increase with dose of the number of activated luminescent centres for instance. Some relevant references are Tite *and* Waine (1962), Tite (1966), Cameron, Zimmerman, *and* Bland (1967), Suntharalingam *and* Cameron (1969), and Zimmerman (1971 b,c.).

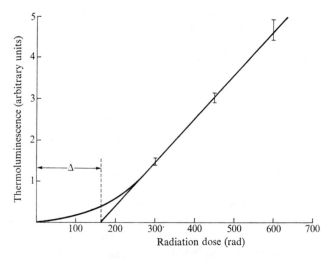

FIG. 3.7. Typical supralinear dependence of TL on radiation dose for pottery samples irradiated with beta or gamma radiation. The degree of supralinearity is measured by the intercept Δ.

In general the increase in sensitivity that occurs during the early part of the growth curve is not erased when the sample is heated to 500°C in the course of measuring the TL. Sometimes it is further enhanced by such heating, and in the case of the 110°C peak in quartz that is used in the dating technique described in section 3.8, there is substantial enhancement despite the absence of supralinearity in growth. Some of the sensitivity change that occurs on heating is due to transparency and reflectivity changes, particularly in samples that change colour on heating. The term *pre-dose effect* is used to signify that part of the sensitivity change that is due to the irradiation dose received previous to the heating, and as a first presumption the change is taken to be proportional to this *pre-dose*.

Whatever the details of the mechanisms involved the pre-dose effect seriously complicates dating—clearly it is not valid to use the value of χ obtained for the sample after it has been heated in the course of measuring the natural TL. Instead the *additive method* illustrated in Fig. 3.8 must be used; three equal samples are required,

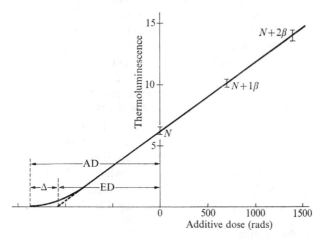

FIG. 3.8. Additive method of evaluating Equivalent Dose (ED). Of three equal samples the first is used to measure N—the natural TL, the second to measure $(N + 1\beta)$—the natural-plus-artificial TL after a dose of β rads, and the third $(N + 2\beta)$; in the above, $\beta = 700$. The supralinearity correction Δ is determined by means of a growth curve such as Fig. 3.7 using samples from which N has been removed. The sum of ED and Δ equals AD, the *Archaeological Dose.*

one is used to measure the natural TL and the other two for combined natural-plus-artificial TL at two levels of additive dose. Although this correctly measures χ in the linear region, because of supralinearity the dose determined by the intercept (ED) is less than the actual dose received. An empirical way of correcting for this is to use already-glowed samples to determine the *second-glow growth curve* (such as Fig. 3.7) and to assume that despite a change in χ on heating there is no change in the intercept. The justification for this procedure is that use of AD ($= $ ED $+ \Delta$) gives improved agreement on tests with known-ages samples—see Table 3.7. An advantage of the quartz inclusion technique is that if attention is restricted to the 'benign' peak at 375°C (as opposed to the 'malign' peak at 325°C) the sensitivity change on heating is often less than 5% and consequently the use of the value given by the second-glow growth curve is then confirmed as valid in each individual case.

Influence of dose-rate

Of necessity the artificial dose is administered at a rate that is about ten million times the rate at which the natural dose was acquired. It is therefore pertinent to ask whether the efficiency of acquiring TL is at all dependent on rate. This is unlikely to be the case until the rate is so high that there is a probability of track volumes overlapping within the lifetime of the ionized electrons; this would need a rate many orders of magnitude greater than those used in dating work. Experiments with lithium fluoride (Tochilin *and* Goldstein, 1966) give no evidence for dose rate dependence until the order of 10^{10} rads per second.

Dose-rate dependence might also occur through one of the supralinearity mechanisms mentioned earlier. For instance, if, in the competition model, the competing traps are shallow their equilibrium population, and hence also the TL sensitivity, will be dependent on the rate at which they are being filled. However, there is as yet no experimental observation of this effect (e.g. Fleming, 1969).

3.8. Pre-dose dating

Conventional TL dating is based on the steady build-up with time of trapped electrons. It is also possible to determine age by making use of the strong pre-dose effect that is exhibited by the 110°C peak in the glow curve of typical quartz inclusions from pottery. The effect is used to evaluate the archaeological dose AD and the age is then obtained in the usual way as

$$\text{Age} = \frac{\text{AD}}{\kappa D_\alpha + D_\beta + D_\gamma + D_c} \tag{3.12}$$

where κ is the pre-dose effectiveness of alpha radiation relative to beta and gamma. In practice κ is usually less than 0·02, as might be expected from the discussion of the previous section, and so the relation effectively reduces to the expression used for the inclusion technique,

$$\text{Age} = \frac{\text{AD}}{D_\beta + D_\gamma + D_c}. \tag{3.13}$$

It turns out that this pre-dose dating is primarily applicable to samples having ages between 50 and 1500 years, thereby complementing conventional TL dating with its lower limit of around 500 to 1000 years.

The 110° TL peak in quartz has a half-life of about $2\frac{1}{2}$ hours. Consequently it is not present in the natural TL. It is however a highly-sensitive peak, and exposure to a dose (the *test-dose*) of around 1 to 10 rads is usually sufficient to induce an accurately measurable TL. The increase in sensitivity (as indicated by the response to the test-dose) consequent on briefly heating the sample to 400°C or 500°C is proportional to the total radiation dose (the *pre-dose*) that the sample has received subsequent to its firing in antiquity. Thus although the traps responsible for the 110° peak carry an insignificant number of electrons there is nevertheless a memory of the radiation dose that has been received, a memory that is unlocked by the brief heating to 400° or 500°C (such as the sample experiences in the course of a normal glow-curve).

The sequence of measurements is essentially as follows:

(i) Give test-dose and measure response, S_0,
(ii) Heat to 500°C (the *activating temperature*),
(iii) Give test-dose and measure response, S_N,
(iv) Give laboratory calibrating dose, β (usually several hundred rads),
(v) Heat to 500°C,
(vi) Give test-dose and measure response, $S_{N+\beta}$.

Since $(S_N - S_0)$ is proportional to the dose received during antiquity, AD, and $(S_{N+\beta} - S_N)$ is proportional to β, we have

$$AD = \frac{S_N - S_0}{S_{N+\beta} - S_N} \times \beta. \tag{3.14}$$

It is of course necessary to check, for each sample, that the proportionality of the sensitivity increase to dose is valid for the range of dose concerned. The effect usually saturates in the region of 500 rads.

The pre-dose phenomenon can usually be observed in any fine-grain or whole-grain sample containing quartz but for accurate results it is best to extract the quartz as in the inclusion technique—though it is important to omit the etching with hydrofluoric acid since for some reason this upsets the pre-dose behaviour. For a 10 mg sample of separated quartz, a typical sensitivity change is in the range 2%–20% per rad of pre-dose and so an equivalent dose of as little as 10 rads can be measured accurately. The effect was first studied by Fleming (1969) and its validity as a dating method has been confirmed by extensive tests with known-age pottery (Fleming 1973)—as already noted in Table 3.7. Not all pottery contains quartz with satisfactory pre-dose characteristics and of the fifty fragments studied in this test only 34 met the criteria laid down for best accuracy. When it is applicable it is a very powerful method, particularly for authenticity testing. It can often give an answer in cases when the conventional method is inapplicable because of too low TL-intensity in the high temperature region of the glow curve or—as already noted in section 3.6—because it is upset by spurious TL or held in doubt because of the possibility that abnormal fading or re-heating has occurred.

The re-heating hypothesis

To understand how rejection of this hypothesis is possible, it is necessary to consider the way in which the sensitivity increase depends on the activating temperature used in step (ii). Two typical temperature characteristics are shown in Fig. 3.9 the difference in behaviour

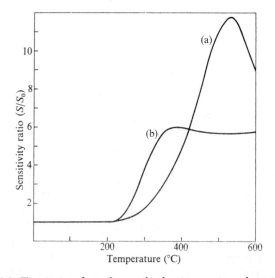

FIG. 3.9. Two types of pre-dose activation temperature characteristic (from Fleming *and* Thompson, 1970). Curve (a) is for geological quartz fired for 18 hours at 1000°C and then given a predose of 1000 rads; curve (b) is for 700°C and a pre-dose of 50 rads. S_0 is the sensitivity before activation; S is the sensitivity after activation by rapid heating to the temperature indicated on the horizontal scale.

being attributable to the different firing conditions used in making the pottery.

Consider now the case of a genuinely ancient object of temperature characteristic type (a) which was reheated to 300°C—just sufficient to erase the high-temperature TL; because only slight activation of the pre-dose will have occurred the equivalent dose deduced from eqn (3.14) will not be seriously low. If the reheating was to a higher temperature then the observed S_0 approaches S_N and a misleadingly low value for AD is obtained; however with the reheating hypothesis in mind we can calculate a value for AD on the assumption that the 'true' value of S_0 (i.e. the value that would have been observed if re-heating had not occurred) is zero. This is an upper limit for AD since S_0 cannot be negative. For a genuine object the age corresponding to this upper limit will be equal to or in excess of the true age. On the other hand for a recent forgery S_N is only slightly greater than the true S_0, and because the latter is usually small the upper limit to the age as derived above will be small also. For some samples S_0 is not small and it is not then possible to exclude the refiring hypothesis.

The mechanism responsible

From studies of the associated radioluminescence, exo-electron emission, and the effect of ultraviolet irradiation Zimmerman (1971b) has established that the sensitivity enhancement is due to an increased availability of charged luminescence centres and has proposed the model shown in Fig. 3.10. In this T_1 and T_2 are electron traps and L and K are hole traps. T_1 is the shallow trap which, with the luminescent centre L, is responsible for the 110° TL peak. Trap T_2 is presumed to be deep enough not to be emptied by heating to 500°C and it is introduced into the model so that charge balance can be maintained. The TL process consists of the thermal release of electrons from the traps T_1 and the capture of some of these into the luminescent centres L. Such capture only occurs for centres which are charged with a hole and so the TL sensitivity is proportional to the number of centres which are so charged.

Firing of the pottery in antiquity is hypothesized to empty nearly all traps and consequently the sensitivity after firing—S_0—is low. Subsequently, the natural radiation dose-rate produces electrons in the conduction band and holes in the valence band; the electrons are trapped in T_2 (because T_1 is too shallow to retain them) and the holes are captured at K (rather than L because of the former's presumed higher capture cross-section). Thus during antiquity the hole population in K gradually builds up.

In step (i) of the pre-dose procedure the test-dose charges the traps T_1 with a small number of electrons and puts a small number of holes into K. On heating through 100° the electrons are released and those that find a charged luminescent centre give rise to TL. Because there has been no change in the number of holes trapped at the centres of type L the observed sensitivity S_0 is the same as if the measurement has been made immediately after firing.

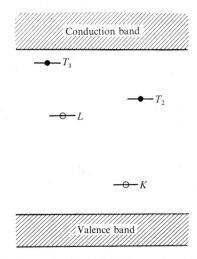

FIG. 3.10. Energy-level model for the pre-dose effect (after Zimmerman 1971 *b*).

The heating to 500°C in step (ii) causes thermal release of holes from K and these are then captured at L (because any recaptured at K are immediately re-ejected). Hence the sensitivity measured in step (iii)—S_N—is proportional to the number of holes that had been accumulated in K during antiquity.

3.9. Other materials

The span of time during which man has been making pottery is roughly the last 10 000 years. In so far as TL is restricted to pottery it is limited to the same span, though by using baked clay and burnt earth from fireplaces some extension is achieved. Because the TL signal increases with age the method is potentially capable of extending back beyond the 50 000 year limit of radiocarbon; from that limit until the order of a million years there is no well-established chronological framework available for archaeology—the period is too recent for potassium–argon dating to be generally applicable and in any case the method dates geological rather than human events. Consequently, although the possible materials for TL are ones that would be ignored on a site where pottery was available, there is strong reason to investigate their reliability as TL clocks. Burnt flint and other burnt stones, volcanic lava, glass, shell, and bone are the most likely possibilities. The most obvious requirement is that there should be sufficient TL sensitivity in the 400° region of the glow curve. Additional criteria for reliability fall under three main headings:

(i) *Zero-age samples should give negligible TL*. For burnt materials the TL traps will have been emptied initially (assuming the temperature was upwards of 300°C) but in the course of sample preparation substantial spurious-TL may be induced. However this is a technical problem and it should be possible to devise means to overcome it—as has been the case with pottery, and also with a hard material such as burnt flint (by means of the slice technique—see section 3.3). A more fundamental barrier with transparent and translucent materials is the possibility that before burial the sample acquired TL through exposure to light.

Biogenic calcium carbonate in the form of shell—even though unburnt—is a possible material as long as the crystals do not contain trapped electrons on formation. Only shells made of calcite are worth considering; it is well-known that aragonite begins to transform (to calcite) around 400°C with the emission of light and this form of spurious TL may be impossible to avoid. An effect in the opposite direction would be that due to recrystallization during burial—this difficulty is also met in radiocarbon dating of shell in which it is essential to discard material of powdery appearance indicative of alteration.

With bone it has so far proved impossible to achieve adequate removal of organic constituents (which give rise to spurious TL) and the only possibility of application seems to be to samples such as dinosaur bone that are old enough for this constituent to have disappeared completely.

(ii) *The growth of TL with dose should be either linear or reproducible.* If the growth is linear the sensitivity can be measured by means of the three-sample additional artificial dose technique (section 3.7). If the sensitivity is not changed by measurement of the natural TL then TL *versus* dose characteristic can be established by laboratory irradiations. It is implicit that the TL must not have reached saturation for the dose range of interest; for pottery, saturation may be reached for a dose of only 10 000 rads but for calcite and flint the level is upwards of 100 000 rads. The levels of radioactivity in the latter two are small so that the dose-rate is mainly environmental; typically this does not exceed ~ 0.2 rads per year, suggesting that as far as saturation effects are concerned the limiting age should be more than half a million years.

This brings us to the question of the lifetime of the trapped electrons. The lifetime corresponding to the trap depth and frequency factor found for the 375°C TL peak in quartz is 40 million years, and in general lifetimes of the order of a million years or more are to be expected for traps responsible for TL in the 400°C region of the glow curve and above. However, in attempting to date 50 000 year-old volcanic lava it was found that for some mineral samples the lifetime may be several orders of magnitude lower than is indicated by the trap depth and the frequency factor. This *abnormal fading* is discussed below.

(iii) *The effective dose-rate can be evaluated.* The same considerations of micro- and macrodosimetry as discussed earlier in the chapter are still relevant but, in extending the time range, uncertainty due to radioactive equilibrium may become of dominant importance. This is particularly likely with unfired material because the event being dated is then a chemical one; for instance, uranium is incorporated in shell on formation but without those of its daughters that are chemically different. This is of course the basis of the uranium-series dating of shell discussed in section 1.2; as in that method, another likely difficulty is the mobile uranium component which migrates in and out of the shell during burial. However, such materials usually have a much lower internal radioactivity than pottery and the consequent greater importance of the environmental dosage may alleviate the situation. On the other hand the environmental dosage may be afflicted with disequilibrium uncertainties too; for instance in marine

sediment there is unsupported thorium-230 of half-life 75 200 years—
the basis of the ionium dating method.

Reported investigations of other materials: shell (Johnson and Blanchard, 1967), volcanic lava (Aitken, Fleming, Doell, and Tanguy,
1968), bone (Jasínka and Niewiadomski, 1970; Christodoulides and
Fremlin, 1971), burnt flint (Göksu and Fremlin, 1972), fired rock
crystal (Wintle and Oakley, 1972), burnt stone (Mejdahl, 1972).

3.10. Abnormal fading

The expected lifetime of an electron in a trap of depth E eV and
having a frequency factor s second^{-1} is given by

$$\tau = s^{-1} \exp(E/kT) \tag{3.15}$$

where k is Boltzman's constant and T K is the storage temperature.
For the 375°C peak in quartz, $E = 1 \cdot 7$ eV and $s = 1 \cdot 5 \times 10^{13}$ sec^{-1}
so that, for storage at 20°C, $\tau = 40 \times 10^6$ years (Fleming, 1969). For
substances having glow curves that do not contain separable peaks the
approximations suggested by Curie (1963) are useful: for a TL peak
at $T^{\star}$K, $E \sim (T^{\star}/500)$ for $s \sim 10^9$ s^{-1}, and $E \sim (T^{\star}/350)$ for
$s \sim 10^{13}$ s^{-1}. On the basis of the former the lifetimes (at 20°C) corresponding to various values of $T^{\star}$ are as given in Table 3.8.

TABLE 3.8

*Typical lifetimes (τ) corresponding to various glow-curve
temperatures ($T^{\star}$), for storage at 20°C*

$T^{\star}$	100°C	200°C	300°C	400°C	500°C
τ	3 h	1 yr	3000 yr	10^7 yr	3×10^{10} yr

These predictions are totally at variance with the behaviour of some
of the feldspar mineral studied by Wintle (1973). For volcanic lavas
of known age the observed TL was significantly too low, sometimes
by an order of magnitude, although the ages were short compared
to the lifetimes associated with the 400°C–500°C region of the glow
curve according to the Table. Very much more anomalous were the
results of short-term stability tests: loss of 10%–40% of the 350°C–
500°C TL in periods varying between a few hours and a few days was
observed for some samples of sanidine, fluorapatite, labradorite,
andesine, zircon, and bytownite. Not all samples of these minerals

showed the effect, and for quartz and limestone the fading was insignificant over months of storage.

Apart from their discouraging implications for geological lava dating these observations call into question the basic validity of pottery dating using fine-grain or whole-grain samples since from these there is a substantial, if not dominant, contribution from feldspar minerals. However, the satisfactory results obtained with known-age samples (Table 3.7) indicate that this behaviour is not common among the minerals constituents of pottery. Also, the short-term stability tests that are now made routinely on fine-grain samples show that it is only the occasional sample which exhibits measurable loss (5%–10%) for a storage period of up to a month. The reason for this fortunate circumstance has not yet been established but presumably it is connected with the extra firing that the constituent minerals experience when pottery is made.

The rate of percentage loss in abnormal fading is initially rapid, getting progressively slower as the time elapsed since irradiation increases. To account for the initial rapid loss in terms of eqn (3.15) requires $E \sim \frac{1}{2}$ eV and $s \sim 10^3$ s^{-1}, and for various reasons it is difficult to accept the model on which (3.15) is based as valid for such values. It seems more likely that the initial rapid fading is due to a subsidiary means of escape available to only a proportion of the electrons in a given type of trap, and that when these have gone the stability of the remainder is characterized by a lifetime of the order of magnitude indicated in Table 3.8. It has been suggested (Garlick *and* Robinson, 1972) that the subsidiary escape is due to overlap of wave-functions—presumably a wave mechanical 'tunnelling' process similar to that involved in the escape of an alpha particle from the nucleus.

3.11. Related techniques

Fission track dating has already been outlined in section 1.2. There are two other solid-state effects induced by nuclear radiation which have been suggested as possibilities for dating. Both of them are ways other than thermoluminescence of measuring the trapped electron population.

Thermally stimulated current (TSC)

Electrons released from traps in the course of a glow curve can give rise to a measurable conductivity in an otherwise insulating solid;

this is due to those electrons which spend a finite time in the conduction band before capture at other traps or centres. By plotting current against temperature a curve similar to a TL glow curve is obtained. In the work on volcanic lava by Hwang *and* Fremlin (1970), the samples used were 1 mm thick and the current due to a few tens of volts was measured with a d.c. amplifier. A difficulty is that a substantial TSC (equivalent to a few megarads of radiation) is observed in an unirradiated sample—possibly due to ionic conduction—and consequently the technique has potential only for old geological samples.

Thermally-stimulated exo-electron emission (TSEE)

Many substances that exhibit TL also show electron emission at about the same temperature. It seems that electrons are able to escape despite the fact that their kinetic energy is insufficient to overcome the surface potential barrier; it is presumed that these are electrons released into the conduction from traps very close to the surface. The effect is measured by heating the sample inside a Geiger–Muller counter.

Because the effective sensitive layer is very thin the technique has the potential advantage in radiation dosimetry of being able to measure short-range particles in the presence of a strong gamma ray background. A difficulty is that the sensitivity is highly dependent on surface condition and liable to change with heating. Rather surprisingly, preliminary reports of investigation into dating application claim that there is no effect analogous to spurious TL, i.e. there is no appreciable TSEE signal from unirradiated material.

REFERENCES

1. *Technical and Developmental*

AITKEN, M. J. (1968). Thermoluminescent dating in archaeology: Introductory review. *Thermoluminescence of Geological Materials* (ed. D. J. McDougal), pp. 369–78. Academic Press, New York.

AITKEN, M. J. (1969). Thermoluminescent dosimetry of environmental radiation on archaeological sites. *Archaeometry*, **11**, 109–14.

AITKEN, M. J. (1970). Dating by archaeomagnetic and thermoluminescent methods. *Phil. Trans. R. Soc. Lond. A.* **269**, 77–88.

AITKEN, M. J. *and* ALLDRED, J. C. (1972). The assessment of error limits in thermoluminescent dating. *Archaeometry*, **14**, 257–67.

AITKEN, M. J., ALLDRED, J. C., *and* THOMPSON, J. (1968). A photon-ratemeter system for low-level thermoluminescence measurements. *Second International Conference on Luminescence Dosimetry* (eds. J. A. Auxier, K. Becker, *and*

E. M. Robinson), 248–65. Avail. as CONF-680920 from U.S. National Bureau of Standards.
AITKEN, M. J. *and* FLEMING, S. J. (1972). Thermoluminescence dosimetry in archaeological dating, *Topics in Radiation Dosimetry Supplement 1* (ed. F. H. Attix), pp. 1–78. Academic Press, New York.
AITKEN, M. J., FLEMING, S. J., DOELL, R. R., *and* TANGUY, J. C. (1968). Thermoluminescent study of lavas from Mount Etna: preliminary results. In *Thermoluminescence of Geological Materials* (ed. D. J. McDougall), pp. 359–66. Academic Press, New York.
AITKEN, M. J., FLEMING, S. J., REID, J., *and* TITE, M. S. (1968). Elimination of spurious thermoluminescence. *Thermoluminescence of Geological Materials* (ed. D. J. McDougall), pp. 133–42. Academic Press, New York.
AITKEN, M. J., TITE, M. S., *and* FLEMING, S. J. (1967). Thermoluminescent response to heavily ionizing radiations. *Luminescent Dosimetry* (ed. F. H. Attix), pp. 490–501. Available as CONF-650637 from U.S. National Bureau of Standards.
AITKEN, M. J., TITE, M. S., *and* REID, J. (1963). Thermoluminescent dating: progress report. *Archaeometry*, **6**, 65–75.
AITKEN, M. J., TITE, M. S., *and* REID, J. (1964). Thermoluminescent dating of ancient ceramics. *Nature*, **202**, 1032–3.
AITKEN, M. J., ZIMMERMAN, D. W., *and* FLEMING, S. J. (1968). Thermoluminescent dating of ancient pottery. *Nature*, **219**, 442–4.
CAMERON, J. R., ZIMMERMAN, D. W., *and* BLAND, R. W. (1967). Thermoluminescence vs. roentgens in lithium fluoride: a proposed mathematical model. In *Luminescence Dosimetry* (ed. F. H. Attix), pp. 47–56. Available as CONF-650637 from U.S. National Bureau of Standards.
CHERRY, R. D. (1964). Alpha particle detection techniques applicable to the measurement of samples from the natural radiation environment. In *The Natural Radiation Environment* (ed. J. A. S. Adams *and* W. M. Lowder), pp. 407–26.
CHRISTODOULIDES, C. *and* FREMLIN, J. H. (1971). Thermoluminescence of biological materials. *Nature*, **232**, 257–8.
CLARK, S. P., PETERMAN, Z. E., *and* HEIER, K. S. (1966). Abundances of uranium, thorium and potassium. *Mem. Geol. Soc. Amer.* **97**, 521–41.
CURIE, D. (1963). *Luminescence in Crystals* (transl. G. F. J. Garlick). Methuen, London; Wiley, New York.
DESAI, V. S., *and* AITKEN, M. J. (1974). Radon escape from pottery: effect of wetness. *Archaeometry*, **16**, 95–7.
FLEMING, S. J. (1966). Study of thermoluminescence of crystalline extracts from pottery. *Archaeometry*, **9**, 170–3.
FLEMING, S. J. (1968). The colour of spurious thermoluminescence in dosimetry phosphors. *Second International Conference on Luminescence Dosimetry* (eds. J. A. Auxier, K. Becker, *and* E. M. Robinson), pp. 266–80. Available as CONF-680920 from the U.S. National Bureau of Standards.
FLEMING, S. J. (1969). The acquisition of radioluminescence by ancient ceramics. Unpublished D.Phil. thesis, Oxford University.
FLEMING, S. J. (1970). Thermoluminescence dating: Refinement of the quartz inclusion method. *Archaeometry*, **12**, 135–46.
FLEMING, S. J. (1971). Thermoluminescent authenticity testing of ancient ceramics: the effects of sampling by drilling. *Archaeometry*, **13**, 59–69.
FLEMING, S. J. (1973). The pre-dose technique: a new thermoluminescent dating method. *Archaeometry*, **15**, 13–30.
FLEMING, S. J. *and* STONEHAM, D. (1973). The subtraction technique of thermoluminescent dating. *Archaeometry*, **15**, 229–38.

FLEMING, S. J. and THOMPSON, J. (1970). Quartz as a heat-resistant dosimeter. *Health Physics*, **18**, 567–8.

GARLICK, G. F. C. and ROBINSON, I. (1972). The thermoluminescence of lunar samples. In *The Moon* (eds. S. K. Runcorn and H. Urey), pp. 324–9. International Astronom. Union.

GÖKSU, H. Y. and FREMLIN, J. H. (1972). Thermoluminescence from unirradiated flints: regeneration thermoluminesce. *Archaeometry*, **14**, 127–32.

GRÖGLER, N., HOUTERMANS, F. G., and STAUFFER, H. (1960). Ueber die Datierung von Keramik und Ziegel durch Thermolumineszenz. *Helv. Phys. Acta*, **33**, 595–6.

HWANG, F. S. W. and FREMLIN, J. H. (1970). A new dating technique using thermally-stimulated current. *Archaeometry* **12**, 67–72.

ICHIKAWA, Y. (1965). Dating of ancient ceramics by thermoluminescence. *Bull. Inst. chem. Res. Kyoto Univ.* **43**, 1–6.

JASÍNKA, M. and NIEWIADOMSKI, T. (1970). Thermoluminescence of biological materials. *Nature*, **227**, 1159–60.

JOHNSON, N. M. and BLANCHARD, R. L. (1967). Radiation dosimetry from the natural thermoluminescence of fossil shell. *Am. Mineral*, **52**, 1297–310.

KENNEDY, G. C. and KNOPFF, L. (1960). Dating by thermoluminescence. *Archaeology*, **13**, 147–8.

LEDERER, C. M., HOLLANDER, J. M., and PERLMAN, I. (1967). *Table of Isotopes*, 6th edn. John Wiley & Sons Inc. New York, London, and Sydney.

MAZESS, R. B. and ZIMMERMAN, D. W. (1966). Pottery dating from thermoluminescence. *Science*, **152**, 347–8.

MEJDAHL, V. (1969). Thermoluminescence dating of ancient Danish ceramics. *Archaeometry*, **11**, 99–104.

MEJDAHL, V. (1970). Measurement of environmental radiation at archaeological excavation sites. *Archaeometry*, **12**, 147–71.

MEJDAHL, V. (1972). Progress in TL dating at Risö. *Archaeometry*, **14**, 245–56.

MEJDAHL, V. (1972a). Dosimetry techniques in thermoluminescent dating. Risø Report no. 261. Danish Atomic Energy Commission, Risø DK-4000, Roskilde, Denmark.

RALPH, E. K. and HAN, M. C. (1966). Dating of pottery by thermoluminescence. *Nature*, **210**, 245–7.

RALPH, E. K. and HAN, M. C. (1969). Potential of thermoluminescence in supplementing radiocarbon dating. *Wld. Archaeol.* **1**, 157–69.

SUNTHARALINGHAM, N. and CAMERON, J. R. (1969). Thermoluminescent response of lithium fluoride to radiations with different LET. *Phys. Med. Biol.* **14**, 397–410.

TANNER, A. B. (1964). Radon migration in ground water: a review. In *The natural radiation environment* (eds. J. A. S. Adams and W. M. Lowder), pp. 164–90. University of Chicago Press.

TOCHILIN, E. and GOLDSTEIN, N. (1966). Dose rate and spectral measurements from pulsed X-ray generators. *Health Phys.* **12**, 1705–13.

TITE, M. S. (1966). Thermoluminescent dating of ancient ceramics: A reassessment. *Archaeometry*, **9**, 155–69.

TITE, M. S. and WAINE, J. (1962). Thermoluminescent dating: A reappraisal. *Archaeometry*, **5**, 53–79.

TURNER, R. C., RADLEY, J. M., and MAYNEORD, W. V. (1958). The α-ray activity of human tissues. *Brit. J. Radiol.* **31**, 397–406.

WINTLE, A. G. (1973). Anomalous fading of thermoluminescence in mineral samples. *Nature*, **244**, 143–4.

ZIMMERMAN, D. W. (1967). Thermoluminescence from fine grains from ancient pottery. *Archaeometry*, **10**, 26–8.

ZIMMERMAN, D. W. (1971). Thermoluminescent dating using fine grains from pottery. *Archaeometry*, **13**, 29–52.

ZIMMERMAN, D. W. (1971a). Uranium distributions in archaeological ceramics: dating of radioactive inclusions. *Science*, **174**, 818–9.

ZIMMERMAN, J. (1971b). The radiation-induced increase of the 100°C thermoluminescence sensitivity of fired quartz. *J. Phys. C.: Solid St. Phys.* **4**, 3265–76.

ZIMMERMAN, J. (1971c). The radiation-induced increase of thermoluminescence sensitivity of the dosimetry phosphor LiF (TLD-100). *J. Phys. C.: Solid St. Phys.* **4**, 3277–91.

ZIMMERMAN, D. W. (1972). Relative thermoluminescence effects of alpha- and beta-radiation. *Radiation Effects*, **14**, 81–92.

2. *Application to archaeological dating and to authenticity testing*

AITKEN, M. J., MOOREY, P. R. S., *and* UCKO, P. J. (1971). The authenticity of vessels and figurines in the Hacilar style, *Archaeometry* **13**, 89–141.

AITKEN, M. J., ZIMMERMAN, D. W., *and* FLEMING, S. J. (1970). Thermoluminescent dating of pottery, Proceedings of the 12th Nobel Symposium at Uppsala, August, 1969, *Radiocarbon Variations and Absolute Chronology* (ed. I. Olsson), pp. 129–40. Almqvist and Wiksell, Stockholm.

BRONSON, B. *and* HAN, M. C. (1972). A thermoluminescence series from Thailand, *Antiquity*, **46**, 322–6.

FAGG, B. E. B. *and* FLEMING, S. J. (1970). Thermoluminescent dating of a terracotta of the Nok culture, Nigeria. *Archaeometry*, **12**, 53–5.

FLEMING, S. J. (1971c). Thermoluminescent dating of sherds. Appendix to P. Warren, Myrtos: An early bronze settlement in Crete). *British School at Athens Supplementary Volume No. 7*, 343–4.

FLEMING, S. J. (1973a). Thermoluminescence and glaze studies of a group of T'ang dynasty ceramics. *Archaeometry*, **15**, 31–52.

FLEMING, S. J., MOSS, H. M., *and* JOSEPH, A. (1970). Thermoluminescent authenticity test of some 'Six Dynasties' figures. *Archaeometry*, **12** (1), 135–46.

FLEMING, S. J. *and* ROBERTS, H. S. (1970). Thermoluminescent authenticity testing of a pontic amphora, *Archaeometry*, **12** (2), 129–34.

FLEMING, S. J., *and* SAMPSON, E. H. (1972). The authenticity of figurines, animals and pottery facsimiles of bronzes in the Hui Hsien Style. *Archaeometry*, **14**, 237–43.

FLEMING, S. J. *and* STONEHAM, D. (1973a). Thermoluminescent authenticity study and dating of Renaissance terracottas. *Archaeometry*, **15**, 239–48.

HUXTABLE, J., AITKEN, M. J., *and* WEBER, J. C. (1972). Thermoluminescence dating of baked clay balls of the poverty point culture. *Archaeometry*, **14**, 269–75.

HUXTABLE, J., ZIMMERMAN, D. W., HASAN, S. N. *and* GAUR, R. C. (1972). Thermoluminescent dates for ochre-coloured pottery from India. *Antiquity*, **46**, 62–3.

SAMPSON, E. H., FLEMING, S. J., *and* BRAY, W. (1972). Thermoluminescent dating of Colombian pottery in the Yotoco style. *Archaeometry*, **14**, 119–26.

WINTLE, A. G. *and* OAKLEY, K. P. (1972). Thermoluminescent dating of fired rock-crystal from Bellan Bandi Palassa, Ceylon. *Archaeometry*, **14**, 277–80.

ZIMMERMAN, D. W. *and* HUXTABLE, J. (1969). Recent applications and developments in fine grain dating, *Archaeometry*, **11**, 105–8.

ZIMMERMAN, D. W. *and* HUXTABLE, J. (1970). Some thermoluminescent dates for linear pottery. *Antiquity*, **44**, 304–5.

ZIMMERMAN, D. W. *and* HUXTABLE, J. (1971). Thermoluminescent dating of upper palaeolithic fired clay from Dolni Vestonice. *Archaeometry*, **13**, 53–7.

4 Archaeomagnetism

4.1. Introduction

The magnetic elements

IF a magnetized needle is suspended at its centre of gravity so that it can swing freely in all directions, it will take up a definite inclination to the horizontal and lie in a definite vertical plane. This plane is called the local magnetic meridian, and the angle which the needle makes with the horizontal is called the inclination *I* or the angle of dip. (See Fig. 4.1(a)).

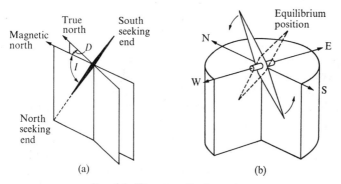

FIG. 4.1. The magnetic elements.

If the needle is now weighted so that it is horizontal, it will still take up a position in the magnetic meridian plane, and the directions defined by the needle are called magnetic north and magnetic south. The angle between magnetic north and geographical (or true) north is called the compass variation, or more commonly, the declination *D*.

Suppose that the weighting is now taken off the needle, and it is fixed onto a horizontal axle at its centre of gravity, the axle pointing magnetic east-west so that the needle can swing freely in the magnetic meridian plane (Fig. 4.1(b)). If unrestrained it will of course take up a direction making the angle of dip with the horizontal. Let the needle now be turned, on its axle, through an angle of 90°; the torque (or couple) required to restrain it from returning towards its equilibrium position is a measure of the magnetic intensity (or field strength), F. If the magnetic moment of the needle is M then the torque equals $M \times F$. It is convenient to represent a magnetic field by means of lines of force. Their direction at any point is identical with that taken up by a freely suspended magnetized needle, and their concentration (number of lines per cm^2 normal to their direction) represents the field strength F.

The values of the three elements, declination (D), dip or inclination (I), and intensity (F), define the magnetic field at any point on the earth's surface. Both I and F are strongly dependent on latitude. The field is approximately the same as would be produced by a short bar magnet at the centre of the earth inclined at an angle of 11° to the axis of rotation (see Fig. 4.2). I varies from 0° at the magnetic equator to 90° at the magnetic poles; the value of F at the equator is half the value of the poles.

Secular variation

It should be understood that the bar magnet of the last paragraph is hypothetical. Except at the centre the core of the earth is a hot liquid under high pressure, and according to the dynamo theory 99% of the earth's field is due to a magneto-hydrodynamic electric current system in this liquid core. Various sources of energy have been suggested for this dyanmo, e.g. convection effects arising from cooling of the earth's surface or from heating of the interior by radioactivity, chemical separations and crystallizations, mechanical torques arising from the 26 000-year precessional motion of the earth's axis.

Excluding local anomalies due to iron-ore deposits in the earth's crust and certain very small transient variations the earth's actual field equals that expected on the bar-magnet model (*the dipole field*) plus additional terms (*the non-dipole field*) which in some regions reach more than 20% of the total field. The 'non-dipole field' of the earth can be subdivided into ten regions, each several thousand miles across. It has been found that at present each region drifts westwards as a whole, on the average at the rate of 0·2° of longitude per year. This has been interpreted as the slow motion with respect to the earth's crust of local irregularities in the current distribution near the surface of the liquid core. Together with any changes in the 'dipole field' as a whole the resulting changes in *D, I,* and *F* are termed *secular variation*.

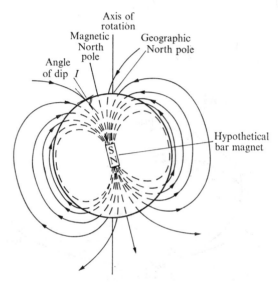

Fig. 4.2. Bar magnet representation of the main part of earth's magnetic field—the dipole field. The *lines of force* represent, at any point, the direction in which a small magnetized needle tries to point. The concentration of these lines is a measure of the *field strength*.

Archaeomagnetism

At the present time the declination (*D*) for London changes by roughly 1° every decade, becoming less westerly. The angle of dip (*I*) also changes and the secular variation of these two elements has been recorded for London, Paris, and Rome over the past four centuries from observations on suspended magnetized needles—see Fig. 4.3. This information is taken from Bauer (1899), who collated early magnetic data from various parts of the world, and from later records (see e.g., Kaye and Laby's Tables of Physical and Chemical Constants).

Besides the written record, this information is also stored in baked clay which has remained in position on cooling down from firing by means of the thermoremanent magnetism (TRM) which is induced by the geomagnetic field in iron oxide minerals in the clay as it cools from 700°C. This means that the baked clay acquires a weak but permanent magnetization in the same direction as the field at the time of cooling (and in the case of successive firings it is the last cooling that is effective).

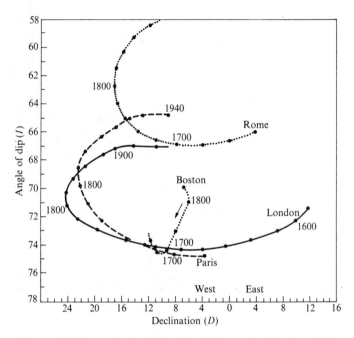

FIG. 4.3. Secular variation from historical records—London, Paris, Rome, and Boston. The time scale is indicated by dots at 20-year intervals. Prior to 1900 the curves shown are those obtained by Bauer (1899) using recorded observations to determine an empirical formula; Bauer's extrapolations into periods when only declination was measured have been omitted.

Clay has been used for thousands of years in the construction of hearths, ovens, and kilns. Hence whenever such a structure can be dated by reference to archaeological chronology, or by radiocarbon or thermoluminescent dating, there is the opportunity to obtain otherwise irretrievable geophysical information. Conversely, once the secular variation curve has been thus extended backwards into archaeologically interesting periods, the direction of remanent magnetization found in a structure can be used to establish its date. Unfortunately the secular variation curve is different for different regions of the earth's surface so that calibration with known-age structures needs to be done for each region in which 'magnetic dating' is to be used. Nor is the behaviour regular and although for Europe during the period covered by Fig. 4.3 the data are approximated by incomplete ellipses, in earlier centuries (see Fig. 4.9) the form is quite different.

It is also possible to determine the ancient intensity of the geomagnetic field by measurements on baked clay. This is because the strength of the magnetization acquired is proportional to the field intensity. If a sample is reheated and allowed to cool in the present day field, the ratio of the original magnetic moment to the new moment gives the ratio of the ancient intensity to the present day intensity. Since records of direct measurement of intensity are only available over the past two centuries this type of archaeomagnetic data is of particular interest geophysically as well as for radiocarbon dating (see section 2.8). Reliable results are not easy to obtain owing to the possibility of mineralogical changes occurring during the reheating. The necessary techniques and criteria for reliable results were established by Thellier *and* Thellier (1959) and their first results showed that substantial variations had indeed occurred in the past— they found that in Roman times the intensity in France was some 60% higher than its present-day value.

For intensity measurements it is not essential that the baked clay should have remained undisturbed. Bricks and tiles can be used, also fragments of pottery. It is possible to use bricks and tiles for determination of the angle of dip since the requirements of stacking in a kiln usually ensures that one face or edge is horizontal (and irregularities in the stacking can be averaged out by measuring a large number of samples). The angle of dip can similarly be found from whole pots if the form is such as to necessitate that they should be baked standing upright. This is the case, for example, with Chinese Yüeh ware on account of the heavy glaze and ornamentation, but unfortunately the more usual technique in other cultures was to pack the pots in the kiln rather irregularly.

The present state of archaeomagnetism derives mainly from the work of Professor E. Thellier at L'Institut de Physique du Globe in Paris from 1933 onwards (and now at Le Laboratoire de Géomagnétisme du Parc-Saint-Maur). Archaeomagnetism has developed in parallel with and as part of the much wider field of paleomagnetism. The former is usually taken to signify some involvement with ancient man whereas the latter covers all geophysical and geological applications. The 'fossilized' magnetic record in rocks is used to give information about the past behaviour of the geomagnetic field on a geological time scale and also to make deductions about the formation and drifting of the earth's crust (see, e.g., Irving, 1964; or McElhinny, 1973; for shorter accounts, see Bullard (1958) or Doell (1969)).

The next three sections outline the physical mechanism responsible for remanent magnetism and methods of measurement. Discussion of results is given in section 4.5 *et seq.*

Units

The centimetre–gram–second electromagnetic system (e.m.u.) is commonly employed in paleomagnetism and this practice will be followed in chapters 4, 6, and 7. Magnetic field strength is measured in *oersted* and intensity of magnetization (magnetic moment per cm^3) in *gauss*, so that *gauss* cm^3 is the unit for magnetic moment and *gauss per oersted* the unit for volume susceptibility. On this basis the unit for specific magnetization is *gauss* cm^3 *per gram* and the unit for specific susceptibility is *gauss* cm^3 *gram*$^{-1}$ *per oersted*; however for the sake of brevity the latter is denoted by *e.m.u. per gram*. In some texts *e.m.u.*, is used more widely, as a general substitute for all units of this system.

For conversion to the S.I. (rationalized M.K.S.) system it is useful to note:

1 oersted of magnetic field strength $= 79.6$ amp/metre
1 gauss of magnetic induction $= 10^{-4}$ tesla
1 gauss of intensity of magnetization $= 10^3$ amp/metre
1 gauss/oersted of volume susceptibility $= 12.6$ SI units
1 gauss cm^3/gram of specific magnetization $= 1$ amp metre^2/kilogram
1 e.m.u./gram of specific susceptibility
  $= 1.26 \times 10^{-2}$ SI units/kilogram.

In the S.I. system there is risk of ambiguity owing to the alternative usage of weber/metre^2 for magnetization instead of amp/metre, the former unit being larger by a factor of 0.796×10^6. Use of amp/metre has now been recommended by the International Association of Geomagnetism and Aeronomy (at its 1973 meeting in Kyoto).

4.2. Remanent magnetism: TRM

The thermoremanent magnetism (TRM) of baked clay results from the magnetic properties of *magnetite* (Fe_3O_4) and *haematite* ($\alpha\text{-}Fe_2O_3$). The average iron-oxide content of the earth's crust is 6·8%, and most

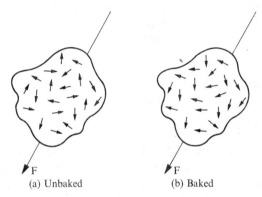

| (a) Unbaked | (b) Baked |

FIG. 4.4. Domain alignment in backed clay.

(a) Unbaked clay. Domains are in random directions and the net magnetic effect is very small.

(b) Baked clay. Elevated temperature has allowed preferential alignment which subsequently remains 'frozen' at normal temperatures.

soil and clay, and some rocks, contain significant quantities of these minerals dispersed as fine grains. The main features of the TRM can be understood by regarding these minerals as ferromagnetic (strictly speaking magnetite is ferri*magnetic, and haematite is described as a canted *anti*ferromagnetic lattice). In a ferromagnetic lattice exchange interactions cause parallel alignment of the atomic magnetic moments and magnetic domains are formed; these are minute volumes within which the mineral is spontaneously magnetized in a uniform direction. The way in which TRM is acquired may be visualized from Fig. 4.4. In raw clay the domains (which can be thought of as little bar magnets) are randomly orientated and the net magnetic effect is zero since on the average every domain is balanced out by another pointing in the reverse direction. If the temperature is raised (to several hundred °C or more) the thermal agitation of the crystal lattice allows some of the domains to be aligned by the earth's magnetic field. On cooling, the domain directions remain fixed and because of the preferential alignment there is now a weak permanent magnetization in the same direction as the earth's field.

Besides being the commonest archaeological material, baked clay is also the most satisfactory for archaeomagnetism. Baked soil is difficult to collect as a coherent sample, and burnt stones, even if sufficiently magnetic (limestone usually contains very little iron), are not as reliable, although 'rock magnetism' is the whole basis of palaeomagnetic studies. Metallic iron is useless; the direction of its magnetization is strongly influenced by the shape of the object and it is not stable.

Properties of TRM

Before giving a more detailed discussion of the way in which TRM is acquired the outstanding properties of this remarkable phenomenon are now listed.

(a) The direction of the TRM is the same as that of the magnetic field (as long as any local field due to the magnetism of the clay itself is small; ideally this requires the intensity of magnetization to be less than 10^{-3} gauss, but in practice much stronger magnetizations are tolerable).

(b) For given thermal treatment the intensity of TRM is proportional to the magnetic field strength (excluding magnetic fields very much stronger than encountered naturally).

(c) The intensity (after cooling) increases with the temperature of baking, up to a limiting value reached when the baking temperature is 675°C (see Fig. 4.5).

(d) A second heating, in a different magnetic field, to the maximum temperature reached during the first (or 675°C, whichever is lower) destroys all trace of the original magnetization.

(e) The partial TRM, $M(T_1, T_2)$, acquired as the sample cooled from T_1 to T_2, is unaltered as long as the temperature subsequently remains below T_2, but is completely destroyed if the temperature reaches T_1. Thus, in Fig. 4.5, if after the first cooling from above 675°C, the sample is subsequently reheated to 500°C (say) and then allowed to cool in a space where the magnetic field strength is zero (by artificial annulment), the TRM remaining is M (675°C, 500°C) as indicated. The dashed curve shows the effect of such demagnetization for successively increasing temperatures.

(f) The carriers that acquire magnetization within a given temperature interval lose it, on demagnetization, in the same temperature interval. This explains why the amount acquired is equal to the amount lost, as stated in (e), but it implies also that if after a first heating with a certain orientation of the sample, there is a second heating to a lower temperature and with a different orientation, the two superposed magnetizations can be separated by careful demagnetization, both in

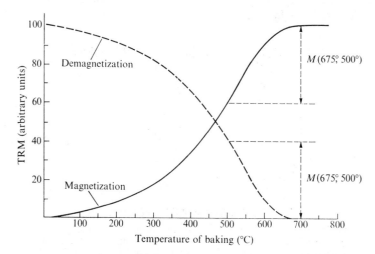

FIG. 4.5. Acquisition of TRM—idealized curve for baked clay. The full curve shows the magnetization (measured at 20°C) acquired in cooling in a magnetic field from the temperature of baking to 20°C. The broken curve shows the gradual demagnetization of a sample that had been fully magnetized; this is by cooling in zero magnetic field and the curve shows the magnetization remaining after coolings from successively increasing temperatures.
The shape of the curve depends on the composition of the sample. However, the demagnetization curve should always be the mirror image of the magnetization curve—if not, then mineralogical change has occurred on in the course of the bakings.

magnitude and direction. The vectors in Fig. 4.6, represent two such magnetizations. Archaeologically, M (675°, 400°) might derive from the initial baking of a vase, the full magnetization having been partially destroyed by a second heating to 400°C, perhaps for the purpose of firing the glaze, but in a different orientation with respect to the magnetic field. Thus M (400°, 20°) is in a different direction to M (675°, 400°) and the resultant, actually observed, is in a different direction still. If the vase is now cooled in zero field from successively increasing temperatures, the direction of remaining magnetization, found after each cooling, gradually swings round to the direction of M (675°, 400°). When the reheating temperature exceeds 400°C there is no further change in the direction of the resultant, only a reduction in the magnitude as M (675°, 400°) is gradually eaten away. Thus, not only can the two directions be found, but also the temperature of the second heating (as long as it did not exceed that of the first, or 675°C, whichever is the lower).

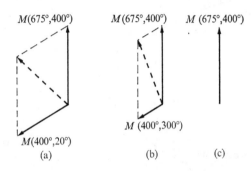

FIG. 4.6. Vector addition of TRM.

(a) The observed magnetization is the resultant of that acquired between 675°C and 400°C during the initial firing, and that acquired between 400°C and 20°C during a second heating when the orientation of the sample was different.

(b) That part of the secondary magnetization acquired between 300°C and 20°C has been removed by cooling from 300°C in zero field.

(c) By cooling from 400°C in zero field, all of the secondary magnetization has been removed.

An extreme case of superposition is two equal TRMs, acquired in different temperature ranges, at 180° to one another. The resultant is nil initially, but as the demagnetization procedure is applied, a magnetic moment develops.

(g) Although the major part of the magnetization is acquired well above normal temperatures, that acquired in cooling between say 50°C and 20°C, is not always negligible; it may account to a few per cent of the total.

(h) The TRM acquired by a sample on cooling from 675°C is usually an order of magnitude larger than the instantaneous magnetization induced in the sample by the same field at normal temperatures.

(i) Stability of direction over thousands of years is demonstrated by pots and bricks which have been stored in a position such that their magnetization is not parallel to the earth's field.

(j) The magnetization is unaltered by the application of opposing magnetic fields unless the applied field strength is several hundred oersteds or more.

Magnetite and haematite

A grain of magnetite is not spontaneously magnetized as a whole because of the strong demagnetizing fields that would result; instead the grain divides into domains, within each of which the magnetization is uniform, and which arrange themselves so that the magnetic flux forms closed paths that as far as possible are within the magnetic material. In magnetite the dimensions of the domains may be as small as 0·03 micron. In haematite, because the saturation magnetization is smaller by a factor of 1000, the domain size can be as large as a millimetre. Consequently, whereas the grains of magnetite are *multi-domain grains*, those of haematite are *single-domain grains*.

The net magnetization of a multi-domain grain in an applied field arises from movement of domain walls such that domains in the direction of the applied field grow at the expense of domains which are opposed to it; for magnetite the coercive force is the order of ten to a hundred oersteds (being largest for small grains). For an assembly of single-domain grains the net magnetization in an applied field arises from domain rotation from one direction of easy magnetization (as determined by the crystalline anisotrophy and by the shape of the grain) to another; for haematite, coercive forces of the order of several thousand oersteds are common. Thus for red highly oxidized baked clay in which haematite predominates the TRM is 'hard' but of a lower specific magnetization than for grey reduced clay in which magnetite is the major constituent. The overall range of specific magnetizations encompassing both types is 0·0001 to 0·1 gauss cm³/g for cooling in a field of 0·5 oersted. Of course for refined clays, such as china clay, the TRM is very much weaker.

Theory of TRM

According to the classic exposition of Néel (1955) the acquisition of thermoremanent magnetism (TRM) can be understood in terms of the blocking temperature T_B. Above T_B the magnetic domains are able to realign as dictated by the direction of the external magnetic field, while below it they are 'frozen'. T_B is of course lower than the temperature at which the alignment of the atomic moments in domains disappears—the Curie point (565°C for magnetite and 675°C for haematite). Because T_B depends on the grain size as well as on the material a sample of baked clay exhibits a continuous spectrum of blocking temperatures. This gives rise to Thellier's law of partial TRM which is incorporated in (e) and (f) above.

For the single-domain grains of haematite the TRM may be understood in comparatively simple terms. In the case of ellipsoidal grains the direction of easy magnetization is along the major axis and the grain is spontaneously magnetized either parallel or antiparallel to that axis. Reversal from one state to the other becomes possible when the thermal agitation energy of the grain is comparable with the potential energy of the constraints tending to keep the magnetization along the preferred axis of the grain. The probability of reversal is a very sharply rising function of temperature and above T_B there is a high probability of reversal within a few seconds, while below T_B reversals is only likely within a very long time. Above T_B the behaviour of the grains is paramagnetic. In the absence of an external field there is no preferential direction but when a field is applied the probability for each grain to be in the state that has a component in the same direction as the field is higher than for the reverse situation. Hence there is a net magnetization in the same direction as the field. When the temperature falls below T_B this magnetization is retained although the applied field may be altered.

Although the intensity of magnetization within a grain is unaffected by the applied field, the net TRM acquired by an assembly of dispersed grains is proportional to it. This is because, although there is a high probability of domain reversal at T_B, the fractional alignment achieved by the field is far from complete—the difference in magnetic potential energy, μF, between the parallel and anti-parallel states being small compared to kT_B. The fractional excess of domains with a component in the field direction is effectively equal to $(\mu F/3kT_B)$, where μ is the magnetic moment of the grain and F the applied field. Thus the TRM of a sample of baked clay is proportional to the field intensity in which it cooled down and archaeomagnetic measurements can be used to determine the ancient geomagnetic field in strength as well as in direction.

The theory of the TRM acquired by multi-domain grains has been developed by Stacey (1963) and by Dickson, Everitt, Parry, *and*

Stacey (1966). It is less straightforward but it leads to the same pattern of behaviour as does the single-domain theory, though with quantitative difference. On the other hand, according to Verhoogen (1959) and to Kobayashi *and* Fuller (1968), the TRM of multi-domain grains really resides in restricted regions displaying properties analogous to those of single-domain grains. A comprehensive account of the theory of rock magnetism has been given by Stacey *and* Banerjee (1974).

Using the parameters suggested by Stacey (1963), grains which become demagnetized by heating for 1 hour at 200°C (for example) have a relaxation time of greater than 200 000 years at 20°C. Hence for the specimen of Fig. 4.5 at least 90% of the TRM is stable over archaeological times; in practice any unstable component can be removed by successive demagnetization to increasing temperatures in zero field until the remanent direction stays the same.

4.3. Other types of remanent magnetization

Archaeomagnetism rests on the assumption that the remanent magnetization of the sample records information about the earth's field existing when the feature cooled down for the last time. If this last cooling did not correspond to the archaeologically assumed use of the feature, that is not a fault of the scientific technique. There is also the possibility of secondary magnetization having been acquired through minor reheatings due, for example, to an accidental fire; such effects can be separated out by thermal demagnetization in zero field, and anyway their occurrence is likely to be suspected from visual inspection of the archaeological feature. However there are in addition three causes from which remanent magnetization can be acquired without heating: time, strong magnetic fields, and chemical changes.

Fortunately such effects are either negligible or absent in most samples of baked clay. But in some cases they may cause small errors, and in others the results may be completely incomprehensible.

Viscous remanent magnetism (*VRM*)

The blocking temperature T_B has been explained as the temperature at which thermal agitation causes continual domain reversal in single-domain grains, and domain rearrangement in multi-domain grains. There will be some grains for which T_B is below normal temperatures. Such grains follow changes in the applied field direction and exhibit no remanent effects. However, grains for which T_B is in the temperature range immediately above room temperature exhibit a sort of magnetic 'viscosity'—a remanent magnetism builds up as the time of application of the external field is prolonged, and if the external field is removed, the remanent magnetism does not disappear instantaneously. This viscosity effect arises because although the average thermal agitation energy of a grain is insufficient to overcome the constraining forces, there is a finite probability that each grain will at some time possess an above-average thermal energy. There is some similarity here with evaporation from a liquid well below its boiling point; on the average the molecules do not have enough kinetic energy to escape from the surface, but, because for short intervals a few of the molecules have energies well in excess of the average, evaporation takes place.

As the time of observation is prolonged, the chance of a given excess thermal energy grows and so more grains are affected, and also those with higher values of T_B. Experimentally it is found that the remanent magnetization is proportional to the logarithm of the time. This has the fortunate consequence that the growth (or decay) of viscous magnetization observed in a sample between $t = 10$ min and $t = 14$ days, is equal to the amount acquired between $t = 14$ days and $t = 90$ years, or between $t = 90$ years and $t = 200\,000$ years. Thus observation of the change of magnetization during a few weeks of laboratory storage indicates whether or not the viscous magnetization acquired since archaeological times is appreciable. Viscous magnetization is removed by heating to around 150°C and cooling in zero field; it can also be removed by alternating-field demagnetization.

Strong magnetic fields

In fields of a hundred oersteds or more, a sample may acquire remanent magnetization because the applied field exceeds the coercive force of some of its grains. This isothermal remanent magnetism (IRM) is acquired instantaneously and does not decay when the field is removed. For the single-domain grains of haematite, fields of several thousand oersteds are necessary, but for the multi-domain grains of magnetite several hundred oersteds are enough to produce an IRM. An IRM can be produced in baked clay by the magnetic field associated with a flash of lightning but fortunately, like VRM, IRM can be removed by application of alternating field demagnetization. Lightning may also produce anhysteritic remanent magnetization (ARM), the effect of a strong alternating field in the presence of a

weak steady field. ARM may be inadvertently produced in the course
of alternating field demagnetization if the earth's field is not precisely
annulled.

Chemical magnetization

The occurrence, within a sample, of a chemical change whereby a
magnetic mineral is formed, results in a remanent magnetization in a
direction dictated by the existing external field direction. Such chemical
remanence shows the high stability of TRM and cannot be separated.
Consequently, the magnetization of a sample in which this has
happened will be mistaken for TRM. The field direction deduced will
not be that corresponding to the time of last cooling but to some later
period.

Fortunately, in well-baked clay such chemical changes are unlikely
to occur spontaneously, since such material is remarkably stable on
reheating. However, excessive weathering, the impregnation of a
sample with organic matter, or prolonged immersion in water could
lead to such parasitic effects.

Detrital remanent magnetism

Although not an interfering effect it is convenient to include this
type of remanent magnetism here. *Detrital* remanent magnetism
(DRM) occurs in sediments deposited in calm water. The magnetic
particles present inherit a remanence from the rocks from which
they have been eroded and tend to be aligned by the geomagnetic field
as they settle. In addition to this 'true' DRM magnetization may be
acquired after deposition by rotation and by chemical change; if this
post-depositional component is strong the direction recorded in the
sediment may correspond to an appreciably later time than the actual
date of deposition.

The DRM of lake sediments and glacial varves is another source of
archaeomagnetic data and the DRM measured in cores obtained
from deep-sea sediments has been important in detecting geomagnetic
reversals. The latter application has been reviewed by Opdyke (1972)
who stresses the importance of alternating-field cleaning of samples
before measurement in order to remove secondary components.

4.4. Practical procedures

The discussion of the next three sub-sections is primarily in respect
of measuring remanent direction, though much of it is also relevant

to measurement of ancient intensity for which the techniques are outlined in the fourth sub-section.

Before embarking on the appreciable labour involved in sample collection and measurement it is wise to ask, in respect of each application, what benefit it is going to be. A date can only be obtained if the secular variation curve has been established for the region in question, and for the purpose of building up the curve, samples are only acceptable if in association with reliable archaeological dating evidence; otherwise they are valueless and misleading.

Sample collection

For an archaeologist faced with the question of which burnt features on his site are suitable for magnetic dating, the prime consideration is whether any movement has occurred since baking. Thus in a pottery kiln, reliable samples would be expected to come from the floor and the lower part of the walls rather than from the superstructure. Before any sample is extracted for measurement it is of course vital that its exact orientation should be marked on it. This is done by partially encasing it in gypsum plaster, or foaming polystyrene, before detaching it from the structure. To do this a miniature square 'ditch' is dug, leaving the sample as a stump in the middle, about 10 cm by 10 cm. A square metal frame is placed in the ditch and levelled. Plaster is then poured in and the top surface smoothed off flush with the top of the frame. When the plaster has set, a line is sighted from a nearby theodolite and marked on the top surface. The theodolite orientation datum is found by shooting the sun at a known time and using suitable astronomical tables. Hence the azimuth of the line of the plaster surface is found with respect to true (geographic) north; the sample's orientation with respect to the horizontal is provided by the plaster surface. When the marking is complete the sample is detached by cutting away underneath the frame and transported to the laboratory for measurement.

Although the precision of measurement (and of marking) is better than 0·5°, the scatter in the individual directions found in samples from the same structure is often of the order of 5° or 10°. This makes it important to take at least a dozen samples from each structure. The most obvious cause of the scatter is that irregular subsidence has taken place, but there is also evidence that it can be due to distortion of the geomagnetic field by the magnetism of the structure itself (Harold 1960; Weaver 1961, 1962; Aitken *and* Hawley, 1971).

Measuring instruments

The astatic magnetometer consists essentially of two bar magnets of equal strength fixed rigidly at either end of a rod about 10 cm long (Fig. 4.7) and suspended by a fine fibre of phosphor-bronze or quartz. Since the two magnets are antiparallel the net torque due to the earth's field is zero. On the other hand, the torque on the lower magnet due to a small sample positioned beneath it is substantially greater than

Fibre

N

S

S

N

Sample

FIG. 4.7. Principle of the astatic magnetometer. The restoring torque due to the earth's field is eliminated by using magnets of exactly equal moment. There is a net torque due to the sample because it is nearer to the lower magnet than to the upper one.

that on the upper one and the resultant deflection is a measure of the horizontal component of the magnetization of the sample. The classic description of this type of instrument, and consideration of its fundamental sensitivity capabilities, has been given by Blackett (1952). A good quality instrument can detect samples having an intensity of magnetization of the order of 10^{-7} gauss.

For archaeomagnetic work the astatic magnetometer has the drawback that for nonuniformly magnetized samples the sample dimensions need to be small compared to the distance from the lower magnet. Samples extracted from archaeological structures are usually inhomogeneous and it is not always practical to obtain small samples because of their weak mechanical strength and because of the difficulty of marking an accurate enough direction on a small sample. On account of these considerations Thellier (1938) developed a magnetometer based on electromagnetic induction; the sample is rotated inside a coil system and its magnetization is determined by measurement of the induced voltage. Early measurements were made by observing the throw of a ballistic galvanometer consequent on 180° rotation of the sample but greater sensitivity is obtained by using continuous rotation (typically at 5 Hz). Essentially, the amplitude of the induced

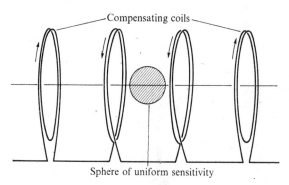

Fig. 4.8. Simple compensated Helmholz coil system for spinner magnetometer. The outer pair of coils is wound in opposite sense to the inner pair thus eliminating the effects of uniform magnetic disturbances and of non-uniform disturbances of constant horizontal gradient.

voltage serves to determine the component of the TRM in the plane of rotation and the phase of the voltage with respect to the driving shaft yields the azimuth of that component.

The continuous rotation system is now usually known as the *'spinner' magnetometer*. In its more sophisticated forms fairly complex coil configurations are used. The objectives of these can be best illustrated by the straightforward system shown in Fig. 4.8. First, in order to avoid interference from external magnetic fields due to moving iron objects (such as passing cars) a pair of compensating coils is connected in series-opposition with the detecting coils; both sets have the same number of area-turns so that the voltages induced in each set by a distant source annul one another. As in the case of the upper magnet of the astatic pair, the outer set is comparatively remote from the sample, and the reduction in sensitivity due to the compensating coils is small. Secondly the detecting coils form a Helmholtz pair so that there is a region within which the detection sensitivity is uniform (a sphere of 20 cm diameter in the case of the 60 cm diameter coils used by Thellier). This uniformity of sensitivity is important when intensity measurements are being made. The direction is determined correctly without uniformity as long as the electronics are such that only the fundamental frequency is accepted.

A spinner magnetometer suitable for archaeomagnetic samples and capable of accommodating samples having dimensions up to 30 cm has been described by Aitken, Harold, Weaver, *and* Young (1967). An alternative to detection by pick-up coils is to use fluxgate detectors and a spinner magnetometer of this type suitable for small samples (2·5 cm diameter) having a minimum detectable moment of order of 10^{-6} gauss cm^3 has been described by Foster (1966). A particularly flexible and convenient development of the fluxgate spinner is the use of an on-line computer for signal analysis (Molyneux, 1971). Also for small samples there is the ultra sensitive spinner using pick-up coils developed by Jelinek (1966).

Magnetometers based on nuclear magnetic resonance (n.m.r.) are not suitable for this type of measurement because they require the field due to the sample to be fairly uniform over the volume of the detector. This means that the sample would have to be at an appreciable distance from the detector and in consequence the sensitivity obtainable would be poor. At the other end of the scale of sophistication is the technique in which the sample is suspended on a fibre (or floated on a pool of mercury) and allowed to orientate itself in a uniform magnetic field; the procedure is simple but slow.

A comprehensive account of measurement techniques will be found in *Methods in paleomagnetism* (Collinson, Creer, *and* Runcorn, 1967). A subsequent development is the superconducting type of magnetometer and it is expected that a new generation of ultra-sensitive instruments will eventually become available (refer, for example, to Zimmerman 1972).

Cleaning techniques

As has been mentioned earlier a sample may carry other remanent magnetizations than the 'true' TRM and before measurement takes place it is necessary, for reliable results, to rid the sample of any such additional magnetizations or at any rate to evaluate their importance. A small viscous (VRM) component is to be expected in most samples, and, since this arises from grains with low blocking temperatures, the obvious way to remove it is the thermal demagnetization procedure in which the sample is heated to the blocking temperature corresponding to the 'hardest' VRM and cooled in zero magnetic field. A suitable gas-fired nonmagnetic oven for use with the bulky samples of archaeomagnetism has been described by Aitken *et al.* (1967); the earth's field is annulled by a single set of coils aligned along the field direction and designed to reduce the field to within 1% of its normal value over a volume of one cubic foot.

The question of what temperature corresponds to the blocking temperature of hardest VRM has been studied by Weaver (1964) who, in respect of archaeomagnetic samples of up to 2000 years old, finds that the major part of the VRM is removed by 100°C but that there is a small further removal by heating to 200°C. In practice, 100°C is usually satisfactory for routine measurements and 200°C is only employed when a sample shows a dramatic shift for the 100°C cleaning. The hardness of the VRM increases slightly with age but on account of the logarithmic law the contribution of the hard VRM is relatively unimportant and the main part of the VRM is acquired in the last few hundred years.

Viscous magnetization can also be removed by alternating-field demagnetization; the earth's field is annulled as before and the sample is subjected to a strong alternating magnetic field which is smoothly and slowly reduced to zero. This randomizes domains having a coercive force less than the maximum value of the alternating field. The normal procedure is to use successively increasing maximum fields until the remanent direction ceases to shift. Because a fairly wide range of blocking temperatures may corrrespond to a given coercive force (Everitt 1961, 1962; Doell *and* Smith, 1969) there may be appreciable removal of 'true' TRM before a field sufficiently strong to remove all VRM has been reached; with thermal washing a much better separation of the two can be achieved. On the other hand, the alternating-field technique is more effective in removal of IRM and ARM (due for instance, to strikes of lightning—see Rimbert 1967, Tanguy 1970).

Intensity measurements

TRM acquired by baked clay is proportional to the intensity of the geomagnetic field in which it cooled so that

$$F_A = \frac{M_A}{M_L} \times F_L \qquad (4.1)$$

where M_A is the moment that the sample acquired by cooling in the ancient field F_A, and M_L is the moment acquired when the sample is reheated and cooled in the present day laboratory field F_L.

The fundamental difficulty with this technique is that during the laboratory reheating mineralogical changes may take place. If so, the effective sample that carries M_L may have TRM properties different from the original sample carrying M_A, and eqn (4.1) is not valid. Such changes may be an actual chemical oxidation or reduction (for example, between magnetite and haematite) or merely an alteration in the condition of the magnetic grains.

Heating in air or in an inert atmosphere as appropriate to the oxidation state of the sample is helpful, but is far from being a complete solution to the problem. Consequently, reliable results can be obtained only if careful tests for stability of TRM properties are incorporated in the experiment and samples thereby found unsatisfactory are rigorously excluded. In the step-by-step heating method of Thellier and Thellier (1959) the sample is successively heated twice to each of a set of increasing temperatures (for instance, 100°C, 200°C, 300°C, etc.). By reversing the orientation of the sample in between the first and second heating it is possible to determine the ancient TRM and the new TRM corresponding to each temperature interval. In the absence of any change in the magnetic characteristics of the sample, the ratio of ancient TRM to new TRM is the same for all temperature intervals; if a significant change is observed the sample is discarded. Alternatively the first heating (and cooling) is carried out in zero magnetic field.

Comment and discussion about these techniques has been given, for instance, by Smith (1967), by Weaver (1966, 1970) and by Bucha (1971) and descriptions of practical utilization by Nagata, Kobayashi, *and* Schwarz (1965). Du Bois *and* Watanabe (1965), Sasajima (1965), and Bucha (1967). It appears that successful application is most to be expected when highly oxidized samples are used. A promising development is the use of alternating field demagnetization as a means of identifying grain categories which have not been affected by the thermal treatment (Shaw, 1974).

4.5. Ancient direction: from archaeological structures

The precision that can be attained under good conditions is illustrated by the measurements made by Thellier *and* Thellier (1951) on orientated samples extracted from a Roman kiln at Carthage of *circa*

A.D. 300—one of the first structures ever sampled for archaeomag-netism. The individual values of *D* and *I* were:

3° 45′ W,	49° 45′	2° 15′ W,	50° 30′	1° 45′ E,	51° 15′
2° 15′ W,	50° 15′	0° 30′ W,	50° 45′	1° 30′ W,	51° 45′
0° 15′ W,	50° 30′	1° 15′ W,	51° 0′	0° 15′ W,	52° 0′

The average values are $D = 1° 15′$ W, $I = 51° 0′$, to be compared with $D = 0° 30′$ W, $I = 58° 0′$ obtained for two Punic kilns contem-poraneous with the sack of Carthage by the Romans in 146 B.C., and $D = 3° 30′$ W, $I = 52°$ for present-day Tunis.

Since this pioneer work archaeomagnetic measurement of ancient direction has been reported for various parts of the world: Arizona and New Mexico (Watanabe *and* Dubois, 1965; Du Bois, 1967, 1969), Australia (Barbetti *and* McElhinney, 1972), Bulgaria (Kovacheva-Nozharova, 1968), Egypt (Du Bois, 1969), England (e.g. Cook *and* Belshé, 1958; Aitken, Harold, *and* Weaver, 1964; Aitken *and* Hawley, 1967), France (e.g. Thellier, 1966), Greece (Belshé, Cook, *and* Cook, 1963; Bammer 1969), Iran (Kawai *et al.*, 1972); Japan (e.g. Watanabe 1958; Kawai *and* Hirooka, 1965; Sasajima 1965; Hirooka 1971) and U.S.S.R. (e.g. Burlatskaya, Nechaeva, *and* Petrova, 1969; Rusakov *and* Zagniy, 1973). The preceding list refers to orientated samples extracted from fired structures thereby allowing determination of both *D* and *I*; some of the results obtained for England, the Ukraine, and Japan are shown in Figs. 4.9, 4.10, and 4.11. The value of *I* can also be obtained from bricks, despite move-ment since baking; this was first demonstrated by Thellier (1936, 1938) and it is possible because of the regular way in which bricks were stacked while being baked. Investigation of the accuracy that can be obtained with bricks has been reported from Denmark (Abraham-sen 1973) and extensive work using bricks has also been carried out in the U.S.S.R. (e.g. Burlatskaya *et al.*, 1970). It is also possible to deduce the ancient value of *I* by measurements on a vase—as was first demonstrated by Folgheraiter (1899)—but only when the orna-mentation or glazing dictates that it must have been baked standing upright on a horizontal surface. This is not the case for most archaeological pottery but results have been reported by Aitken (1958) for Chinese Yüeh ware and by Clarke *and* Connah (1962) for British beaker pottery of the Late Neolithic and Early Bronze Ages.

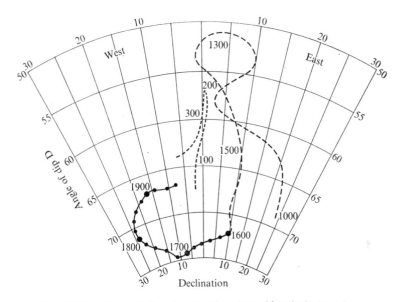

FIG. 4.9. Secular variation for London from historical data (continuous line) and archaeomagnetic data (dashed line). The dates indicated are A.D. The historical curve shown in Fig. 4.3 was the ellipse fitted to the recorded data whereas the historical part of the curve shown above is a better fit (from Aitken 1970).

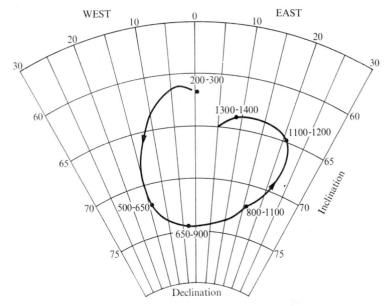

FIG. 4.10. Secular variation in the Ukraine, from archaeomagnetic data (after Rusakov and Zagniy 1973). The dates indicated are A.D.

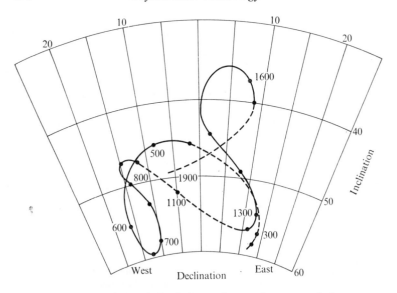

FIG. 4.11. Secular variation in Japan, from archaeomagnetic data (from Hirooka 1971). The dates indicated are A.D.

Precision and accuracy: circle of confidence

In quoting the average values of D and I for a structure it is usual to express the likely error in terms of the 95% circle of confidence. This is derived from the deviations of the individual sample directions from the average direction by means of the statistical method given by Fisher (1953), If the *Fisher index* at the 5% level of confidence is quoted as $\theta_{95}°$, this means that there is a 95% probability that the true vector direction of the magnetization lies within a cone of semi-angle $\theta°$ coaxial with the vector direction defined by the average values for D and I. It is useful to note that an approximate value for θ_{95} can be obtained in terms of the standard errors, α_D and α_I calculated from the deviations of the individual values of D and I from the average values, $\bar{D}$ and $\bar{I}$; this is

$$\theta_{95} = 1 \cdot 6 \, \theta_{68} = 0 \cdot 75 \, (\alpha_I + \alpha_D \cos I), \qquad (4.2)$$

where

$$\alpha_I{}^2 = \frac{\Sigma(I_1 - \bar{I})^2 + (I_2 - \bar{I})^2 + \dots}{N(N-1)}$$

and similarly for α_D. N is the number of samples.

For the kiln at Carthage mentioned above $\theta_{95} = 0\cdot8°$. For another kiln, at Trèves (Thellier *and* Thellier, 1952), the spread of individual sample directions was appreciably greater—between 5° W and 10° E for *D*—giving $\theta_{95} = 1\cdot3°$. The average specific magnetizations for the two kilns were $0\cdot6 \times 10^{-3}$ and $2\cdot6 \times 10^{-3}$ gauss cm^3/g respectively and it is to be presumed that the wider spread in the kiln at Trèves was due to local distortions of the field direction by the structure itself. In considering similar deviations in Romano-British circular pottery kilns, it was realized by Harold (1960) that although there was a substantial degree of randomness in the deviations, a systematic feature was present too. This was a first harmonic sinusoidal dependence of the deviation on the azimuth of the sample with respect to magnetic north; *I* was too steep in northerly parts of the circumference and too shallow in southerly parts, *D* was too westerly in eastern parts and too easterly in western parts. The amplitude of the deviation for *D* was approximately twice that for *I*. Because of the observed dependence on azimuth it was initially thought that the effect was due to 'kiln wall fall-out'—a uniform outward tilting of the walls subsequent to the last firing, typically by about 3°. However, when a replica kiln was fired experimentally the samples taken from it showed a substantial systematic variation although during and after the firing no evidence for an actual physical movement of sufficient magnitude had been indicated by the various monitoring devices employed (Weaver, 1962).

The above experiment does not rule out the possibility that substantial physical movement may have occurred in ancient kilns, but it does confirm that magnetic distortion can be a significant effect in increasing sample-to-sample scatter. In practice, as would be expected from either cause, the scatter is usually less if the samples are taken from the flat floor of the structure—when available. However, there is then risk that the average value of *I* obtained may be less steep than the true value. Table 4.1 shows average values for six ancient kilns in which both floors and walls were available for sampling and it will be seen that on average the value for the floors, I_F, is less steep than that for the walls, I_W, by 3° or 4°. This is the expected effect of magnetic refraction and the true value should lie in between. These considerations stress the importance of comprehensive sampling. If samples are obtained from only a restricted position of the structure the result is liable to be misleading. Of course this does not apply to weakly magnetized material and in any case the

TABLE 4.1

*Comparison of remanent inclination in walls and floors of six
pottery kilns* (from Aitken *and* Hawley, 1971)

Kiln	Walls		Floors		$I_W - I_F$
	No. of samples	I_W	No. of samples	I_F	
Mancetter/1	12	66·3 ± 1·2	5	62·7 ± 0·4	+3·6 ± 1·3
Mancetter/2	12	62·2 ± 1·2	10	60·9 ± 1·6	+1·4 ± 2·0
Mancetter/9	7	68·1 ± 1·5	7	63·2 ± 1·0	+5·0 ± 1·8
Gloucester	15	67·0 ± 0·9	13	62·7 ± 0·4	+4·3 ± 1·0
Thetford/46	22	66·6 ± 1·0	11	63·6 ± 1·3	+2·9 ± 1·7
Thetford/115	29	67·7 ± 1·0	12	63·2 ± 0·6	+4·5 ± 1·2

The limits quoted are the standard errors of the mean value calculated according to (4.2).

degree to which the result is 'misleading' depends on the size of error that is significant.

As long as the movement and distortion effects are not serious it is well-established that to within experimental limits (of about 1°), the remanent direction obtained does indeed represent the true earth's field direction at the time of firing. This is from the basic work of Thellier (1938), from measurements on experimentally-fired replica kilns (Weaver 1961, 1962), and by measurements on ancient kilns lying within the period covered by historical data (Aitken *and* Weaver, 1962; Aitken *and* Hawley, 1966).

Magnetic dating

From time to time in archaeological literature reference is made to magnetic dating as an absolute method of age determination. This point of view overlooks the fact that, except for the restricted period during which the ancient direction is known from historical records, the time-scale of the calibrating reference curve for a region is based on the existing archaeological chronology. While there are certainly circumstances in which magnetic dating provides the archaeologist with useful information, unfortunately this is not the general rule, and to avoid false expectations it is important that the limitations are appreciated. These are:

(i) The calibrating reference curve needs to be set up for each region of (say) 500 to 1000 miles across in which it is to be used for dating. Besides the need for an existing chronology already noted, this setting up takes several years of sample collection and measurement as well as requiring the availability of an adequate number of structures under excavation.

(ii) The recurrence in time of the same pair of values of D and I—as for England in the twelfth and fourteen centuries and more frequently for Japan (see Figs. 4.9 and 4.11).

(iii) There are periods when the change in direction is rather slow— e.g. Roman times in England.

(iv) Although for some structures the accuracy is good and the uncertainty in the average direction is less than 1°, there is an appreciable proportion of cases for which the uncertainty is 3° or 4°— due either to movement since firing or to magnetic distortion effects. The latter uncertainty is comparable with the change in geomagnetic direction that occurs over a century; also, there may be doubt as to which branch of the reference curve is appropriate.

(v) If the sampling is comprehensive, as is necessary for a reliable result, the structure is destroyed; also, the work of sampling may take up to a full day and added to this there are one or two days of laboratory measurement. (These remarks do not apply to sampling for intensity measurements—such sampling can be less destructive and less time-consuming.)

Despite the above limitations useful archaeological results can be achieved and there is plenty of scope for its application (see, e.g., Hurst 1963, 1966; Crossley 1967). Also, an archaeologist excavating a burnt structure should appreciate that although it may not yield a magnetic date, it may nevertheless be a source of unique geophysical information.

The above discussion refers to direct archaeological application; the use of magnetic dating for lake-sediment studies, and perhaps indirectly for archaeology, will be mentioned shortly. Archaeological magnetic dating based on ancient intensity is discussed in section 4.8.

4.6. Ancient direction: from sediments and volcanic lava

Sediments

Figure 4.12 shows the declination and inclination changes found by measuring the remanent magnetization in a long core (of diameter

6 cm) taken from the bed of Lake Windermere, England (Mackereth, 1973; Thompson, Molyneux, *and* Mackereth, 1972; Molyneux, Thompson, Oldfield, *and* McCallan, 1972; Thompson 1973). The declination and inclination values for England derived from historical

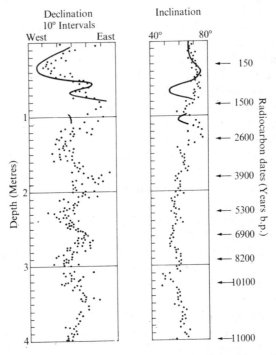

FIG. 4.12. Declination and inclination values (·) obtained for sediment cores from Lake Windermere, together with secular variation curves from historical recording and archaeological structures. The sediment data are from Thompson (1973) plus later additions and are composite points from several cores; the declination scale is relative rather than absolute and the age scale for the curves has been adjusted so as to match the first westward and eastward maxima of the sediment declination values.

records and archaeological structures are also shown and it is seen that for declination the two records compare well.

In the declination changes shown by the lake core record there is an element of regularity and spectral analysis of the data shows there to be a single significant periodity, of about 2800 years. The time scale is from radiocarbon dating. Similar measurements have been made on cores from Lough Neagh and Lough Gall in Ireland and linked to the changing spectrum of pollen types obtained from the same cores. Although there are differences in the details of the declinations curves there is good agreement in the broad features. Hence it seems likely that magnetic dating may be a useful tool for limnological research; this is in the sense that magnetic measurements allow the transfer of the radiocarbon time-scale obtained for Lake Windermere (and Lough Neagh) to other parts of the lake and to other lakes; the deposits need to be lacustrine rather than fluviatile (i.e. the sediment needs to have been deposited in still water). From the archaeological point of view, although the core makes available the broad features of the reference curve over a long time span, it is not feasible to use it to date isolated structures; dating is possible in the limnological case because a long sequence of variation is utilizable. Hence there is possible application as a stratigraphical tool in Paleolithic archaeology once the magnetic pattern has been related to the pollen sequence for the period concerned. This has been done for a 2-metre deposit of the Hoxnian interglacial period; the directions observed are similar to those recorded for the recent past in the Windermere sediments (Thompson *et al.*, 1974).

It will be noted that the amplitude of the variation shown by the lake core in Fig. 4.12 is less than that shown by the archaeological structures. The presumed reason for this is that the remanent magnetization is predominantly a post-depositional chemical magnetization acquired over an appreciable time interval, perhaps of the order of a century; such an effect would smooth out the record. The inclination values do not show any periodicity, nor do they match the archaeological record. This could be because the inclination values are upset by compaction as the coring tool is driven in, and because of smoothing out. Measurements were also made of the intensity of magnetization of susceptibility; these provide a further means of relating different cores. The intensity correlates with the carbon content and is a measure of biological activity; this confirms that the magnetization, which is carried largely by haematite, is chemical rather than depositional in origin. A possible source of the haematite is that it is derived from magnetite which is precipitated from iron hydroxides due to the reducing environment produced by bacteria living near the sediment–water interface.

The importance of deep-sea sediments in detecting geomagnetic reversals is mentioned later (section 4.9). Such sediments are also valuable in establishing long-term trends, as discussed by Opdyke (1972). The sedimentation rate is not usually sufficiently rapid to give any detail, secular variation changes with periods of a few thousand years or less being averaged out. However, in the case of two Aegean cores spanning the last 27 000 years that were measured by Opdyke, Ninkovitch, Lowrie, *and* Hays (1972), the sedimentation rate was such that 2-cm long samples cut from one of the cores represented only 30 years. Inclination values from these cores showed a 6000-year periodicity. Mineralogical investigation of the core material suggested that the dominant ferromagnetic mineral was very fine-grain detrital magnetite; it was considered that the depositional magnetization of this was sufficient to account for the observed intensity and that a secondary chemical magnetization was not necessarily present.

In early work with sediments there were indications that the recorded inclinations were systematically too shallow—the rather low inclination values obtained for New England varved clays spanning 5000 years around 10 000 B.C. by Johnson, Murphy, *and* Torreson (1948) were ascribed to this. Laboratory redeposition of glacial varve sediments does indeed give inclination values that are too shallow—by about 20° according to the work of Griffiths, King, Rees, *and* Wright (1960); it was hypothesized that as a non-spherical grain settled on the bottom there was a tendency for its long axis— which is also the preferred direction of magnetization—to become horizontal. However, where results from natural sediment can be compared with direct record, as in the recent varved clays from Sweden measured by Griffiths (1955), the inclination error indicated is much smaller, not more than 5°–10°. The explanation could be that in the natural sediments the dominant magnetization is post-depositional. Varved clays from Sweden have also been used to determine ancient inclinations and declinations over the periods 1100 B.C. to A.D. 750, and A.D. 1300 to A.D. 1900 (Griffiths, 1955); distortions by bottom currents and by the slope of the surface are considered to be the main obstacles in the way of good accuracy.

Volcanic lava flow

These are another source of information about secular variation; historically-dated flows in Iceland have been used by Brynjólfsson (1957) and the historically dated flows of Mount Etna have been used both by Chevallier (1925) and by Tanguy (1970). As with kilns, there is some magnetic distortion, causing both scatter and systematic error. Both are reduced by comprehensive sampling; the latter author usually obtained a standard error of less than 1° for the mean direction of a flow but notes evidence that inclinations are consistently too shallow by 2° (in reasonable correspondence with specific magnetization in the range 10^{-3}–10^{-2} gauss cm^3/g). Although systematic errors of this magnitude are not too serious, there are other volcanic contexts in which they may be much larger; for instance, direct measurements of I on Mt. Mihara in Japan (Rikitake, 1951) indicate that although the value on the lower slopes is not anomalous the value at the summit is some 10° too steep. According to Tanguy the main obstacle to work on Etna is that even though an eruption may be well-documented historically it is often difficult to identify the corresponding lava flow with certainty. The lava flows of Hawaii have also been extensively sampled, the results indicating that the secular variation there has been remarkably slight over many thousands of years (see Doell *and* Cox, 1971). Here again age determination is a difficulty and the extension of thermoluminescent dating to lava would be valuable.

4.7. Geophysical discussion

The archaeomagnetic results shown in Figs. 4.9–4.11 show that in the short-term at any rate the secular variation does not follow any simple worldwide pattern. In particular the curve for England disposes of the nineteenth-century notion that the secular variation curve repeatedly traces out an ellipse with a period of about 450 years—a notion contrary to the established geophysical presumption that the secular variation is mainly due to transient irregularities, near the core–mantle boundary, in the dynamo current system that generates the main field.

Westward drift

Compared to the precise and detailed knowledge that we have of present-day spatial variations the data available from the past is still inadequate and fragmentary when considered from the point of view of what is desirable to characterize the phenomenon—let alone theorize about its mechanism. About the only well-established systematic feature of the secular variation is the tendency of non-dipole features of the field to drift westward—at any rate for the past three centuries or so. This westward drift was first discussed by Halley (1692) who noted among other indications that the position of zero declination in the South Atlantic had moved 23° to the West in 90 years. Detailed analysis by Bullard, Freedman, Gellman, *and* Nixon (1950) of the change in the worldwide pattern of the field between 1907 and 1945 gave a value for the drift of the non-dipole field as a whole of close to 0·23° of longitude per year. Analysis of changes in various other recorded features of the field by various authors indicate a drift-rate in the range 0·1° to 0·2° per year to have been going on since A.D. 1600 (for a summary, see Skiles (1970)).

The geophysical interpretation of this drift is that it is due to relative motion between the outer part of the core and the mantle— the mantle rotates faster than the core and so magnetic features associated with irregularities in the current pattern at the surface of core appear to an observer on the mantle to be drifting westward. Hence the past secular variation at a particular station should be given by the present-day spatial irregularities observed on looking westward along the line of latitude running through the station. Obviously, if the form of the irregularity remained unchanged for long enough then the secular variation would repeat itself each time the mantle made one revolution relative to the core (every 1600 years). However, the lifetime of the irregularities is expected to be only of the order of a few hundred years and so the correlation should not extend back for more than that length of time. For London there is in fact a credible correlation for the past few centuries, as was pointed out by Bauer (1899), but before that the archaeomagnetic data show—as expected— a complete breakdown of correlation (Aitken *and* Weaver, 1964).

An additional implication of the observed time variation of D and I is that whenever the curve is describing a clockwise motion the direction of the drift is westward and that for counter-clockwise curvature it is eastward (Runcorn, 1959; Skiles, 1970); this may be demonstrated by moving a small bar magnet underneath a suspended magnetized needle. Thus the prolonged period of distinctively anticlockwise curvature, from the third to the fourteenth centuries in Fig. 4.10 and from the fifth to the eighth centuries in Fig. 4.11 implies eastward drift (i.e. mantle rotating more slowly than the outer part of the core) whereas the clockwise curvature of Fig. 4.9, from the sixteenth century onwards implies westward drift, in agreement with the direct observations mentioned above. Of course the ideal way to derive information about the direction of the drift is by comparison of archaeomagnetic data from different parts of the world. Comparative data is at present rather too sparse for a clear cut conclusion but the analyses of Yukutake (1967) suggest that for the past thousand years the drift has always been westward (partially contradicting the inference drawn from Fig. 4.10). This is also the viewpoint of the Soviet investigators Burlatskaya, Nechaeva, *and* Petrova (1969) who point to the observed retardation of the last maximum of the angle of dip as one moves from Japan (last maximum *circa* A.D. 1300) to Britain (last maximum A.D. 1700).

The way in which irregularities in the current pattern might be generated has been considered by Hide *and* Malin (1970) who suggest that they arise from the relative motion through the core of protruding bumps on the mantle at the interface, a kilometre or so high. Support for this is given by the observed correlation between features of the non-dipole field and irregularities in the gravity field of the earth. The best fit for correlation is obtained by rotating the present non-dipole field eastward by 160° of longitude; on account of the westward drift of the field it is conjectured that 500 or 600 years ago the best fit for correlation would have been obtained with zero longitude displacement and that the main features of the non-dipole field might have been generated at this time. It is possibly significant that the change from eastward drift to westward drift suggested by the archaeomagnetic data of Fig. 4.9 occurred then too.

Dipole movement

Analysis of the data on a worldwide basis has led to a somewhat different interpretation (Kawai, Hirooka, Sasajima, Yashawa, Ito, *and* Kume, 1965; Kawai *and* Hirooka, 1967; Kawai, Hirooka, *and* Tokeida, 1967; Hirooka, 1971). Although the archaeomagnetically observed secular variation curve observed for Japan bears little resemblance to that for England, when the data are expressed in terms of *virtual pole positions* there are some broad trends in common (see Fig. 4.13). The virtual pole position for an observing station is the orientation of a dipole placed at the centre of the earth which would produce a magnetic field at the station having the observed values of D and I. Kawai *et al.* (1967) have calculated the virtual pole motion that best fits the archaeomagnetic data for England, Japan, and Arizona, and the volcanic lava data for Iceland. They propose as a working model that over the past 2000 years the representative dipole has executed a 'quasi-hypotrochoidal' movement around the rotational axis of the earth; this movement is a basic anticlockwise precession of the dipole around the rotational axis, at an inclined

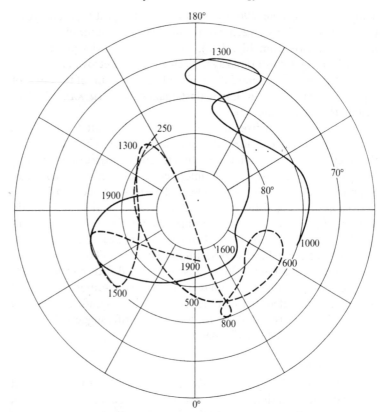

Fig. 4.13. Virtual pole positions derived from archaeomagnetic data for
England (solid line) and for Japan (dashed line). The virtual pole for an
observing station is the orientation of a dipole at the centre of the earth
such that the magnetic field would have the values of *I* and *D* observed at
the station. Although the pole positions do not superimpose, it is to be
noted that there is a broad similarity in the movement. Data used are
from Aitken (1970) and Hirooka (1971).

angle of 11° and with a period of 1500 years, together with a superimposed smaller and more rapid clockwise precession, at an inclined
angle of 7° and period 400 years. When both motions reinforce there
is a net rapid anticlockwise motion, and when they are in opposition
the motion is slow and clockwise. Because of the limited time-span
of the data used the model is bound to be approximate, and indeed
because of the sparseness of the observing stations the basic inference
of worldwide correlation could be due to coincidence. However, it is

interesting to consider what this model suggests in terms of physical reality. It is reasonable to interpret the basic anticlockwise motion as an actual precession of the main current system; indeed such precession has also been inferred from the 27 000-year record of inclination provided by the Aegean sediment cores (Opdyke *et al.*, 1972), though the different period ascribed to the motion—6000 years—is a difficulty in using one set of data to support the other. Also, in the 11 000-year record from Lake Windermere there was a single periodicity of 2800 years in the declination values but no periodicity in the inclination values (see Fig. 4.12).

As regards the clockwise motion, the explanation for this could be along the lines already used in discussion of westward drift. The effect of an irregularity in the current pattern near the core-mantle boundary spreads over approximately 120° of longitude (Skiles, 1970) so that if it is assumed that the earth's surface has always been rotating faster than the outer part of the core by 0·23° of longitude per year, a clockwise motion with a period of around 500 years is to be expected. The difficulty in using this explanation is that the model implies not only that there is worldwide correlation of these localized disturbances but also that they are due to a central dipole.

In the above discussion care has been taken to specify the outer part of the core when mentioning relative movement of the earth's surface. This is because there may be relative motion between the outer part of the core and the main current system; such motion is indicated by the fact that although the analyses by Bullard *et al.* (1950) indicate appreciable westward drift of the non-dipole field over a forty year period, there is negligible movement of the dipole field.

In essence the model of Kawai *et al.* is a return to the pre-twentieth century notion that the secular variation is regular and predictable. This fell into disrepute because of the rapid motion of the main current system that was implied. However the rapid motion does not seem unreasonable in view of the agile behaviour that is implied by geomagnetic reversal events and excursions (section 4.9).

Before closing this discussion there are two other points to be noted. First, that averaged over periods of a hundred thousand years or more the angular displacement of the virtual dipole from the earth's axis of rotation is zero—as would be expected if the dipole is precessing around the axis at a fixed angle. The evidence for this is from analysis of worldwide paleomagnetic measurement (e.g. Opdyke *and* Henry, 1969). Secondly, that from the analysis of the Windermere core results, there is indication of a slow counter-clockwise precession which could be an effect associated with the 25 800-year precession of the equinoxes. In noting this Creer *et al.* (1972) point out that it would be consistent with the suggestion by Malkus (1968) that the geomagnetic dynamo is driven by torques arising from the precession of the earth's rotational axis.

4.8. Ancient intensity

Variation in the magnetic intensity observed at a particular site may be due to:

(i) a change in the magnetic dipole moment of the earth, i.e. in the strength of the main current system in the core;

(ii) a change in the orientation of the main current system. As illustrated in Fig. 4.2 the intensity at the geomagnetic poles is twice that on the geomagnetic equator; a 10° tilt of the magnetic dipole axis towards a measuring station would cause an increase in intensity by about 13% for latitude 35° but less elsewhere and by a negligible amount at the poles and equator; or

(iii) an alteration in the local non-dipole field arising from irregularities in the current pattern near the surface of the core. The likely magnitude of variations from this cause can be estimated by taking ±10° as typical of the angular deviation of the total force vector from the direction corresponding to a dipole field— deviations of this order are indicated by the observed secular variation of direction (remembering that in middle latitudes the declination change is about twice the deviation of the total force vector). An angular deviation of ±10° implies a non-dipole field that is about 20% of the dipole field in strength. The direction of this disturbing vector is variable; the resultant total intensity will be 20% high when the disturbing vector is parallel to the dipole field vector, and 20% low when it is anti-parallel.

The intensity variations produced by (ii) and (iii) give the possibility of additional data in respect of secular variation; where data closely spaced in time are available there are certainly indications of appreciable short-term variations though inspection of some of these results suggests that the fluctuations may be due in part to incomplete elimination of the effect of mineralogical change during reheating. Because they are less reliable than direction measurements, and also more tedious, intensity measurements are subsidiary as a means of studying secular variation and the primary interest is in the evidence obtainable about (i)—both because of its bearing on the mechanism of geomagnetic reversals (section 4.9) and because of the effect on radiocarbon dating (section 2.8). The latter is not affected by (ii) and (iii).

Intensity data are obtainable from kilns, hearths, ovens, etc. as well as from bricks and pottery fragments. Although pottery fragments do not allow determination of the ancient inclination they have the advantage of being abundant. Baked clay—particularly if highly oxydized—is superior to volcanic lava in respect of unreliability due to mineralogical change; even so, as implied above it is by no means immune to this risk (see, e.g., Thellier *and* Thellier, 1959). Archaeomagnetic intensity results have been reported by Nagata, Arai, *and* Momose (1963), Nagata, Kobayashi, *and* Schwarz (1965), Du Bois *and* Watanabe (1965), Athavale (1966), Schwarz *and* Christie (1967), Kitazawa *and* Kobayashi (1968), Athavale (1969) ,Burlatskaya *et al.* (1970), Bucha, Taylor, Berger, *and* Haury (1970), Kitazawa (1970), Bucha (1971), and Rusakov *and* Zagniy (1973a).

Evaluation of the geomagnetic dipole moment

It is not possible, by measurements restricted to one region of the earth's surface, to determine the relative contributions of (i), (ii), and (iii) to the observed intensity changes. If ancient inclination values are available as well then an upper limit is obtained of the extent to which (ii) could have been important—change in inclination is also attributable to (iii). To establish definitively the past values of the geomagnetic dipole moment requires intensity measurements on a network of sites distributed over the earth's surface so that the dipole component can be evaluated by spherical harmonic analysis. In default of this the best that can be done is to interpret available measurements in terms of (i): obviously the more widely spaced the sites the more reliable is the average moment so obtained, and the spread of values is a measure of the validity of the interpretation.

The quantity actually measured for each sample is the ratio (F_A/F_L) where F_A is the ancient intensity and F_L is the laboratory intensity in which the sample was remagnetized. Many experimenters express their results as the ration (F_A/F_0), where F_0 is the present-day value at the site, and there is much to be said for the simplicity of this form of presentation.

An alternative approach is that used in the review and listing of intensity data carried out by Smith (1967, 1967a, 1967b, 1968). In cases where the associated ancient inclination, I_A, has been obtained the *virtual dipole moment* (VDM), M_A, is calculated according to the relation

$$F_A = \frac{2M_A}{R^3 \sqrt{(1 + 3 \cos^2 I_A)}}, \qquad (4.3)$$

where R is the radius of the earth. This relation is valid as long as the non-dipole field contribution to F_A and I_A is unimportant. If this is not the case then there will be a scatter in the values of M_A obtained from sites in different parts of the world. When the ancient inclination is not available, the *reduced dipole moment* (RDM) is calculated: this is obtained from the relation

$$F_A = \frac{M_A}{R^3} \sqrt{(4 - 3 \cos^2 \lambda)}, \qquad (4.4)$$

where λ is the geomagnetic latitude as determined by the position of the site relative to the position of the dipole axis (78·3° N, 69° W) obtained from spherical harmonic analysis of present-day worldwide data. This relation assumes as before that there is a negligible non-dipole contribution to F_A but the use of I_A is replaced by the assumption that the angle of tilt of the dipole was the same in antiquity as today.

Figure 4.14 shows available RDM values averaged over 500-year intervals, together with the standard error derived from the scatter of the individual values. It seems well-established that the ancient geomagnetic moment was substantially higher than at present from A.D. 1500 to 1000 B.C., reaching a 50% increase around A.D. 500, and that it was somewhat less than the present-day value from 200 B.C. to 5000 B.C. The data points from Turkey suggest that around 6000 B.C. the moment was high again, but until data from other parts of the world are available the possibility that the high intensity observed in Turkey was due to a combination of (ii) and (iii) cannot be ruled out. However, in view of the difficulty of obtaining suitable samples it is reasonable to interpret the data as indicative of (i) provisionally; the best-fit sine wave has a period of about 8000 years and the remarkable

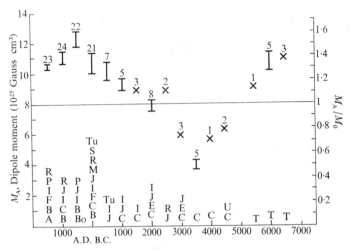

FIG. 4.14. Variation of the geomagnetic dipole moment according to archaeomagnetic data (from Cox 1968, with additional data from Bucha *and* Mellaart 1967, and Athavale 1969). M_A is the ancient value of the reduced dipole moment (RDM) as derived by Smith (1967a, 1968) using the present-day geomagnetic colatitude of the site from which the sample was obtained; M_0 is the present-day value of the dipole moment from spherical harmonic analysis. The data have been averaged over 500-year intervals and where shown the vertical bars represent the standard error of the mean value; the numerals indicate the number of data contributing to each interval; the letters indicate the countries in which the sites were located: *A*—Central Asia, *B*—Bulgaria, *Bo*—Bolivia, *C*—Czechoslovakia, *E*—Egypt, *F*—France, *I*—India, *J*—Japan, *M*—Mexico, *P*—Peru, *R*—Russia, *S*—Switzerland, *T*—Turkey, *Tu*—Tunisia, *U*—United States.

correlation with the observed fluctuations in atmospheric carbon-14 concentration (section 3.8) lends support to the validity of the interpretation.

Evidence for intensity variations due to dipole tilt

For a dipole field the inclination at geomagnetic latitude λ is given by

$$\tan I = 2 \tan\lambda. \tag{4.5}$$

If, at a site where the ancient intensity was high, the ancient inclination was greater than predicted by this relation then there is the possibility that the enhanced intensity arose from a tilt of the dipole towards the site—(ii)—rather than from an increased dipole moment. Of the sites contributing to Fig. 4.14, among the few that have accompanying inclination data are those measured by Thellier *and* Thellier (1959) which gave the first indication that the intensity had been greater in the past. The data are given in Table 4.2 and it will be seen that there is

TABLE 4.2

Ancient intensity and inclination values (from Thellier *and* Thellier, 1959)

Place	Date	F_A/F_0	I_A	I_D
Lille	A.D. 1460	1·19	63·0°	69·4°
Paris	A.D. 200	1·54	62·2°	68·6°
Fréjus	A.D. 200	1·44	60·5°	63·5°
Basle	A.D. 175	1·57	63·5°	66·5°
Carthage	146 B.C.	1·65	58·0°	57·3°

F_A—ancient intensity
F_0—present day intensity at the site
I_A—ancient inclination
I_D—inclination derived from (4.5), λ being measured relative to dipole axis at 78·3°N, 69° W.

no evidence that high values of (F_A/F_0) are associated with tilt of the dipole axis towards the measurement sites.

In section 4.7 the possibility that the geomagnetic dipole slowly precesses around the earth's axis of rotation at a fixed angle of 11° or 12° was discussed—with a period of 1500 years according to the model based on archaeomagnetic data of the last 2000 years (Kawai *et al.*), and with a period of 6000 years according to the 27 000 deep-sea sediment record (Opdyke *et al.*) According to eqn (4.4) the associated intensity variations are only $\pm 14\%$ at latitude 35°, and less elsewhere; since the observed intensity variations amount to about $\pm 50\%$ there is no question of the predicted dipole movement being sufficient to account for them. However it has been suggested both by Sasajima *and* Maenaka (1966) and by Hirooka (1971) that the dipole movement indicated by the model of Kawai *et al.* does contribute significantly to the deviation of observed intensity values from the average curve. In Fig. 4.15 the intensity variations observed in Central Europe are compared with the predictions of the model (superimposed on the effect of (i) only). This comparison suggests that dipole movement accounts

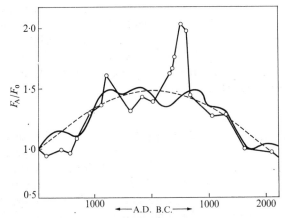

Fig. 4.15. Comparison of geomagnetic intensity variation observed for Central Europe with variation of resultant intensity obtained by adding effect of dipole movement to effect of variation of dipole strength. (F_A/F_0) is the ratio of ancient intensity to present day intensity at the sampling site. Open circles joined by straight lines are data for Central Europe (from Bucha 1971); dashed curve is $\{1 + \frac{1}{2}\sin(2\pi/8000)\}$, an approximate fit to the worldwide average data of Fig. 4.14; the full curve is the resultant after addition of intensity variations due to dipole movement predicted by the model of Kawai *et al.* (1967).—See section 4.7.

for only a small part of the deviation; for this locality the dominant cause of deviation is presumably (iii)—the non-dipole fields.

Magnetic dating using intensity

It is sometimes suggested that the worldwide average intensity variations shown in Fig. 4.14 can be used for magnetic dating, e.g. that pottery fragments with $(F_A/F_0) = 0.5$ can be attributed to *circa* 3500 B.C. However in view of the substantial short-term deviation from the worldwide average behaviour indicated by Fig. 4.15, it would seem that such a value of (F_A/F_0) could occur as a deviation from average behaviour at any time between say 2000 B.C. and 5000 B.C.

This conclusion may also be reached by considering the standard deviation implied by the standard errors shown in Fig. 4.14. For the 500-year period having the widest geographical spread of data, i.e. the period A.D. 250 to 250 B.C. the standard error is $\pm 4.5\%$; since 21 values contribute the corresponding standard deviation of the individual values is $\pm 21\%$.

On the other hand the strong short-term variations shown in Fig. 4.15 suggest that used as an adjunct to dating by direction measurements, intensity data could be valuable. For instance, intensity values could be used to distinguish between two dates for which the direction is the same. As with direction a prerequisite would be a detailed reference curve for the region concerned.

4.9. Geomagnetic reversals

It is now well-established from paleomagnetic studies that during certain periods of the geologic past the earth's field direction was reversed by 180° with respect to its present direction. When reversely magnetized rocks were first found one explanation put forward was that the minerals involved were abnormal in that they acquired remanent magnetism in the opposite direction to the applied field— and indeed a few such minerals do exist. However this explanation cannot account for reversed magnetization in deep-sea sediments nor for the worldwide synchroneity that is in general observed for the ages of reversely magnetized rocks; this synchroneity implies also that it is a reversal of the dipole field (i.e. of the main current system) rather than an abnormally strong irregularity in the non-dipole field. Reversal of magnetic polarity on the part of the earth should not be regarded as too remarkable since this is known to happen with many stars, sometimes within a matter of days.

The present polarity epoch is termed the *Brunhes* and this was preceded by the *Matuyama* reversed epoch, the transition occurring around 0·7 million years ago. The lengths of the last four polarity epochs (*Brunhes*, *Matuyama*, *Gauss*, and *Gilbert*) have been of the order of a million years but within an epoch there are the occasional occurrences of abnormal polarity lasting one or two hundred thousand years and sometimes very much less. These are termed *events* or *excursions* depending on the degree of reversal achieved. Within the last two million years there is at present evidence for seven or eight of these. The provisional nomenclature that has developed is as follows:

   (i) *Olduvai* (at 1·8 million years b.p., lasting about 0·2 million years).
  (ii) *Gilsa* (at 1·6 million years b.p.)
 (iii) *Jaramilo* (at 0·9 million years b.p., lasting about 50 000 years).
 (iv) '*V zone*' (at 340 000 b.p. lasting about 20 000 years).
  (v) *Blake* (at 110 000 b.p., lasting about 5000 years).

(vi) *Mungo* (at 30 000 b.p., lasting about 4000 years).

(vii) *Laschamp* (in progress sometime between 20 000 b.p. and 9000 b.p., duration unknown).

(viia) *Gothenburg* (having an end date of 12 400 b.p.).

The data for this list have been drawn from Cox (1969), Stacey (1969), Opdyke (1972), and the literature references cited later.

The distinction between event and excursion is often uncertain, particularly when the magnetic record of the occurrence is either incomplete—as in the case of isolated lava flows, or poorly resolved—as in the case of slowly-deposited sediment. Strictly speaking, to qualify as an event there should be complete reversal of the field direction, i.e. 180° change both in I and in D. According to Opdyke (loc. cit.) a full reversal appears to take about 10 000 years to complete (using abnormal intensity as the criterion) and so it is to be expected that a true event would occupy at least 20 000 years; hence shorter occurrences for which the available record indicates abnormal polarity rather than full 180° reversal should be regarded as excursions —and presumed to be aborted reversals. On this basis only (i), (iii) and (iv) qualify as events though in default of a term to cover both alternatives it seems likely that looser usage of 'event' will occur. According to the model developed by Cox (1968) the shorter the duration of an 'occurrence' the higher its probability and so it is to be expected that many additional events and excursions will be discovered as research proceeds. On the other hand, from the practical point of view, the shorter the duration the lower the likelihood of detection.

Events and excursions with archaeological connotations

The Olduvai event is a short period of normal polarity in the middle of the Matuyama reversed epoch; as implied by its name evidence for this event was first obtained from lava underlying the volcanic ash in which the hominid remains at Olduvai were found. The age of the lava was determined by potassium–argon dating and subsequently by fission-track dating. So far the only occurrence detected directly in archaeological remains is the polarity excursion recorded in the aboriginal fireplaces at *Lake Mungo*, Australia (Barbetti *and* McElhinney, 1972). The remanent direction found in one of the nine fireplaces implied a shift in the virtual pole position by about 120° and the directions in five others were grossly abnormal; charcoal from the fireplaces was dated by radiocarbon (Barbetti *and* Polach, 1973). This work points the way to a new branch of archaeomagnetism: the finding of abnormal magnetizations in Mesolithic and Paleolithic hearths will not only serve as valuable time-markers but will also provide opportunity to study the progress of associated intensity changes.

The Laschamp excursion is of particular interest in this context. The primary evidence for this excursion is the almost completely reversed magnetization—such as to imply a virtual pole shift of about 150°—found in four lava flows of the Chaîne des Puys in the French Massif Central, near the village of Laschamp (Bonhommet *and* Babkine, 1967). Radiocarbon dating of material overlying the volcanoes responsible for the flows gives 9000 b.p. as the most recent possible date for the lava, and potassium–argon dating of the lava itself sets 20 000 b.p. as the other limit (Bonhommet *and* Zähringer, 1969). The measurements on sediments from Lake Windermere shown in Fig. 4.13 give no indication of abnormal direction back to 11 000 b.p. Also, in a 14-metre core from a Swedish glacial deposit at *Gothenburg* the direction of magnetization is normal until the very lowest layer (Morner, Lanser, *and* Hospers, 1973). Presumably the reversed magnetization in this layer is another manifestation of the Laschamp excursion; the radiocarbon date for the upper boundary of the layer is 12 400 b.p.

With regard to the other age limit for the Laschamp excursion, Denham *and* Cox (1971) have pointed out that sediments from Mono Lake, California, indicate normal polarity from 30 000 b.p. to 13 300 b.p.; the latter is a direct radiocarbon date (± 500 years), the former is extrapolated from a radiocarbon date of 23 300 b.p. by assuming that the sediment deposited at a uniform rate. Hence there is circumstantial evidence that the Laschamp–Gothenburg excursion occurred around 13 000 b.p.; however the deposition rate of the Mono sediment was such that an excursion having a duration of less than 1700 years might have gone undetected. A very brief period of abnormal direction, probably lasting for less than 1000 years, is indicated by measurements on sediment from Lake Biwa-ko, Japan (Nakajima *et al.*, 1973). Radiocarbon dating places it earlier than 15 000 b.p., probably by several thousand years. Evidence of the Laschamp excursion has also been noted in deep-sea and terrestrial sediments (Wollin, Ericson, Ryan, *and* Foster, 1971; Clark *and* Kennett, 1973; Bucha, 1970); on the other hand there is no good evidence for it in the 27 000-year-long Aegean cores mentioned in section 4.6. Although it is well-established that a proper reversal is worldwide, this is not necessarily so for an excursion.

Except for the Lake Mungo fireplaces, directional results from archaeological material do not at present extend further into the past than about 5000 B.P. (e.g. Aitken *and* Hawley, 1967; Kawai *et al.*, 1972). There is no evidence of abnormality from measurements on orientated samples taken from structures and the inference of reversed polarity around 2700 B.P. from measurements on pottery (Folgheraiter 1899) is presumed to be erroneous.

Mechanism

Although when first considered, a reversal of the main current system seems to be a cataclysmic event, it is less so when it is realized that reversal of mechanical motion is not implied. The double-disc self-excited dynamo is one of various systems that have been proposed as useful models of the current system in the core (Rikitake, 1958). Since the dynamo is self-excited the direction of current flow can be reversed without reversal of the mechanical rotation; furthermore, solution of the appropriate electrical and mechanical equations shows that with the current in one direction there can be oscillations about a mean value which increase in amplitude until a minimum approaches zero, whereupon the current reverses in direction and the process is repeated. In the probabilistic model developed by Cox (1968) the sequence is made less regular on account of 'noise' introduced by turbulent motions in the fluid core; fluctuations due to this noise may trigger off a reversal at any time when the current is near zero, thus giving an element of randomness in the durations of successive polarity cycles.

These ideas are consistent with the general picture that has been built up from paleomagnetic observations: before a polarity transition there is a gradual decrease in intensity over a period approaching ten thousand years, during the transition itself the intensity is down to one-fifth or less of the normal value, and after the transition the intensity gradually increases. The period of low intensity may last for ten times as long as the period of abnormal direction.

It is presumed that the usual mode of reversal is by collapse of the main dipole and subsequent regrowth in the opposite direction; during the transition period the observed field is thought to represent either the continuation of the non-dipole field while the dipole field is going through zero, or the rotation of a much reduced main dipole (Lawley, 1970; Dagley *and* Wilson, 1971). The alternative mode of main dipole rotation without collapse or diminution seems to be ruled out as common behaviour by the low intensity that is generally observed during a transition. However it is to be noted that during the early part of the Mungo excursion the observed intensity was six times the present-day value (see section 2.8).

The probabilistic model referred to above predicts that short polarity intervals will be much more common than long polarity intervals. The same conclusion is drawn by Nagata (1969) from the supposition that collapse of the main current system occurs whenever there is symmetry about the earth's rotational axis, and that after collapse there is equal probability of regeneration in either direction.

Consequences

The effect that polarity transitions might have on radiocarbon dating has already been discussed in section 2.8. It has also been suggested that the increased cosmic ray dose-rate associated with low magnetic field intensity might cause an acceleration of biological mutation rates and so give rise to a discontinuity in evolutionary process (Uffen, 1963). However, whereas the comparatively low energy cosmic rays responsible for radiocarbon production in the upper atmosphere are strongly deflected by the geomagnetic field, the high-energy component which reaches the surface of the earth is not much affected (Harrison, 1968). For instance, whereas at the top of the atmosphere the cosmic ray intensity decreases by a factor of ten on going from pole to equator, at ground level the change is only 14%. In addition, cosmic rays are responsible for somewhat less than half of the total radiation dosage received by an organism on earth so that the effect of any change tends to be diluted. Apart from this, radiation is by no means the main agency responsible for mutations. A possible explanation of the correlation between reversals and evolutionary discontinuities that are observed in deep-sea sediments (e.g. Opdyke, Glass, Hays, *and* Foster, 1966) is that the effect is indirect, via climate. This is substantiated by the correlation observed between paleotemperature and magnetic intensity, also in deep sea sediments (Wollin, Ericson, Ryan, *and* Foster, 1971; see also Wollin, Kukla, Ericson, Ryan, *and* Wollin, 1973); colder climate correlates with higher intensity.

REFERENCES

ABRAHAMSEN, H. (1973). Archaeomagnetic tilt correction on bricks. *Archaeometry*, **15**, 267–74.

AITKEN, M. J. (1958). Magnetic dating. *Archaeometry*, **1**, 16–20.

AITKEN, M. J. (1970). Dating by archaeomagnetic and thermoluminescent methods. *Phil. Trans. R. Soc. Lond. A.* **269**, 77–88.

AITKEN, M. J., HAROLD, M. R., and WEAVER, G. H. (1964). Some archaeomagnetic evidence concerning the secular variation in Britain. *Nature*, **201**, 659–60.

AITKEN, M. J., HAROLD, M. R., WEAVER, G. H., and YOUNG, S. A. (1967). A "big-sample" spinner magnetometer. In *Methods in Palaeomagnetism* (eds. D. W. Collinson, K. M. Creer, and S. K. Runcorn), pp. 301–5. Elsevier, Amsterdam.

AITKEN, M. J. and HAWLEY, H. N. (1966). Magnetic dating III. Further archaeomagnetic measurements in Britain. *Archaeometry*, **9**, 187–97.

AITKEN, M. J. and HAWLEY, H. N. (1967). Archaeomagnetic measurements in Britain, IV. *Archaeometry*, **10**, 129–35.

AITKEN, M. J. and HAWLEY, H. N. (1971). Archaeomagnetism: evidence for magnetic refraction in Kiln structures. *Archaeometry*, **13**, 83–5.

AITKEN, M. J. and WEAVER, G. H. (1962). Magnetic dating: Some archaeomagnetic measurements in Britain. *Archaeometry*, **5**, 4–22.

AITKEN, M. J. and Weaver, G. H. (1964). Recent archaeomagnetic results in England. *J. Geomagn. Geoelect.* **17**, 393–6.

AITKEN, M. J., WEAVER, G. H., and HAWLEY, H. N. (1963). Magnetic dating. Further archaeomagnetic measurements in Britain. *Archaeometry*, **6**, 76–80.

ATHAVALE, R. N. (1966). Intensity of the geomagnetic field in India over the past 4000 years. *Nature*, **210**, 696–701.

ATHAVALE, R. N. (1969). Intensity of the geomagnetic in prehistoric Egypt. *Earth Planet. Sci. Lett*, **6**, 221–4.

BAMMER, A. (1969). Die gebrannten Mauerziegel von Ephesos und ihre Datierung. *Jahresheften des Österrichischen ärchaologischen Institutes*, **47**, 290–9.

BARBETTI, M. and McELHINNEY, M. W. (1972). Evidence for a geomagnetic excursion 30 000 years B.P. *Nature*, **239**, 327–30.

BARBETTI, M. and POLACH, H. (1972). ANU radiocarbon date list V. *Radiocarbon*, **15**, 241–51.

BAUER, L. A. (1899). On the secular variation of a free magnetic needle. *Phys. Rev. 3*, 34–8.

BELSHÉ, J. C., COOK, K., and COOK, R. M. (1963). Some archaeomagnetic results from Greece. *Annu. of Bri. Sch. at Athens*, **58**, 8–13.

BLACKETT, P. M. S. (1952). A negative experiment relating to magnetism and the earth's rotation. *Phil. Trans.* 250A, 309–70.

BONHOMMET, N. and BABKINE, J. (1967). Sur la présence d'aimantations inversées dans la chaine des Puys. *C.r. Acad. Sci., Paris*, **264**, 92–4.

BONHOMMET, N. and ZAHRINGER, J. (1969). Paleomagnetism and potassium argon age determinations of the Laschamp geomagnetic polarity event. *Earth Planet. Sci. Lett.* **6**, 43–6.

BRYNJÓLFSSON, A. (1957). Studies of remanent and viscous magnetism in the basalts of Iceland. *Advances in Physics.* **6**, 247–54.

BUCHA, V. (1967). Intensity of the earth's magnetic field during archaeological times in Czechoslavakia. *Archaeometry*, **10**, 12–22.

BUCHA, V. (1970). Geomagnetic reversals in Quaternary revealed from a paleomagnetic investigation of sedimentary rocks. *J. Geomagn. Geoelect.* **22**, 253–271.

BUCHA, V. (1971). Archaeomagnetic dating. *In Dating Techniques for the Archaeologist* (eds. H. N. Michael *and* E. K. Ralph), pp. 57–117. MIT Press, Cambridge, Massachusetts and London, England.

BUCHA, V. *and* MELLAART, J. (1967). Archaeomagnetic intensity measurements on some Neolithic samples from Catal Huyuk (Anatolia). *Archaeometry*, **10**, 23–5.

BUCHA, V., TAYLOR, R. E., BERGER, R., *and* HAURY, E. W. (1970). Geomagnetic intensity: changes during the past 3000 years in the Western hemisphere. *Science*, **168**, 111–114.

BULLARD, E. C. (1958). The secular variations of the Earth's magnetic field. *Year Book of the Physical Society*, 47–60.

BULLARD, E. C., FREEDMAN, C., GELLMAN, H., *and* NIXON, J. (1950). The Westward Drift of the earth's magnetic field. *Phil. Trans. R. Soc. Lond.* **243**, 67–92.

BURLATSKAYA, S. P., NACHASOVA, I. E., UECHAEVA, T. B., RUSAKOV, O. M., ZAGNIV, G. F., TARHOV, E. N., *and* TCHELIDZE, Z. A. (1970). Archaeomagnetic research in the U.S.S.R.: recent results and spectral analysis. *Archaeometry*, **12**, 78–88.

BURLATSKAYA, S., NECHAEVA, T., *and* PETROVA, G. (1969). Some archaeomagnetic data indicative of the westward drift of the geomagnetic field. *Archaeometry*, **11**, 115–30.

CHEVALLIER, R. (1925). L'aimantation des laves de l'Etna et l'orientation du champ terrestre on Sicile du XII an XVIII siécles. *Ann. Phys., Paris*, **4**, 5–162.

CLARK, H. C. *and* KENNETH, J. P. (1972). Paleomagnetic excursion in latest Pleistocene deep-sea sediments. *Earth Planet. Sci. Lett.* **19**, 267–74.

CLARKE, D. L. *and* CONNAH, G. (1962). Remanent magnetism and beaker chronology. *Antiquity*, **36**, 206–9.

COLLINSON, D. W., CREER, K. M., *and* RUNCORN, S. K. (1967). *Methods in Paleomagnetism*. Elsevier, Amsterdam.

COOK, R. M. *and* BELSHÉ, J. C. (1958). Archaeomagnetism: a preliminary report on Britain. *Antiquity*, **32**, 167–78.

COX, A. (1968). Lengths of geomagnetic polarity intervals. *J. geophy. Res.*, **73**, 3247–60.

COX, A. (1969). Geomagnetic reversals. *Science*, **163**, 237–45.

CREER, K. M., THOMPSON, R., MOLYNEAUX, L., *and* MACKERETH, F. J. H. (1972). Geomagnetic secular variation recorded in the stable magnetic remanence of recent sediments. *Earth Planet. Sci. Lett.* **14**, 115–27.

CROSSLEY, D. W. (1967). Glassmaking in Bagot's Park, Staffordshire in the sixteenth century. *Post-Medieval Archaeology*, **1**, 44–83.

DAGLEY, P. *and* WILSON, R. L. (1971). Geomagnetic field reversals—a link between strength and orientation of a dipole source. *Nature Physical Science*, **232**, 16–18.

DENHAM, C. R. *and* COX, A. D. (1971). Evidence that the Laschamp polarity event did not occur 13 300–30 400 years ago. *Earth Planet. Sci. Lett.* **13**, 181–90.

DICKSON, G. O., EVERITT, C. W. F., PARRY, L. G., *and* STACEY, F. D. (1966). Origin of themoremanent magnetization. *Earth Planet. Sci. Lett.* **1**, 222–4.

DOELL, R. R. (1969). History of the geomagnetic field. *J. appl. Phys.*, **40**, 945–54.

DOELL, R. R. *and* COX, A. (1971). Pacific geomagnetic secular variation. *Science*, **171**, 248–54.

DOELL, R. R. *and* SMITH, P. J. (1969). On the Use of Magnetic Cleaning in Paleointensity Studies. *J. Geomagn. Geoelect*, **21**, 579–94.

Du Bois, R. L. (1967). Some features of the secular variation of the geomagnetic field. *Space Magnetic Exploration and Technology Symposium*, Remo: University of Nevado.

Du Bois, R. L. (1969). Archaeomagnetism from sites in Southwestern United States, dated 2000–1000 B.P. *Gen. Sci. Assembly in Madrid of the Int. Ass. of Geomagn. and Aeronomy*, III–19.

Du Bois, R. L. and Watanabe, N. (1965). The use of Indian Pottery to Determine the Paleointensity of the Geomagnetic Field for United States 600–1400 A.D. *J. Geomagn. Geoelect.* 17, 417–23.

Dunlop, D. J. and West, S. (1969). A experimental evaluation of single domain theories. *Rev. Geophys.* 7, 709–55.

Everitt, C. W. F. (1961). Thermoremanent magnetization, 1. Experiments on single domain grains. *Phil. Mag.* 6, 713–26.

Everitt, C. W. F. (1962). Thermoremanent magnetization II. Experiments on multidomain grains. *Phil. Mag.*, 7, 583–616.

Fisher, R. (1953). Dispersion on a sphere. *Proc. R. Soc. Lond.* 217A, 295–305.

Folgheraiter, G. (1899). Sur les variations seculaire de l'inclinaison magnetique dans l'antiquité. *Archs. Sci. phys. nat.* 8, 5–16.

Foster, J. (1966). A paleomagnetic spinner magnetometer using a fluxgate gradiometer. *Earth Planet. Sci. Lett.* 1, 463–6.

Griffiths, D. H. (1955). The remanent magnetism of varved clays from Sweden. *Mon. Not. Roy. Astr. Soc., Geophys. Suppl.* 7, 103–14.

Griffiths, D. H., King, R. F., Rees, A. I., and Wright, A. E. (1960). The remanent magnetization of some recent varved sediments. *Proc. R. Soc. A.* 256, 359–83.

Halley, E. (1962). An account of the cause of the change of the variation of the magnetical needle; with an hypothesis of the structure of the internal part of the earth. *Phil. Trans. R. Soc. Lond.* 17, 563.

Harold, M. R. (1960). Magnetic dating: Kiln wall fall-out. *Archaeometry*, 3, 45–7.

Harrison, C. G. A. (1968). Evolutionary processes and reversals of the earth's magnetic field. *Nature*, 217, 46–7.

Hide, R. and Malin, S. C. R. (1970). Novel correlations between global features of the earth's gravitational and magnetic fields. *Nature*, 225, 605–9.

Hirooka, K. (1971). Archaeomagnetic study for the past 2000 years in Southwest Japan. *Memoirs Fac. Sci. Kyoto Univ., Series of Geol. and Mineral*, XXXVIII. 167–207.

Hurst, J. G. (1963). Post-Roman archaeological dating and its correlation with archaeological results. *Archaeometry*, 6, 81–2.

Hurst, J. G. (1966). Post-Roman archaeological dating and its correlation with archaeomagnetic results. *Archaeometry*, 9, 198–9.

Irving, E. (1964). *Paleomagnetism*, Wiley & Sons, New York, London, and Sydney.

Jelinek, V. (1966). A high sensitivity spinner magnetometer. *Studia Geophysica et Geodoetica* (Prague), 10, 58–78.

Johnson, E. A., Murphy, T., and Torreson, O. W. (1948). Pre-history of the earth's magnetic field. *Terr. Magn. Amos. Elect.* 53, 349–72.

Kawai, N. and Hirooka, K. (1965). Archaeomagnetic Studies in S. W. Japan. *Ann. Géophys.* 21, 574–7.

Kawai, N. and Hirooka, K. J. (1967). Wobbling motion of the geomagnetic dipole field in historic time during these 2000 years. *J. Geomagn. Geoelect.* 19, 217–27.

Kawai, N., Hirooka, K., Nakajima, I., Tokieda, K., and Tosi, M. (1972). Archaeomagnetism in Iran. *Nature*, 236, 223–4.

KAWAI, N., HIROOKA, K., SASAJIMA, S., YASHAWA, K., ITO, H., *and* KUME, S. (1965). Archaeomagnetic studies in southwestern Japan. *Am. Geophys.* **21**, 574–8.

KAWAI, N., HIROOKA, K., *and* TOKEIDA, K. (1967). A vibration of geomagnetic axis around the geographic North pole in the historic time. *Earth Planet. Sci. Lett.* **3**, 48–50.

KITAZAWA, K. (1970). Intensity of the geomagnetic field in Japan for the past 10 000 years. *J. geophys. Res.* **75**, 7403–11.

KITAZAWA, K. *and* KOBAYASHI, K. (1968). Intensity variation of the geomagnetic field during the past 4000 years in South America. *J. Geomagn. Geoelect.*, **20**, 7–19.

KOBAYASHI, K. *and* FULLER, M. (1968). Stable remanence and memory of multi-domain materials with special reference to magnetite. *Phil. Mag.* **18**, 601–24.

KOVACHEVA-NOZHAROVA, M. (1968). Ancient magnetic field in Bulgaria. *C.r. Acad. Bulgare des Sci.* **21**, 761–3.

LAWLEY, E. A. (1970). The intensity of the geomagnetic field in Iceland during Neogene polarity transitions and systematic deviations. *Earth Planet. Sci. Lett.* **10**, 145–9.

LOWES, F. J. (1955). Secular variation and the non-dipole field. *Ann. Geophys.* **11**, 91–112.

MACKERETH, F. J. H. (1971). On the variations in direction of the horizontal component of remanent magnetization in lake sediments. *Earth. Planet. Sci. Lett.* **12**, 332–8.

MALKUS, W. V. R. (1968). Precession of the Earth as the course of geomagnetism. *Science*, **160**, 259–264.

MCELHINNY, M. W. (1973). *Paleomagnetism and Plate Tectonics*. Cambridge University Press, London and New York.

MOLYNEUX, L. (1971). A complete result magnetometer for measuring the remanent magnetization of rocks. *Geophys. J.R. astron. Soc.* **24**, 429–33.

MOLYNEAUX, L., THOMPSON, R., OLDFIELD, F., *and* MCCALLAN, M. F. (1972). Rapid measurement of the remanent magnetization of long cores of sediment. *Nature Physical Science*, **237**, 42–43.

MORNER, N. A., LANSER, J. P., *and* HOSPERS, J. P. (1971). Late Weischselian Paleomagnetic reversal. *Nature*, **24**, 173–4.

NAGATA, T. (1969). Length of geomagnetic polarity intervals. *J. Geomagn. Geoelect.* **21**, 701–4.

NAGATA, T., ARAI, Y., *and* MOMOSE, K. (1963). Secular variation of the geo-magnetic total force during the last 5000 years. *J. geophys. Res.*, **68**, 5277–81.

NAGATA, T., KOBAYASHI, K., *and* SCHWARZ, E. J. (1965). Archaeomagnetic intensity studies of South and Central America. *J. Geomagn. Geoelect.*, **17**, 399–405.

NAKAJIMA, T., YASKAWA, K., NATSUHARA, N., KAWAI, N., *and* HORIE, S. (1973). Very short period geomagnetic excursion 18 000 yr BP. *Nature Physical Science*, **244**, 8–10.

NÉEL, L. (1955). Some theoretical aspects of rock magnetism. *Advances in Physics*, **4**, 191–243.

OPDYKE, N. D. (1972). Paleomagnetism of deep-sea cores. *Rev. Geophys. Space Phys.* **10**, 213–49.

OPDYKE, N. D., GLASS, B., HAYS, J. D., *and* FOSTER, J. H. (1966). Paleomagnetic Study of Antarctic deep-sea cores. *Science*, **154**, 349.

OPDYKE, N. D. *and* HENRY F. W. (1969). A test of the dipole hypothesis. *Earth Planet. Sci. Lett.* **6**, 139–51.

OPDYKE, N. D., NINKOVICH, D., LOWRIE, W., *and* HAYS, J. D. (1972). Paleomag. of two Aegean deep-sea cores. *Earth Planet. Sci. Lett.* **14**, 145–59.

RIKITAKE, T. (1951). The Distribution of Magnetic Dip is Ooshima Island. *Bull. Earthq. Res. Inst.* **29**, 161–81.

RIKITAKE, T. (1958). Oscillations of a system of disk dyanamos. *Proc. Cambridge Phil. Soc.* **54**, 89–105.

RIMBERT, F. (1957). Sur l'aimantation rémanente anhystérétique des ferrimagnétiques. *C.r. Acad. Sci., Paris*, **245**, 406–8.

RUNCORN, S. K. (1959). On the theory of the geomagnetic secular variation. *Ann. Géophys.* **15**, 87–92.

RUSAKOV, O. M., *and* ZAGNIY, G. F. (1973a). Intensity of the geomagnetic field in the Ukraine and Moldavia during the past 6000 years. *Archaeometry*, **15**, 275–85.

RUSAKOV, O. M. *and* ZAGNIY, G. F. (1973). Archaeomagnetic secular variation study in the Ukraine and Moldavia. *Archaeometry*, **15**, 153–8.

SASAJIMA, S. (1965). Geomagnetic secular variation revealed in the baked earths in West Japan. *J. Geomagn. Geoelect.*, **17**, 413–16.

SASAJIMA, S. *and* MAENAKA, K. (1966). Intensity studies of the archaeosecular variation in West Japan, with special reference to the hypothesis of the dipole axis rotation. *Mem. College Science, Kyoto*, **B33**, 53–67.

SCHWARZ, E. J. *and* CHRISTIE, K. W. (1967). Original remanent magnetization of Ontario potsherds. *J. geophys. Res.* **72**, 3263–9.

SHAW, J. (1974). A new method of determining the magnitude of the palaeomagnetic field. *Geophys. J.R. astron. Soc.* **27**, (in press).

SKILES, D. D. (1970). A method of inferring the direction of drift of the geomagnetic field from paleomagnetic data. *J. Geomagn. Geoelect.* **22**, 441–62.

SMITH, P. J. (1967). The intensity of the ancient geomagnetic field: a review and analysis. *Geophys. J.R. astron. Soc.* **12**, 321–62.

SMITH, P. J. (1967a). Ancient geomagnetic field intensities—I. Historic and archaeological data. *Geophys. J.R. astron. Soc.* **13**, 417–9.

SMITH, P. J. (1967b). Ancient geomagnetic field intensities—II. *Geophys. J.R. astr. Soc.* **13**, 483–6.

SMITH, P. J. (1968). Ancient geomagnetic field intensities—III. Historic and archaeological data. *Geophys. J.R. astron. Soc.* **16**, 457–460.

STACEY, F. D. (1963). The physical theory of rock magnetism. *Advances in Physics*, **12**, 45–133.

STACEY, F. D. (1969). *Physics of the Earth*. Wiley & Sons, New York, London, Sydney, and Toronto.

STACEY, F. D., *and* BANERJEE, S. K. (1974). *The Physical Principles of Rock Magnetism*. Elsevier, Amsterdam.

TANGUY, J. C. (1970). An archaeomagnetic Study of Mount Etna. *Archaeometry*, **12**, 115–128.

THELLIER, E. (1936). Aimantation des briques et inclinaison du champ magnétique terrestre. *Ann. Inst. Phys. Globe*, **14**, 65–70.

THELLIER, E. (1938). Sur l'aimantation des terres cuites et ses applications géophysiques. *Annls. Inst. Phys. Globe*, **16**, 157–302.

THELLIER, E. (1966). Le champ magnétique terrestre fossile. *Nucleus*, **7**, 1–35.

THELLIER, E. *and* THELLIER, O. (1951). Sur la direction du champ magnetique terrestre, retrouvée sur des parois de four des époques punique et romaine, à Carthage. *C.r. Acad. Sci., Paris*, **233**, 1476–9.

THELLIER, E. *and* THELLIER, O. (1952). Sur la direction du champ magnétique terrestre, dans la région de Trèves, vers 380 après. *J.C. C.r. Acad. Sci., Paris*, **234**, 1464–6.

THELLIER, E. *and* THELLIER, O. (1959). Sur l'intensité du champ magnétique terrestre dans le passé historique et géologique. *Ann. Geophys.* **15**, 285–376.

THOMPSON, R. (1973). Paleoliminology and paleomagnetism. *Nature*, **242**, 182–4.

THOMPSON, R., AITKEN, M. J., GIBBARD, P., *and* WYMER, J. J. (1974). Paleomagnetic study of Hoxnian lacustrine sediments. *Archaeometry*, **16**, 233–7.

UFFEN, R. J. (1963). Influence of the Earth's Core on the Origin and Evolution of Life. *Nature*, **198**, 143–4.

VERHOOGEN, J. (1959). The origin of thermoremanent magnetization. *J. geophys. Res.* **64**, 2441–9.

WATANABE, N. (1958). Secular variation in the direction of geomagnetism as the standard scale in geomagnetochronology in Japan. *Nature*, **182**, 383–4.

WATANABE, N. *and* DUBOIS, R. L. (1965). Some Results of an Archaeomagnetic Study on the Secular Variation in the Southwest of North America. *J. Geomagn. Geoelect.* **17**, 395–7.

WEAVER, G. H. (1961). Magnetic dating measurements. *Archaeometry*, **4**, 23–28.

WEAVER, G. H. (1962). Archaeomagnetic measurements on the second Boston experimental kiln. *Archaeometry*, **5**, 93–107.

WEAVER, G. H. (1964). The development of apparatus for the analysis of thermoremanent magnetism in archaeological samples. Unpublished B.Sc. thesis, Oxford University.

WEAVER, G. H. (1966). Measurement of the past intensity of the earth's magnetic field. *Archaeometry*, **9**, 174–186.

WEAVER, G. H. (1970). Some temperature related errors in palaeomagnetic intensity measurements. *Archaeometry*, **12**, 87–97.

WOLLIN, G., ERICSON, D. B., RYAN, W. B. E., *and* FOSTER, J. H. (1971). Magnetism of the Earth and climatic changes. *Earth Planet. Sci. Lett.* **12**, 175–83.

WOLLIN, G., KUKLA, G. J., ERICSON, D. B., RYAN, W. B. F., *and* WOLLIN, J. (1973). Magnetic intensity and climatic changes 1925–1970. *Nature*, **242**, 34–7.

YUKUTAKE, T. (1967). The westward drift of the magnetic field in historic times. *J. Geomagn. Geoelect.* **19**, 103–16.

ZIMMERMAN, J. E. (1972). Josephson effect devices and low-frequency field sensing. *Cryogenics*, **12**, 19–31.

5 *Location of Buried Remains*

5.1. Introduction

As with an iceberg, only a small fraction of a country's archaeology is visible above the surface; the rest has been buried by gradual accretion of soil to depths varying between a few inches and some tens of feet. Often there is no surface indication until deep ploughing or building activity throws up fragments and there may be little time between the first discovery of an archaeological site and its total obliteration. This puts a premium, first on techniques for site *discovery*, and secondly, on techniques for rapid *exploration* of a site so as to reduce to a minimum the amount of fruitless trial trenching.

Experience and intuition enable an archaeologist to see relationships between surface features and reliefs which are often insigificant to the layman and new sites continue to be discovered in this way. Of course there are many sites too which are known by local tradition or legend, or which show themselves by obviously man-made disturbances, e.g. the circular banks and ditches of an Iron Age hill-fort. However, by far the most powerful weapon of site discovery is aerial photography, and because a site may only show up in this way at a particular time of day in a particular season in a particular climatic sequence, each year's aerial surveying brings its new revelations.

The rôle of geophysical techniques is in site exploration, by detecting abnormalities in the physical properties of the ground. These techniques should not be overestimated; they do not usually relieve the archaeologist of the need to use his spade—but they do suggest the most fruitful spots in which to insert it. Of course there are occasions when a geophysical survey produces such a complete plan that valid archaeological interpretation is possible without excavation, but such occasions are rare and interpretations made without confirmatory excavation should be used cautiously. Aerial photography sometimes produces such a complete and clear-cut plan for a site that a geophysical survey is redundant; however the situation is more often that the two are complementary—the geophysical survey gives a more detailed plan, or gives precise location of features seen from the air only vaguely. Sometimes a site which records strongly on geophysical survey may be completely unseen from the air—and vice versa.

The geophysical techniques routinely used in archaeology are magnetic and electrical resistivity surveys; an outline of these is given in the present chapter and a fuller discussion in Chapters 6, 7, and 8. Also in the present chapter is a brief discussion of aerial photography and of what can at present be described as 'subsidiary' geophysical techniques. Some of these are possibilities which have not yet proved efficacious, some are effective techniques which are only applicable in special circumstances. Although one can say that for a given type of site on given soil conditions a certain technique is best (e.g. magnetic surveys for the interior of hill-forts on sedimentary geology) it is misleading to think of any one technique as being universally paramount.

5.2. Aerial photography

Visual indication arises from *crop-marks*, *soil-marks* and from slight differences in relief (*shadow-marks*); these are meaningless to an observer on the ground in the same way that to a man lying on a carpet the pattern is a confused blur. This presumes that there is a pattern to recognize and aerial photography is most powerful for large-scale features of significant geometry; isolated features such as kilns and pits do not show up so clearly and it is a fortunate circumstance that these are just the features most easily detectable magnetically.

Crop-marks result from different moisture conditions. The crop above a buried wall will ripen prematurely, showing up as a lightened line, while above a buried ditch the crop is richer and therefore darker in appearance; it is also slightly higher than elsewhere and this will be particularly noticeable when the sun's rays are oblique. Features need to be within about a metre of the surface in order to have an effect. The state of the crop, the type of crop, the previous rainfall sequence and the angle of the sun are all critical factors; in some conditions reversed crop-marks are seen, i.e. walls are dark and ditches light. Full exploitation of aerial photography requires a lot of trial of different conditions and consequently routine military photographs are of limited value.

A feature seen on an aerial photograph is not easy to fix on the ground unless recognizable landmarks are nearby; this is particularly true of oblique shots, which are often the most revealing archaeologically. Hence the need to use one of the ground techniques for pinpointing.

Although tremendous technical advances have been made in recent years in aerial photography from satellites and for military purposes these have not so far produced a corresponding order of magnitude advance in type of archaeological information obtained, though the ease and efficiency of application has been very much improved. Some features reveal themselves by *snow-marks*; these usually appear in a light cover of melting snow and are due to differences in ground surface temperatures arising from thermal conductivity and heat capacity variations. These snow-marks can be photographed conventionally, but exploitation of long infra-red photographic techniques to detect such features in the absence of snow, or on sites in hot parts of the world where thermal effects are more marked, has not yet been achieved.

5.3. Magnetic prospecting

The detection of iron-ore deposits by means of magnetic measurements has been used in geological prospecting since the end of the nineteenth century. From archaeological remains the magnetic disturbances are very much weaker, and a highly sensitive instrument is required. In addition, to be of practical value, speed, simplicity, and portability are essential. These requirements are met by the *proton magnetometer* and magnetic location in archaeology began in 1958, in England, when a transistorized version of that instrument became available.

Although iron is the most obvious and powerful cause of magnetic disturbance, this is not of much archaeological importance because association of iron with a feature is comparatively rare, even in Iron-Age archaeology. It was the much weaker permanent magnetization (the *thermoremanent* magnetism already discussed in Chapter 4) known to be acquired by the baked clay of pottery kilns on cooling down from firing that suggested archaeological application of magnetic prospecting. However, during early attempts to locate pottery kilns with this technique it was found that a number of magnetic *anomalies*, having a strength of the order of magnitude expected for kilns, turned out on excavation to come from filled-in pits. This extended the scope of the technique from burnt feature detection to general surveying of archaeological sites, for nearly all cultures have dug holes in the ground for one reason or another—food storage, rubbish, etc. The magnetic disturbance from a pit is due to the enhanced magnetic *susceptibility* of the soil-filling compared to the adjacent rock or subsoil into which the pit has been dug. This enhancement, which is a fortunate chance of soil chemistry, results from involvement of the soil with man's occupation; it depends both on the concentration of organic matter in the soil and on the degree of burning to which the soil has been exposed, as well as on the iron content. Ditches are detectable too, but with less certainty because of the possibility of their filling being sterile sub-soil or rock, rather than cultivated top-soil. In special circumstances walls, roads, building foundations, and cavities show up magnetically.

The greatest drawback to magnetic prospection is the interfering effects of extraneous iron such as horseshoes, buried pipes, wire-netting, and iron fencing. Such handicaps usually occur anywhere bordering present-day human habitation, but in open country the magnetic technique is generally the quickest and surest method of site exploration—as long as the geological structure is sedimentary. On igneous geology the thermoremanent magnetism of the rock itself may be so strong as to mask the anomalies from the archaeological features.

Besides the proton magnetometer, magnetic disturbances can be located with the differential fluxgate magnetometer and with the caesium magnetometer. Variations in magnetic suceptibility of the soil can also be detected with the so-called Soil Conductivity Meter (SCM) and with the Pulsed Induction Metal Detector (PIM) although these instruments were developed with other objectives. These instruments are discussed later in the chapter. Both the SCM and the PIM have the disadvantage that they are much more sensitive to near-surface features than magnetometers, but on the other hand, the SCM type of instrument can be sophisticated so as to discriminate against iron and thus allow prospection in a locality that may be impossible for magnetometers.

5.4. Electrical resistivity surveying

Like the magnetic technique, resistivity surveying in archaeology is a scaled-down version of a geological technique. Its first archaeological use was in England in 1946 by R. J. C. Atkinson. Resistivity is largely dependent on water content and one intuitively expects wide differences between stone, clay, wet soil, dug soil, sand, etc. Walls, building foundations, roads, and ditches show up clearly with this technique; tombs, pits, underground cavities have also been detected.

The instruments available for resistivity measurements are more tedious in operation than those for magnetic prospecting. In particular, probes have to be temporarily inserted a few inches into the ground in order to make electrical contact. However, the drawback of interference from iron and igneous rocks is absent, though on the other hand resistivity measurements are seriously affected by rainfall. In general with this technique and also to some extent with the magnetic one, while some archaeological features show up sharply whatever the terrain, it is not always possible to distinguish others from small-scale geological effects.

The induced polarization technique

An unwanted effect in resistivity surveying is the occurrence of electrolytic polarization at the probes and this necessitates the use of an alternating voltage source. In the Induced Polarization technique (IP) developed by Aspinall *and* Lynam (1968, 1970) the varying degrees to which polarization occurs in soil, clay, rock, etc. is utilized; limited field experience suggests that the types of feature detectable are roughly the same as for resistivity surveying but that in some cases features show up with greater clarity. However, like the resistivity method, the technique requires the insertion of probes into the ground, except that each probe has to incorporate copper sulphate gel; the associated electronics are considerably more sophisticated too.

5.5. Electromagnetic techniques

The soil conductivity meter (SCM)

As just mentioned a serious drawback with conventional techniques for resistivity measurement is the need to insert steel probes into the ground—for the purpose of injecting electric current and measuring voltage. In principle, variations in ground resistivity should be detectable using the transmitter-receiver device sketched in Fig. 5.1, which does not require any contact with the soil. This is in fact a simple metal detector and also the basis of the Soil Conductivity Meter (SCM); it consists of a transmitter coil and a receiver coil mounted on the same shaft about a metre apart. The transmitter coil is fed with a continuous sinusoidal current, at a frequency of 4 kHz in the standard SCM. The plane of the transmitter coil is vertical whereas that of the receiver coil is horizontal; the receiver coil is

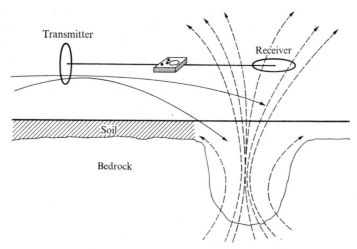

FIG. 5.1. Operation of SCM-type instrument.

orientated relative to the transmitter coil so as to avoid any pick-up of the primary transmitter field, and the only signals received are due to the secondary fields from eddy currents and magnetizations, induced in the ground by the primary field.

Field trials with the SCM have shown that although it can detect pits and ditches this is due to the induced magnetization signal rather than the eddy-current signal. Consequently it is not a substitute for conventional resistivity measuring techniques; as substitute for the proton magnetometer it has the advantages of simplicity, cheapness and convenience of operation, but the disadvantage that its depth of detection is less and so it is only effective for shallow, near-surface features. This is because with the SCM there is both a 'go' and 'return' signal and the sensitivity falls off as the sixth power of the depth (d^{-6}) whereas with the proton magnetometer there is no transmitted signal and the sensitivity falls off only as the third power (d^{-3}).

Theoretical considerations and model experiments (Tite *and* Mullins, 1969, 1970) confirm that at the standard frequency of 4 kHz the SCM response is dominated by the magnetic signal, and indicate that in order to make the instrument respond to resistivity variations it would be necessary to increase the frequency to 100 kHz. However, the limitation to near-surface features becomes more severe (typically to shallower depth than 30 cm), and such an instrument is only useful in special circumstances. The reduced detection depth is associated with the change from magnetic response to resistivity response, rather than due to increased ground absorption at the higher frequency. The penetration distance in wet soil is of the order of 30 metres up to 30 MHz though it decreases rapidly for higher frequencies.

Use of microwaves

This rapid fall-off prevents the routine use of microwave frequencies— otherwise these would be a powerful tool because in that frequency region the radiation can be formed into torch-like beam. However in very dry, desert-like, conditions the use of microwaves may be feasible; limited field trials on rocks on the shores of the Dead Sea indicated a penetration distance of 10 cm for microwaves of wavelength 3 cm. This was less than expected for completely dry rocks, and it was presumed that there was a residual water content of a few parts per million due to overnight dew.†

Use of radio transmissions

The depth of detection with an instrument of the SCM type would be increased by positioning the transmitter coil at a greater distance from the receiver coil, given that the transmitter power could be appropriately raised. However, any significant increase beyond the usual separation of about a metre would make the instrument unwieldy, particularly since the rod carrying the two coils must be rigid enough to keep the mutual orientation of the coils sufficiently precise to avoid linkage of the primary field. The need to have the receiver rigidly linked to the transmitter is avoided if the transmitter is at a sufficient

† I am indebted to Prof. G. R. Nicoll for the information of this paragraph.

distance from the site for the primary field to be uniform in strength and direction over the whole area of the site. This has been achieved in a novel way by using the routine transmissions of radio broadcasting stations (Tabbagh, 1972).

In the field trials carried out, the sites were at distances of the order of 500 kilometres from the transmitters, which were on frequencies of 164 kHz and 180 kHz and had power of about a megawatt. The transmitter primary field has its magnetic vector horizontal, so by having the axis of the receiver coil vertical, pick-up of the primary field is avoided. The receiver coil is made compact by using a ferrox core and the axis kept vertical simply by allowing it to hang freely under gravity. Magnetizations and eddy currents induced in the ground by the primary field (strength about 1 gamma†) produce a localized secondary field having a vertical magnetic component, and this gives rise to a signal in the receiver coil. If there is variation in the magnetic or electrical characteristics of the ground, the strength of the signal varies from point to point. Fig. 5.2(a) shows the profiles obtained in traversing across a tumulus.

Strong signals are to be expected from long linear features (such as walls, ditches, and roads) but the signal becomes zero if the feature is perpendicular to the direction of the transmitter; it is therefore desirable to utilize two transmitter stations having bearings from the site that differ by about 90°. Calculations show that for a circular cylinder of diameter 1 metre buried so that its axis is 1 metre deep, the vertical secondary field strength is 4 % of the primary field strength for a resistivity contrast of 100 ohm-metre.

Metal detectors

Electromagnetic instruments (such as the type shown in Fig. 5.1) can be used for detection of metal, both ferrous and non-ferrous— for a review see Lancaster (1966). The sensitivity to iron is high because in addition to the eddy-current signal there is a magnetization signal which is usually much stronger. The two can be distinguished if, in addition to amplitude, the phase with respect to the transmitter is measured also. Metal detectors have been the subject of a great deal of electronic sophistication by military and civil authorities and by treasure hunters both on land and underwater. One variant is to use a single or double coil forming part of a sharply-tuned oscillator

† For definition see section 6.1.

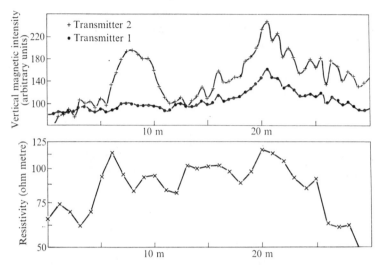

F<small>IG</small>. 5.2. (a) secondary magnetic fields (vertical component) due to radio transmissions observed in traversing through centre of tumulus surrounded by stone-faced bank and ditch (from Tabbagh, 1972). The traverse made an angle of 84° with the direction of one transmitter (1) and 63° with the direction of the other (2); the frequencies were 164 kHz (Allouis) and 180 kHz (Europe 1) respectively.
(b) Resistivity measurements along the same traverse using Wenner configuration with an interelectrode spacing of 1 m (see Chapter 8).

circuit; the proximity of a metal object destroys the condition for resonance and subsidiary circuits indicate this.

In archaeology, metal detection is only of use in special cases, e.g. when large metal objects are among the primary objectives of the excavation—such as in an Iron-Age chariot burial—or in obtaining prior warning of small metal objects during actual excavation. The limited utility stems partly from the short range of detection, and partly from the frequent occurrence of unwanted metal objects. Nevertheless, in the hands of over-enthusiastic amateurs metal detectors constitute a serious threat to the intact preservation of archaeological sites; this is not because large quantities of archaeological objects are actually detected, but because random holes are dug into sites in following up false indications. Besides iron litter on the surface, such indications may arise because of the magnetic response from the soil mentioned above. This response ultimately limits the sensitivity that can be utilized.

The size of the signal from non-ferrous objects depends on the conductivity and on the effective projected area; a coin that is 'end-on' to the instrument will give negligible signal. For ferrous objects the optimum shape is that of a nail, the optimum orientation being with the axis of the object pointing at the instrument; this is because of demagnetizing effects.

The pulsed induction metal detector (PIM)

In the types of metal detector outlined above any slight flexure of the coil system gives rise to a spurious signal; in the SCM-type instrument this is because disorientation of the receiver coil relative to the

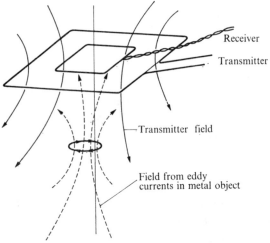

Fig. 5.3. Pulsed induction metal detector: coil system.

transmitter coil allows linkage of the primary field. This is a serious limitation for some applications, e.g. underwater use by a diver, or, searching for skiers buried in an avalanche by means of an ultra-large coil system. In the Pulsed Induction Metal detector pick-up of the primary field is avoided by keeping the receiver circuitry inactive for the duration of the transmitter pulse and no reliance is placed on the rigidity of the coil system; it can also be of whatever shape best suits the application.

The operation of the instrument is as follows (see Figs. 5.3 and 5.4). The primary field transmitted into the ground consists of a d.c. magnetic pulse lasting for about $\frac{1}{2}$ millisecond. Although this induces a voltage in the receiver coil both at switch-on and at switch-off, by keeping the receiver electronics inactive until 50 microseconds after switch-off there is no indicated signal from the receiver. (The coil inductances are low so switch-off can be achieved in a few tens of microseconds.) However if a metal object is linked by the transmitter field, eddy currents will be induced in the object at switch-off (as well as at switch-on). These eddy currents persist after switch-off, decaying

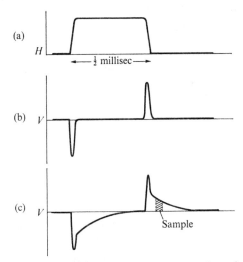

Fig. 5.4. Pulsed induction metal detector: waveforms (after Colani 1966).

(a) Primary magnetic field pulse produced by the transmitter coil.
(b) Receiver response in absence of metal object.
(c) Receiver response with metal object present. The shaded area indicates the time during which the voltage is sampled.

away slowly for a good conductor and rapidly for a bad one. Thus in this case the receiver coil is linked by a secondary d.c. magnetic field, and a voltage is generated due to the changing magnetic linkage as this field decays.

A block diagram of the instrument developed by Colani (1966) is shown in Fig. 5.5. The transmitter is pulsed at a repetition rate of 11 times per second (it is important to avoid sub-multiples of 50 Hz); during each pulse a current of 15 amp is passed through the transmitter coil, which consists of 6 square turns of side about 1 metre and has an overall inductance of about 200 microhenries. The receiver loop is of 14 turns, of side about 0·6 metres and having an overall inductance of about 400 microhenries. The receiver is controlled by means of a sampling pulse which activates it 50 microseconds after each transmitter switch-off for a duration of 25 microseconds. The receiver pulses are integrated over a second, and the output displayed on a meter. Various dimensions of coil can be used and considerable development of the circuitry has taken place since the prototype model just outlined. A later design has been described by Foster (1968).

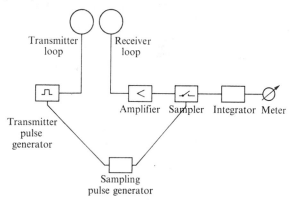

FIG. 5.5. Pulsed induction metal detector: block diagram (from Colani 1966).

Besides the advantage of flexibility in coil design, the PIM is more sensitive than commercially available metal detectors of the conventional type; for instance a brass disc of diameter 0·3 m and thickness of 3 mm can be detected at a distance of 1·5 m. Like the conventional detectors its usable sensitivity is ultimately limited by magnetic response in the soil, though by a more subtle phenomenon (magnetic 'viscosity'—see section 6.4) and less seriously. In underwater use (Foster 1970) it is less affected by the conductivity signal from sea water. In early years of use it went by the name DECCO—Decay of Eddy Currents in Conducting Objects.

5.6. Radioactivity

Most soils contain significant amounts of uranium, thorium, and potassium, typical concentrations being in the range 2–4 ppm (parts per million), 6–18 ppm and 1–3%. The associated gamma rays give rise to a count-rate of the order of 50 per second in a 1·5″ × 2″ sodium iodide scintillation-crystal counter held near the ground, almost an order of magnitude larger than the contribution from cosmic rays. Since the radioactive content of sedimentary rocks (see Table 3.3) such as limestone and chalk is negligible by comparison with that of the soil it might be expected that the count-rate above a soil-filled pit or ditch cut into rock, would be abnormally high. However, because of absorption, the count-rate is determined predominantly by the radioactive content of the upper layers and the contribution from soil or rock deeper than 0·3 metres is small. Consequently, this is unlikely to be an effective means of surveying except when the soil cover is very thin (and even then it has no obvious advantages to offer over magnetic location), though it might be useful in special circumstances— e.g. detection of blocks of granite building stone. Certainly it has the disadvantage that measurement times of the order of half a minute are required.

Detection of a ditch and a wall has been reported by Peschel (1967). It is possible that the depth limitation may be eased by the upward diffusion of radioactive salts and radon. Also, by discriminating against low energy gamma-rays electronically the effective absorption coefficient could be reduced; however, a much larger (and more expensive) sodium iodide crystal is then required in order to obtain a practical count-rate.

Cosmic rays

The absorption coefficient for high-energy cosmic rays (muons) in several orders of magnitude lower than for gamma rays and measurements utilizing this radiation are being used by Alvarez *et al.* (1970) in an attempt to detect a possible second burial chamber in the pyramid of Chephren near Cairo. A directional detector has been set up in the small unfinished chamber located centrally in the pyramid at about ground level and the flux of particles coming from different directions is being measured. The presence of a burial chamber would cause the flux from that direction to be higher than expected; it is estimated that an abnormality of one metre in the thickness would be just detectable. The experiment is very slow because the overall count-rate inside the 450-foot-high pyramid is only about one-sixth of the outside count-rate of about 1 per cm^2 per second.

Neutron scattering

This has been tried as a means of detecting buried walls and cavities by Alldred *and* Shepherd (1963). The probe, which was laid on the ground, consisted of a source of fast neutrons and a detector of slow neutrons. The extent of the slowing-down and scattering is much stronger for hydrogen atoms than for any other elements in soil, so that count-rate in the detector is a measure of the moisture content of soil, within a hemisphere of roughly 20 cm. When the probe was placed on top of stone the count-rate was less than half that from soil, due to the lower moisture content of stone. However, if 10 cm of soil intervened between stone and probe the count-rate was barely distinguishable from that for soil only; consequently it seems unlikely that the effect would be of use except on sites with very thin soil cover. There is also the possibility that in dry conditions the moisture content of the soil itself is lower above a wall than elsewhere but this was not investigated. In respect of cavities in walls it was concluded that a cavity behind a single thickness of brick would be detectable. This also seemed possible using a density probe based on gamma ray backscattering.

5.7. Miscellaneous

Gravity

The use of gravity surveys has been considered by Linington (1966), particularly in respect of locating large empty chambers; these latter are one of the most likely types of feature to have sufficient density contrast to make detection possible. Even so the estimated anomaly is only 0·1 milligals,† i.e. a change in the force of gravity by 1 part in 10^7. Field measurements failed to locate any significant anomalies over known chambers though this may have been due to instrumental difficulties (the overall spread in repeated measurements being 0·03 milligals). Another limiting factor is the extreme sensitivity to distance from the centre of the earth: a change of about 0·25 milligals occurring for a change in height of 1 metre.

Probing and augering

These two simple methods can be very effective given a strong-armed operator, and they should not be overlooked. A useful form of probe is a sharpened steel rod 10–15 mm diameter and 1–1½ metres long. This can be used to detect pits and ditches cut into chalk as long as the top-soil is not too stony.

† 1 gal corresponds to an acceleration due to gravity of 0·01 metre per (second)².

Actual samples at varying depths can be obtained using a soil auger.† This is a useful confirmatory tool when the indications from a magnetic or resistivity survey are indecisive. Both augering and probing are open to the objection of risk of damage.

Seismic and sonic

When used for a primary survey the last two methods, besides being slow and strenuous, have the disadvantage that the evidence can be somewhat subjective unless very strictly controlled. This criticism applies also to *bosing* in which the ground is thumped with a heavy rammer; over filled-in pits, tombs, and ditches a distinctive resonant note is heard, the intensified wavelength being governed by the size of the feature beneath. Bosing is successful where the top-soil is thin and firm, with an unstratified rock such as chalk beneath.

There has been little success however in attempting to exploit seismic effects instrumentally. Seismic techniques are powerful in geophysical exploration but they do not lend themselves to the smaller and more detailed scale required for archaeology. A more promising development is the 'sonic spectroscope', for the detection of cavities in walls and possibly also in the ground (Carabelli, 1966, 1968). The resonant frequency of a wall of solid brickwork is very low, in the range 5 to 20 Hz, but where there is a cavity the resonant frequency is higher. The wall is caused to vibrate by means of a loudspeaker emitting sound-waves of gradually increasing frequency (e.g. from 20 to 3000 Hz). The response of the wall is detected with an accelerometer or geophone, and recorded on a magnetic tape as a function of frequency; in order to improve the signal-to-noise ratio the first recording at any given spot is then used to control the relative amplitudes of the frequencies emitted by the loudspeaker on a second run, and by repeating the whole cycle several times the occurrence of any abnormal resonant frequencies can be detected.

In underwater prospecting, side-looking sonar is the most promising of any of the prospecting techniques. A Roman wreck at a depth of 100 metres has been located with this technique by the Scripps Institute of Oceanography (McGehee, Luyendyk, *and* Boegeman, 1968). The equipment, which was towed at a depth of about 50 metres, consists of two transmitting hydrophones fed every $\frac{1}{2}$ second with 200-watt pulses of 100 kHz carrier frequency, together with two

---

† Obtainable for instance from: H. J. Eykelkamp, 1 Rivierweg, Lathium, Holland.

associated receivers linked to recorders in the surface craft, the recorder trace being triggered by the transmitter pulses. The transmitting hydrophones provide a vertical fan of sound energy (of horizontal width $\frac{3}{4}°$) on either side of the towed vehicle at right angles to the direction of motion. The maximum range of the device is about 400 metres. In a smooth-bottomed region, a more or less steady response is seen on the recorder trace, mainly from the sea-bottom fairly close-in. A wreck above the bottom gives rise to an additional response and its range can be determined by the distance of the response along the time-axis of the recorder.

Phosphate and pollen

Calcium phosphate is the main constituent of bone, and human occupation may lead to an enhanced phosphate content in the soil. Hence, chemical analysis of regularly spaced soil samples can be used to locate regions of habitation. The application of a rapid and simple analysis technique, covering phosphate values from 0·08% to 0·8% has been described by Schwarz (1967), who also gives a summary of other reports.

The species of plant-life growing in archaeological times can be identified by microscopic examination of the pollen left behind (see Dimbleby 1969). The presence of pollen of cultivated plants indicates the proximity of a farming community. Pollen is preserved in peat bogs and in acid soils (e.g. woodland and heathland).

Dowsing

Reports are made from time to time about the location of archaeological remains after the manner of water-diviners (see e.g., Scott-Elliott, 1958). Much hearsay evidence exists both for and against the efficacity of this technique; the author's opinion is that where success is not due to coincidence (on many archaeological sites it is difficult to dig and find *nothing*), it represents a high degree of archaeological intuition on the part of the dowser. Certainly a carefully controlled test for correlation between dowsing response and magnetic disturbance yielded a negative answer (Aitken, 1959).

5.8. Computer analysis

When a successful detection technique is applied to the survey of an appreciable area of an archaeological site, the presentation and analysis of the readings obtained is a serious task. Of course if the objective is to pin-point a single feature (say a pottery kiln) in an area that is otherwise blank of strong anomalies, there is no problem; it is a matter of inserting a stake at the point of strongest disturbance and handing over to the excavating team. On the other hand, if the site comprises a complex of pits, roads, and ditches, etc. some insight into its archaeological nature may be obtainable from a study of the readings; in favourable circumstances an archaeological interpretation to be tested by digging at selected points may be possible, whereas in other cases the survey results may only be useful in influencing the sequence in which different areas are excavated.

To give sufficient resolution for satisfactory interpretation it is usually necessary to take readings at a spacing not exceeding a metre. This is equivalent to 10 000 readings per hectare, an area which would be covered in a few days using the magnetic method. Manual treatment and presentation of the data is liable to take about the same time again, and so where large areas are being surveyed utilization of a computer for this task is worthwhile. Various methods of data presentation are used; e.g. a succession of symbols each expressing a given strength of disturbance, contours, isometric drawings, and random dots having a density proportional to the disturbance strength. Pattern recognition techniques using filtering systems of varying complexity have been developed (Scollar, 1968, 1969, 1970; Linington, 1968, 1969, 1970; Wilcock, 1969, 1970). A particular need is the accentuation of linear features so that weakly showing ditches (for example) can be recognized amid a random background of comparable strength; Linington (1970) describes a comparatively simple system of linear filtering for this purpose.

A highly desirable feature of any computer system is automatic recording of the readings on punched tape (Scollar 1968a) together with associated indications of detector position in the field. This is specifically in respect of instruments with digital output such as the proton magnetometer. On the other hand instruments such as the fluxgate magnetometer and the soil conductivity meter have an analogue output and lend themselves to direct presentation on a portable X-Y plotter.

Model studies

In the interpretation of survey results, a fundamental need is to know the strength and shape of the anomaly produced by a given type of feature. This is particularly important with magnetic surveying because there can be significant displacement of the main anomaly to the south of the feature itself, and there is also the complication of an associated reverse anomaly a little to the north. (This is for the Northern Hemisphere; in the Southern Hemisphere the directions of displacement are reversed.) Continued experience of surveys followed by excavation is the most reliable basis for interpretation, but this takes a long time, nor does it help when a new type of site and feature are being tackled. It is therefore valuable to simulate real situations by means of models; these can be by computation (e.g. Linington, 1964; Scollar, 1969), or more instructively, by means of analogue models in which a scaled-down version of the feature is built in the laboratory and surveyed with a scaled-down detector (e.g. Aitken *and* Alldred, 1964; Carabelli, 1967; Aspinall *and* Lynam, 1968; Tite *and* Mullins, 1970).

5.9. Underwater surveying

Ocean equivalents of the plough and aerial photographs are sponge divers and fishermen's trawling nets. Localization of wrecks, of which the general whereabouts is known by these means, is very much more difficult than the corresponding problem on land however. Steel-hulled vessels, such as the battleships sunk in the Dardenelles, can be reliably found using a proton magnetometer with a towed detector head (Hall, 1966), but wrecks of which only the fittings and perhaps the cannon are ferrous are not detectable in this way unless in shallow water. One successful use of sonar for wrecks in a smooth-bottomed region has been mentioned already. The exploration of a located wreck with the objective of finding metal objects is a more rewarding application and both the proton magnetometer and the pulsed induction metal detector have been used in this context (e.g., Hall, 1966; Green, Hall, *and* Katsev, 1967; Green *and* Martin, 1970, 1970a). With the proton magnetometer the detector head only is carried by a diver, the instrument remaining in a surface craft with which the diver is in telephone communication.

A major difficulty even when a wreck is located is in fixing its position, particularly since the position of the towed detector with respect to the boat is liable to be somewhat uncertain. A novel way of avoiding this difficulty was used by Wilson (1970) in surveying (successfully) in shallow water for wrecks of a French fleet sunk off Quebec in 1760. This was to carry out the survey on ice, thereby allowing the same grid positioning techniques to be used as on land. For warmer climes a sonar–radio system has been used (Hall, 1966a).

REFERENCES

AITKEN, M. J. (1959). Test for correlation between dowsing response and magnetic disturbance. *Archaeometry*, **2**, 58–9.
AITKEN, M. J. and ALLDRED, J. C. (1964). A simulator-trainer for magnetic prospection. *Archaeometry*, **7**, 28–35.
ALLDRED, J. C. and SHEPHERD, A. (1963). Trial of neutron scattering for the detection of buried walls and cavities. *Archaeometry*, **6**, 89–92.
ALVAREZ, L. W., ANDERSON, J. A., EL BEDWEI, F., BURKHARD, J., FAKHRY, A., GIRGIS, A., GONEID, A., HASSAN, F., IVERSON, D., LYNCH, G., MILIGY, A., MOUSSA, A. H., SHARKAWI, M., and YAZOLINO, L. (1970). Search for hidden chambers in the Pyramids. *Science*, **167**, 832–9.
ASPINALL, A. and LYNAM, J. (1968). Induced polarization as a technique for archaeological surveying. *Prospezioni Archeologiche*, **3**, 91–3.
ASPINALL, A. and LYNAM, J. T. (1970). An induced polarization instrument for detection of near surfaces features. *Prospezioni Archaeologiche*, **5**, 67–76.
BRADFORD, J. S. P. (1957). *Ancient Landscapes*, p. 297, Bell, London.
CARABELLI, E. (1966). A new tool for archaeological prospecting: the sonic spectroscope for the detection of cavities. *Prospezioni Archeologiche*, **1**, 25–35.
CARABELLI, E. (1968). Ricerca delle cavità superficiali con l'impiego di vibratori: primi esperimenti. *Prospezioni Archeologiche*, **3**, 37–43.
COLANI, C. (1966). A new type of locating device. I—the instrument. *Archaeometry*, **9**, 3–8.
DIMBLEBY, G. W. (1969). Pollen analysis. In *Science in Archaeology* (eds. D. Brothwell and E. S. Higgs), pp. 167–77. Thames and Hudson, London.
FOSTER, E. I. (1968). Further developments of the pulsed induction metal detector. *Prospezioni Archeologiche*, **3**, 95–9.
FOSTER, E. and HACKENS, T. (1969). Decco metal detector survey on Delos. *Archaeometry*, **11**, 165–72.
FOSTER, E. J. (1970). A diver-operated underwater metal detector. *Archaeometry*, **12**, 161–6.
GREEN, J. N., HALL, E. T., and KATZEV, M. L. (1967). Survey of a Greek shipwreck off Kyrenia, Cyprus. *Archaeometry*, **10**, 47–56.
GREEN, J. N. and MARTIN, C. (1970). Metal detector survey of the wreck of the Armada ship 'Santa Maria de la Rosa.' *Prospezioni Archeologiche*, **5**, 95–100.
GREEN, J. N. and MARTIN, C. (1970a). Metal detector survey at Dun an Oir. *Prospezioni Archeologiche*, **5**, 101–6.
HALL, E. T. (1966). The use of the proton magnetometer in underwater archaeology. *Archaeometry*, **9**, 32–44.
HALL, E. T. (1966a). A sea-going sonar position-fixing system. *Archaeometry*, **9**, 45–50.
HOWELL, M. (1966). A soil conductivity meter. *Archaeometry*, **9**, 20–3.
LANCASTER, D. E. (1966). Electronic metal detectors. *Electronics World*. December 1966, pp. 39–62.
LININGTON, R. E. (1964). The use of simplified anomalies in magnetic surveying. *Archaeometry*, **7**, 3–13.
LININGTON, R. E. (1966). Test use of a gravimeter on Etruscan chamber tombs at Cerveteri. *Prospezioni Archeologiche*, **1**, 37–41.
LININGTON, R. E. (1968). The Rome computer system for treating archaeological survey results. First Part. *Prospezioni Archeologiche*, **3**, 19–36.

LININGTON, R. E. (1969). The Rome computer system for treating archaeological survey results, second part. *Prospezioni Archeologiche*, 4, 9–58.

LININGTON, R. E. (1970). A first use of linear filtering techniques on archaeological prospecting results. *Prospezioni Archeologiche*, 5, 43–54.

MCGHEE, M. S., LUYENDYK, B. P., *and* BOEGEMAN, D. E. (1968). Location of an ancient Roman shipwreck by modern acoustic techniques. *A Critical Look at Marine Technology*. (4th Annual Conference Marine Technology Society, Washington, D.C. July 1968).

MUSSON, C. R. (1968). A geophysical survey at South Cadbury Castle, Somerset, using the Howell soil conductivity anomaly detector (SCM). *Prospezioni Archeologiche*, 3, 115–21.

PESCHEL, G. (1967). Radiometrische Messungen zum Nachweis verdeckter archäologisher Objecte. *Ausgrabungen and Funde*, 12, 287–97.

SCHWARZ, G. T. (1967). A simplified chemical test for archaeological field work. *Archaeometry*, 10, 57–63.

SCOLLAR, I. (1962). Electromagnetic prospecting methods in archaeology. *Archaeometry*, 5, 146–53.

SCOLLAR, I. (1968). Progam package for the interpretation of magnetometer data. *Prospezioni Archeologiche*, 3, 9–18.

SCOLLAR, I. (1968a). Automatic recording of magnetometer data in the field. *Prospezioni Archaeologiche*, 3, 105–10.

SCOLLAR, I. (1969). Some techniques for the valuation of archaeological magnetometer surveys. *Wld. Archaeol.* 1, 77–89.

SCOLLAR, I. (1970). Fourier transforms methods for the evaluation of magnetic maps. *Prospezioni Archeologiche*, 5, 9–41.

SCOTT-ELLIOT, J. (1958). Archaeological detection. *J. Brit. Soc. Dowsers.* 14, 338–9.

TABBAGH, A. (1972). Méthode de prospection électromagnétique S.G.D. *Prospezioni Archeologiche*, 7, 125–34.

TITE, M. S. *and* MULLINS, C. (1969). Electromagnetic prospecting: a preliminary investigation. *Prospezioni Archeologiche*, 4, 95–102.

TITE, M. S. *and* MULLINS, C. (1970). Electromagnetic prospecting on archaeological sites using a soil conductivity meter. *Archaeometry*, 12, 97–104.

WILCOCK, J. D. (1969). Computer analysis of proton magnetometer readings from South Cadbury 1968. A long distance exercise. *Prospezioni Archeologiche*, 4, 95–102.

WILCOCK, J. D. (1970). Some developments in the portrayal of magnetic anomalies by digital incremental plotter. *Prospezioni Archeologiche*, 5, 55–8.

WILSON, A. E. (1970). A winter survey with proton magnetometers of an underwater site. *Prospezioni Archeologiche*, 5, 89–96.

6 *Magnetic Prospecting*

6.1. Introduction

IN section 4.1 we noted that the main features of the earth's magnetic field are the same as would be produced by a bar magnet placed at the centre of the earth. This field is modified first by irregularites in the current system near the core–mantle boundary, and secondly by variations in the magnetic properties of the rock structures forming the mantle and crust. The resultant field varies only slowly in space and time; in Europe the average change in magnetic field intensity over a half-a-kilometre, or over a month, is of the order of 50 parts per million. Superimposed on this smooth basic field are irregular and small-scale variations. It is with these that we are concerned in the present chapter.

In volcanic regions there are strong spatial irregularities arising from thermoremanent magnetism which the lava acquired on cooling from the molten state. On sedimentary geology on the other hand there are no such effects, the types of magnetism involved being very much weaker; there is a significant change on going from one type of surface geology to another, but in general the changes in magnetic intensity across an archaeological site are due to natural variations in thickness of top-soil, and to the activities of man—whether ancient or modern.

Top-soil carries a much higher magnetic susceptibility than the rock or sub-soil from which it has been derived, for reasons that are discussed in section 6.4. As long as the rock surface (or the sub-soil surface) is smooth the magnetic intensity change across the site will be smooth too, and if within the site there are man-made pits dug into the rock that have silted up with top-soil these will produce well-defined magnetic anomalies that can be detected given a sensitive enough magnetometer. Of course if there has been strong natural erosion of the rock surface, such as may occur in Mediterranean regions, the size and shape of these can simulate man-made features; however in general this circumstance is uncommon.

Besides soil features, magnetic anomalies can be produced by burnt structures such as pottery kilns (section 6.3), by iron objects (section 6.6), and in special circumstances by roads, wall foundations, and cavities (section 6.5). Iron objects left by ancient man are fairly rare finds, but modern man's discarded litter is all too frequent and represents a severe handicap to magnetic prospecting.

Measurement

Associated with an anomaly in magnetic intensity there is an anomaly in magnetic direction, both in angle of declination and angle of dip. Early mineral prospectors used false compass readings—checked by reference to the sun or to the pole-star—as an indication of iron-ore deposits. However the strength of anomaly with which we are now concerned is, for some features, a change in intensity of only 100 parts per million, and the corresponding change in direction is of the order of 0·01°. Measurement to this accuracy is certainly possible, but the setting-up time rules it out as a practical method. The advantage of measuring intensity is that instruments are available with which sufficiently accurate measurements can be made easily and rapidly— the order of twenty per minute with a proton magnetometer, which is as fast as they can be recorded. The need for rapidity is dictated by the large number of readings that have to be taken in order to cover a site: a spacing of not more than a metre is usually necessary, and this implies 10 000 readings per hectare (100 m × 100 m).

The proton magnetometer was the first instrument available that fulfilled the practical requirements, and it continues to be the standard instrument for this work. The present chapter assumes it to be the instrument in use and a simplified explanation of its operation is given in the next section. It is discussed further in Chapter 7 together with other relevant instruments. Some of these are widely used in mineral prospecting, for geophysical measurements, and in space rockets. Over land the detecting element may be towed behind an aircraft, and on sea behind a ship. In general the sensitivity required for the archaeological work is not as demanding as for these applications. On a typical archaeological site, random variations due to irregularities in the top-soil ('*soil-noise*') are of the order of ten or twenty parts per million, and this limits the usable sensitivity.

Units

The traditional unit used in geophysics for measurement of variations in the earth's magnetic field strength is the *gamma*, no distinction being made between field strength and magnetic induction. In the e.m.u. system,

$$100\,000 \text{ gamma} \equiv 1 \text{ oersted of field strength}$$
$$\equiv 1 \text{ gauss of magnetic induction.}$$

In the S.I. system,

$$1 \text{ gamma} \equiv 0\cdot79 \text{ milliamp/metre of field strength,}$$
$$\equiv 1 \text{ nanotesla of magnetic induction}$$
$$(1 \text{ tesla} \equiv 1 \text{ weber/metre}^2)$$

The field intensity in Britain is around 48 000 gamma so that a change of 10 parts per million corresponds to approximately $\frac{1}{2}$ gamma.

The e.m.u. system is used for magnetic moment, specific magnetization, and susceptibility, as discussed in section 4.1.

Frequency will be quoted in Hertz (Hz) and 1 Hz = 1 cycle per sec, 1 kHz = 10^3 Hz, 1 MHz = 10^6 Hz.

Transient variations

The slow secular variation arising from changes in the earth's core of 2 or 3 gamma per month is unimportant here. However, there are shorter-term variations due to ionization current changes in the upper atmosphere that matter a great deal. Sun-spot activity, variations in solar ionization, daily and monthly atmospheric tides all play a part. About 30% of the transient variations arise indirectly, from eddy currents induced in the earth's crust by primary currents in the upper atmosphere. Some of the transient variations are worldwide, some are localized to regions of 100 kilometres across.

The variations are somewhat erratic, but there is a strong daily ('diurnal') component and it is this that is of most concern in magnetic surveying. The magnetic field intensity decreases rapidly during the early morning soon after sunrise, reaches a minimum at noon, and increases during the afternoon and night. Whereas during the winter the overall variation may amount to only 5 gamma, which is barely significant, during the summer it may reach 50 gamma and this cannot be ignored. The variation is too irregular, both from day to day and from hour to hour, to allow readings to be corrected by some generalized formula, and the ideal solution is to make simultaneous measurement at a fixed reference point, or, to use a gradiometer type of instrument. A simpler alternative is to complete the survey of each sub-area (typically a 10-metre square) in a time short enough for the transient variation to be negligibile; for typical sites a change of several gamma is barely significant and on normal days the change within ten minutes does not often exceed this. However, there are *magnetic storm days*, associated with strong sun-spot activity, when the overall variation may reach 1000 gamma, and on such days surveying is only possible if a reference detector or a gradiometer is used. The likelihood of magnetic storms varies with the eleven-year periodicity of the sun-spot cycle, the next maximum being around 1980.

In addition to the diurnal variation, there is a variety of much faster types usually referred to as *micropulsations*. The amplitudes of these are much smaller than that of the diurnal variation, and decrease as the periodicity under consideration is reduced. Thus for a period of a few minutes the amplitudes are of the order of a few gamma but for periods below 10 seconds the amplitudes are less than 0·1 gamma. These micropulsations are a serious difficulty only on sites for which the soil-noise is low enough to permit detection of very weak anomalies, and for which a high-sensitivity magnetometer is being used—either a proton magnetometer adjusted to read to better than 1 gamma sensitivity, or, a caesium magnetometer.

6.2. The proton magnetometer (see also Chapter 7)

A conventional magnetometer measures magnetic intensity (field strength) by the torque which tends to turn a delicately balanced magnetized needle until it points along the lines of force (see Fig. 4.1(b)). Delicate instruments of this type are sufficiently sensitive for archaeological work but the speed of operation is severely limited by the need to make the instrument precisely level before measurement. The proton magnetometer on the other hand requires no such setting-up and has more than sufficient sensitivity.

The operation of the instrument is based on a subtle effect experienced by the nuclei of atoms when in a magnetic field. For measurement of the intensity of the earth's magnetic field the most suitable nucleus is that of the hydrogen atom; this consists of a single elementary particle, the proton. Its behaviour in a magnetic field can be understood by regarding it as a tiny gyroscope that carries a bar magnet aligned along the axis of rotation. This magnet tries to point along the lines of force of the earth's field but the gyroscopic effect prevents this temporarily, and it precesses around the direction of the lines of force during the gradual process of achieving alignment along this direction. This precession is similar to that of a

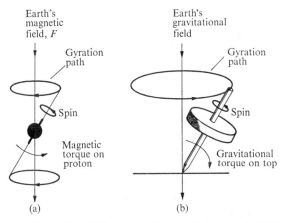

Fig. 6.1. Precession of (a) a proton in a vertical magnetic field, and (b) a spinning top under the influence of gravity.

spinning top under the influence of gravity (see Fig. 6.1). The important thing is that the frequency of precession (the number of gyrations per second) is exactly proportional to the magnetic intensity. The frequency is about 2000 per second for an intensity of 48 000 gamma (typical figure for Northern Europe and the southern part of the U.S.A.). Supposing it to be exactly 2000·00 Hz at one measuring point, at another point where the magnetic intensity is higher by 5 gamma the frequency will be 2000·20 Hz.

Since hydrogen is a constituent part of water, and of organic liquids, a large number of protons (about 10^{25}) are conveniently obtained in a quarter-pint bottle, and this forms the detecting element. The combined magnetic moment of the protons precessing together induces an alternating voltage of about a microvolt in a coil of 1000 turns wound around the bottle, and a long flexible cable feeds this to an electronic instrument for amplification and frequency measurement.

The detector bottle, encapsulated in a suitable resin (such as araldite) is carried on an aluminium staff, usually at a height of 1 foot, and moved by an operator from point to point over the area being surveyed. A second operator controls the instrument and records the digits which are indicated either by meters or visual display tubes. The five-figure number formed by these digits ('*the count*' or '*the reading*') is a measure of the magnetic intensity wherever the bottle is placed. The circuitry is usually designed to give a sensitivity such that 1 unit in the last digit corresponds to 1 gamma. The readings are usually recorded directly in plan form and for convenience only the last three digits are written down—representing hundreds, tens, and units—unless very strong anomalies are being encountered.

Each measurement involves two stages: the *polarizing period* (usually about 2 seconds) and the *counting period* (about $\frac{1}{2}$ second). These are automatically sequenced by timing circuits. At the conclusion of the counting period the reading is indicated and this indication remains until the next polarizing period. During the polarizing period a current of about 1 amp is fed through the coil around the bottle creating a strong magnetic field (of several hundred oersted) along its axis. This ensures that there is a preferred phase at the start of the measurement, i.e. a majority of the protons point along the bottle axis. By orientating this axis roughly East–West, maximum signal *amplitude* is obtained during the subsequent counting period. This counting period is initiated by the polarizing current being turned off; the protons, now freed from the restraint of the strong field, perform their lining-up gyrations as already described. The reading is determined by the *frequency* of gyration and this is *independent of bottle orientation* (as long as the amplitude of the signal is sufficient for accurate measurement).

As a check of correct functioning, most types of the instrument give indication of signal amplitude also. During each counting period this amplitude decays, reaching one half of its initial value in one or two seconds. The cause of this decay is two-fold: first, there is gradual alignment in the earth's field, and secondly, the protons get out of step because molecular fields cause slight differences in gyration frequency. Differences in frequency can also arise in different parts of the water sample because the *external* magnetic field is not the same across the whole volume of the bottle. This similarly causes loss of phase among the protons and a gradient of 200 gamma per metre reduces the decay time to less than a second; observation of such 'fast decay' gives useful additional information (see section 6.6).

With the instrument used by the Oxford University Archaeological Research Laboratory in the early development of magnetic surveying —now the Elsec 592†—the electronic circuitry is such that the indicated reading is inversely proportional to the magnetic intensity. Hence an *increase* in intensity gives a *decrease* in reading. This is no disadvantage for archaeological work, but since with later designs the reading gives the intensity directly in gammas there is risk of confusion as to what is meant by 'positive' and 'negative' in discussing anomalous readings. To avoid this it is better to use 'normal anomaly' as meaning an increase above the average intensity, and 'reverse anomaly' for a decrease below average; i.e. with the early design 'normal anomaly' means a decrease in the *reading*.

The electronics are fairly complex and commercial instruments cost upwards of £800; a simplified and much cheaper version that is adequate for archaeological work is described in section 7.4. All these instruments are conveniently portable and are powered either from miniature accumulators or from dry-cell batteries. Inclusive of these the weight is usually in the range 3 to 10 kilogram. Accumulator or battery capacity is sufficient for at least a long day's work; with accumulators a convenient system is to recharge overnight from the operators' automobile accumulator. The primary rôle of commercially available instruments is in mineral exploration and geophysics; current developments have been reviewed by Hood (1973).

† Some available instruments are:

PPM-1 *from* Austral Exploration Services Pty. Ltd., 5 Deloraine Road, P. O. Box 16, Edwardstown, South Australia.

GM-122 *from* Baringer Research Ltd., 304 Carlingview Drive, Metropolitan Toronto, Rexdale, Ontario.

G-816 *from* Geometrics, 914 Industrial Avenue, Palo Alto, California 94303.

Elsec 592 and 595 *from* Littlemore Scientific Engineering Co., Railway Lane, Littlemore, Oxford OX4 4PZ, England.

GP-70 *from* McPhar Geophysics Ltd., 139 Bond Avenue, Don Mills, Toronto, 404, Ontario.

NPM-3 *from* Sandar Geophysics Ltd., 1305 Richmond Road W., Ottawa, Ontario K2B 7Y2.

Askania Gpr 1 *from* Siemens Aktiengesellschaft, Abt. E. 61 D-75 Karlsruhe 21, Postfach 211080.

M-50 *from* Varian Associates, 611 Hansen Way, Palo Alto, California 94303 *or from* Static Devices Ltd., North Bar Place, Banbury, Oxfordshire, England.

6.3. Burnt features

Pottery kilns

The first proton magnetometer for archaeological use was built for the specific purpose of locating Romano-British pottery kilns under threat of obliteration by road construction (Aitken, Webster, Rees, 1958). This was seen as a vital archaeological need because of the special place that kilns have in the archaeology of N.W. Europe for Roman and later times. Pottery fragments (*sherds*), being durable and common, often form the main evidence about a site's history. The occurrence of similar types of pottery on two different sites form a link between them, and dating evidence obtained on one can be carried over to the other—sherds are rather similar to sub-standards in physics. A kiln is the source of these sub-standards, and its excavation immediately yields geographic information about the pottery types found in it. Also, since the useful life of a kiln was probably less than a few years, if several types are found in it their contemporaneity is established. As a special bonus there is sometimes a load of complete pots in the kiln—left when the potter abandoned the kiln because he was dissatisfied with the quality of product.

Besides all this there is now enhanced interest in the pottery because it can be dated by thermoluminescence, and in the kiln structure itself because of the recorded evidence it holds for archaeomagnetic studies.

Anomaly strength

Although kilns of different civilizations may differ in construction, they all have the common feature that they are constructed with clay—because of its unique refractory properties. Sometimes the clay is used directly in raw form, sometimes as prefabricated bricks; the amount varies from type to type but probably about 1000 kilograms is present in a substantial structure. On cooling down from firing this clay acquires permanent magnetization—the thermoremanent magnetism (TRM) that has already been discussed in Chapter 4. In that context we were concerned with the retrieval of data about the magnetic direction and intensity recorded in the clay, by means of laboratory measurements on extracted samples. We are now concerned with the magnetic field produced by the magnetization of the remains of the kiln as a whole.

Although on a weight for weight basis, the magnetization of baked clay is much weaker than that of iron, the total magnetic moment of a kiln is comparable with that carried by an iron object. Taking the specific TRM magnetization to range from 0·0001 gauss cm³ per gram for red oxidized clay to 0·1 gauss cm³ per gram for grey reduced clay, the total magnetic moment of a kiln should lie in the range 50–50 000 gauss cm³. In terms of the moment induced in average quality iron these limits correspond to weights of a few ounces and several hundred pounds.

Because what remains of a kiln is usually irregular in shape, a precise calculation of the resultant magnetic field is not possible. In some types however, Roman kilns in particular, a substantial fraction of the baked clay is contained in a central pedestal that supports the floor carrying the pottery. If this pedestal is assumed to be spherical, then its magnetic field is given by that of a short bar magnet having the same moment, and aligned along the direction of magnetization (i.e. along the lines of force of the earth's field). In this direction the strength of the anomaly is given by

$$\Delta F = \frac{0\cdot 2 \times M}{d^3} \text{ gamma,} \qquad (6.1)$$

where M gauss cm³ is the moment and d metres the distance from it. Taking $M = 1000$ gauss cm³,

$$\text{for } d = 1 \text{ m,} \qquad F = 200 \text{ gamma}$$
$$d = 2 \text{ m,} \qquad F = 25 \text{ gamma}$$
$$d = 3 \text{ m,} \qquad F = 7 \text{ gamma.}$$

The anomaly of 7 gamma represents a change in total magnetic intensity of just over 1 part in 10 000. Although this is comfortably detectable with a proton magnetometer it is not a lot greater than random variations from point to point on a typical site due to soil-noise.

Many pottery kilns have now been detected and, as a general rule, when the top of the pedestal is about 1–1½ metres below the detector the anomaly strength is in the range 100–200 gamma. This is for substantial kilns, such as Romano-British types; such strong anomalies cannot be expected from kilns of civilizations less advanced in ceramic technology.

Anomaly shape

The quantity measured by the proton magnetometer is the resultant of the normal earth's field **F** and the additional field due to the kiln

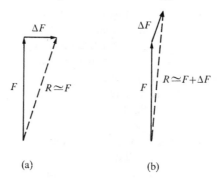

FIG. 6.2. Vector addition.

(a) Anomaly field perpendicular to main field.
(b) Anomaly field nearly parallel to main field.

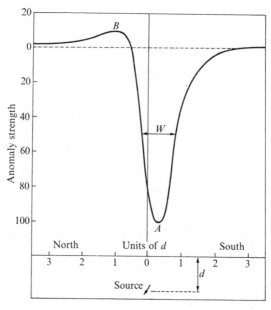

FIG. 6.3. Idealized kiln anomaly. The magnetization of the kiln has been approximated by a short bar magnet at a depth d. The angle of dip, I, is taken to be 68°. The anomaly strength represents the deviation from the normal field strength. The scale has been inverted so as to correspond to a proton magnetometer giving reciprocal indication—an increase in field strength causes a decrease in the reading.

ΔF. These are vectors and the magnitude of the resultant is not easy to calculate except when **F** and **ΔF** are parallel. If **F** is perpendicular to **ΔF** then the resultant **R** differs in magnitude from **F** only slightly (see Fig. 6.2).

The calculated anomaly along a north–south line passing over a short bar magnet is shown in Fig. 6.3; as mentioned above this is the same as due to a uniformly magnetized sphere. The angle of dip has been taken as 68° both for **F** and for the axis of the magnet. The distance scale (horizontal), is in units equal to the depth d of the magnet below the level of the detector. The ordinate scale represents the deviation from normal intensity. It is useful to note the following:

(a) The maximum of the anomaly (A) lies to the south of the source. The displacement is approximately one-third of the depth d.

(b) The separation, W, between the two points at which the anomaly has half its maximum value, is equal to d.

(c) The extreme of the reverse anomaly (B) is 10% of the maximum, and lies one depth unit to the north of the magnet.

(d) The anomaly is very small (less than 2%) at distances greater than 3 times d.

In latitudes where the angle of dip is outside the range 60°–70° these rules and Fig. 6.3 need progressive modification. Figure 6.4 shows the anomaly shape for various angles of dip and Fig. 6.5 the ratio of burial depth to anomaly width. On the magnetic equator the reverse anomaly is dominant and has its maximum directly above the magnet; this has been observed in practice for iron smelting furnaces in Nigeria (Tite, 1966).

The foregoing strictly applies only to sources which can be approximated by a short bar magnet, i.e. compact features of dimensions small compared to the detector distance, d. The effect of a more extended source is to widen the anomaly. In practice rule (a) is reasonably valid, but in rule (b) the distance W usually represents *either* the depth *or* the width of the feature, whichever is the greater. The reverse disturbance referred to in rule (c) is often absent. The localization of the anomaly implied by rule (d) still holds but the anomaly is never less wide than the feature from which it emanates.

Another reason why observed anomalies differ from the ideal shape is the contiguity of a secondary one, e.g. the stokehole of a kiln may

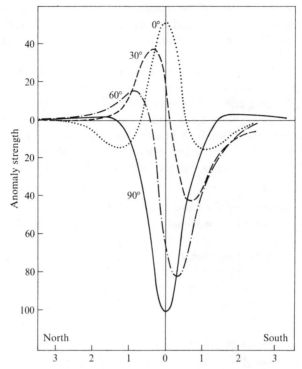

FIG. 6.4. Effect of latitude on anomaly shape. The anomalies are from short bar magnets for the angles of dip indicated. The horizontal scale, representing a north–south traverse through the centre of the anomaly, is in units of burial depth.

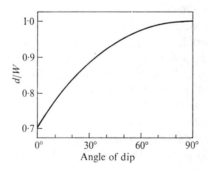

FIG. 6.5. Effect of latitude on anomaly width. d—burial depth; W—distance between points on north–south traverse through the centre of the anomaly at which the strength has fallen to half the maximum.

produce an anomaly for the same reason as a pit; an example of how this can distort the anomaly shape is given in Fig. 6.6.

Other burnt features

The anomalies from furnaces, ovens, domestic hearths, etc. are weaker than from kilns because the amount of baked clay is less, but

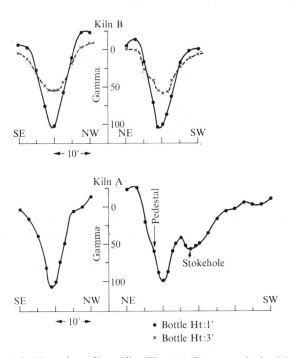

FIG. 6.6. Magnetic profiles—kilns. These readings were obtained during the survey of the Romano-British kiln site at Water Newton, Huntingdonshire. The curves above represent perpendicular traverses through the maximum. On excavation, kilns were found, about 5 ft in diameter and with floors $4\frac{1}{2}$ ft below the present ground surface; each had a substantial central pedestal.

they are usually detectable as long as the depth of burial is not too great.

The magnetic effect of a burnt feature is seriously attenuated by disarrangement. Magnetism is a directional effect and, in the same way that the random orientations of magnetic domains (see Fig. 4.2(a)) cause mutual annulment in unbaked clay, so too, on a larger scale but to an incomplete degree, with the constituent parts of a structure if they have been jumbled since firing. The extreme case of this is a dump of pottery sherds; although the magnetization (TRM) of each individual sherd may be high, the anomaly detected is comparatively weak. This 'weakening by jumbling' effect only applies in the case of permanent magnetization.

6.4. Soil features

There is an anomaly from a filled-in pit or ditch when the magnetic susceptibility of the filling is higher than that of the surrounding strata into which the feature has been dug. The specific susceptibility defines the magnetization induced by a magnetic field per unit mass, the sample remaining at its ordinary temperature. Unlike the permanent magnetization of TRM this induced magnetization is temporary; if the magnetic field is removed the magnetization disappears, and, if the field remains but the orientation of the sample is altered, the direction of magnetization continues to lie along the lines of force of the field. In terms of magnetic domains the effect is explained, in the case of multi-domain grains, as a slight growth of those domains which have a component in the same direction as the field at the expense of those which do not. For single-domain grains the effect is due to a slight decrease in the angle that each domain's magnetization makes with the field. The above discussion ignores viscous magnetization which is mentioned shortly.

The enhanced susceptibility of soils

The susceptibilities of some miscellaneous samples of soil collected from a number of archaeological sites are given in Table 6.1. With two exceptions the susceptibilities of samples taken from the filling of an archaeological feature are higher than from elsewhere on the site. Without exception, all samples of topsoil have a higher susceptibility than the underlying substratum. The actual strength of the specific magnetization (obtained by multiplying the susceptibility by the magnetic field intensity, which is about 0·5 oersted for most of the sites) of some soil samples is comparable with the TRM magnetization of oxidized baked clay; hence the field observation referred to earlier that pit anomalies can be of comparable strength to kiln anomalies.

The foregoing observations are not unexpected in view of the investigations made by Le Borgne (1952, 1955, 1960, 1965), on soils from non-archaeological contexts in Brittany, mainly derived from schist and granite. The susceptibility decreases with depth over the first metre, often by two orders of magnitude, and there is correlation between the susceptibility and the content of organic matter. The explanation given is in terms of the conversion of the iron oxide in the soil from the very weakly magnetic form haematite (α-Fe_2O_3), in which it exists in 'raw' soils and rocks, to the form maghaemite (γ-Fe_2O_3) which has a susceptibility greater by two orders of magnitude. The conversion proceeds by reduction to magnetite (Fe_3O_4) and subsequent re-oxidation. Two possible mechanisms have been proposed:

(i) *Fermentation* (Le Borgne, 1955). This occurs at ordinary temperatures and is favoured by alternating periods of humidity (giving anaerobic conditions suitable for oxidation). The alternation must be sufficiently rapid since a long period of high humidity may cause removal of iron by leaching if the drainage is sufficient.

(ii) *Burning* (Le Borgne, 1960). This is the cumulative effect over the centuries of fire—ground clearance by burning being postulated as an integral part of ancient methods of cultivation. During the burning of vegetable matter, air is excluded from the underlying soil so that reduction occurs; during cooling, air reaches the soil and allows re-oxidation. Consequently, a thin layer of soil underlying the fire acquires an enhanced susceptibility and subsequent disturbance of the soil through cultivation, followed by further fires, ultimately produces enhancement throughout the top-soil. It is to be noted that, although heat is necessary to produce the required chemical changes, the magnetization is still of a temporarily induced type and is not a thermoremanent magnetization.

The results of an extensive study of English soils, mainly from archaeological sites on sedimentary geology (Tite *and* Mullins, 1971; Tite 1972) are consistent with the above. One of the laboratory treatments is to heat each soil in hydrogen at 500°C for several hours; the subsequent a.c. susceptibility χ_H is used as a measure of the maximum susceptibility of which the soil is capable. In a number of cases the percentage by weight of ferric oxide was measured before heating, and with one or two exceptions it was found that χ_H is proportional to this percentage; for 1% ferric oxide the specific susceptibility is 4×10^{-4} e.m.u. per gram. The ratio of the initial susceptibility

TABLE 6.1

Soil susceptibilities and anomalies from unburnt features

Site	Sub-stratum	Soil susceptibilities[a] (e.m.u./g $\times 10^6$)		Typical anomaly[b]
		(a) Samples not associated with archaeological features	(b) Samples from fillings of archaeological features	
Arras, Yorkshire (Iron-Age barrow site)	Chalk	Plough-soil: 1·1, 1·5	Barrow ditch: 0·2, 0·15	5 gamma from barrow ditch 7 ft across, 3 ft deep. Height 2 ft
Barley, Hertfordshire (Iron-Age domestic site)	Chalk	Plough-soil: 0·7, 0·8 Chalk: < 0·05	Pits: 2·6, 2·1, 1·4, 1·0, 0·7	30 gamma from pit 5 ft across and 4 ft deep. Height 2·5 ft
Burrough, Leicestershire (Iron-Age hill fort)	Ferruginous limestone	Soil 6 in. below turf: 2·2, 2·4, 2·6	Pits: 7·6, 6·9, 6·8, 6·2	150 gamma from pit 3 ft across, 3 ft deep. Height 2 ft
Cox Green, Berkshire (Roman villa)	Clay	—	Ditch: 1·5 (rich black filling)	10 gamma from ditch 8 ft wide, 2–3 ft deep. Height 2 ft
Dane's Camp, Worcestershire (Iron-Age hill fort)	Limestone	Turf-layer: 7 to 11 (15 samples) Limestone: < 0·05	Pits: 2 to 12 (13 samples)	100 gamma from pit 4 ft across, 5 ft deep. Hehtig 1·5 ft (see Table 6.2)

Site	Soil type	Soil susceptibility	Feature susceptibility	Notes
Dorchester, Oxon. (Roman)	Gravel	Soil at 1 ft: 0·6, 0·8 Gravel: < 0·05	Ditch: 1·2, 1·2, 1·1	15 gamma from ditch 10 ft wide, 3 ft deep. Height 3 ft
Enkommi, Cyprus (Bronze Age)	Limestone and clay	Soil at 6 in: 0·7, 0·65, 0·5, 0·45	Tomb: 1·1 Well: 3·3 Road: 2·6	10 gamma from thick sun-baked road. Height 6 ft
Hod Hill, Wiltshire (Iron-Age hill fort)	Chalk	Soil 2 in. below turf: 0·6	Ditch of hut: 0·9	(4 gamma from ditch presumed 1 ft deep. Height 1 ft)
Madmarston, Oxon. (Iron-Age hill fort)	Clay	Soil 6 in. below turf: 4·0, 3·5	Pits: between 9 and 22	100 gamma from pit 6 ft across, 5 ft deep. Height 4 ft (see Table 6.2)
Water Newton, Hunts. (Roman kiln site)	Clay	Plough-soil: 1·3, 1·4, 1·6	Pit: 6·4, 5·0, 3·0	70 gamma from pit, 7 ft across, 3 ft deep. Height 3 ft

[a] Susceptibilities were measured by moving the sample into the centre of a coil system and observing the throw of the ballistic galvanometer having a time constant of about 5 seconds.

[b] 'Depth' refers to lowest point of feature below *old* ground surface.
'Height' refers to height of detector-bottle above *old* ground surface.

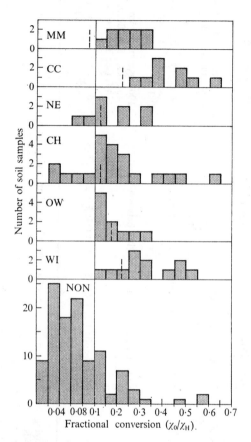

FIG. 6.7. Histograms showing the distribution of values for fractional conversion (χ_0/χ_H) for soil samples from pits and ditches on archaeological sites and for samples of normal agricultural topsoil (from Tite, 1972). The values for the topsoil from archaeological sites are indicated by the vertical dashed lines. Note change of horizontal scale at 0·10.

Key: MM—Madmarston, Oxon (clay: Jurassic—Upper Lias).
    CC—S. Cadbury, Somerset (Limestone: Jurassic—Inferior Oolite).
    NE—N. Elmham, Norfolk (sand, gravel, clay: Glacial Drift).
    CH—Colchester, Essex (sand, gravel: Postglacial Drift).
    OW—Owlesbury, Hampshire (chalk: Cretaceous).
    WI—Winchester, Hampshire (chalk: Cretaceous).
    NON—normal agricultural topsoil.

to the susceptibility after heating in hydrogen (χ_0/χ_H) is termed the 'fractional conversion'. It will be seen from Fig. 6.7, first, that for a given site there is a tendency for the fractional conversion in soils from archaeological features to be greater than in top soil, and secondly, that in general both of these exceed the fractional conversion values found for soils not associated with an archaeological site.[†] This confirms that the high values of susceptibility (χ_0) found in soils from archaeological sites and features is due to an enhancement mechanism such as (i) or (ii) above, rather than some mechanism that leads to an increased concentration of iron oxide.

Of the two enhancement mechanisms (i) and (ii), it is usually assumed that the burning mechanism is predominant. This is because the latter can be easily demonstrated, whereas attempts to achieve comparable enhancement with the fermentation mechanism have not been successful (e.g. Le Borgne, 1955). However, such attempts are inevitably very short-term compared to the actual situation, and the observation that the soil-fill from pits is usually higher than that of the surrounding topsoil suggests that the fermentation mechanism does make a significant contribution. The feature responsible for one of the strongest pit anomalies detected by the author was, on excavation, declared by the archaeologist to have been an Iron-Age latrine. Similarly, on one or two occasions a magnetic survey has duly located last year's Elsan pit.

Whatever the mechanism, the higher susceptibility (χ_0) of archaeological topsoil compared to non-archaeological topsoil suggests field susceptibility surveys as a technique for discovering the existence of new sites. An instrument of the SCM-type (see section 5.5) is appropriate, and convenient, for this. It is to be expected that sites most effectively detected in this way will be those that have been intensively occupied over long periods.

The influence of geology

Although man's activity may determine the fractional enhancement (χ_0/χ_H), the actual value of χ_0 is determined also by χ_H, i.e. by the iron oxide concentration. Figure 6.8 shows the results obtained by Tite (1972) in a survey of agricultural topsoils collected in England from

[†] Recent measurements by M. S. Tite and R. E. Linington indicate for the *terra rossa* which develops from calcareous deposits under Mediterranean conditions the fractional conversion is high irrespective of whether or not the soil is from an archaeological site.

various geological regions lying south and east of a line running from the Bristol Channel to the Humber estuary. The actual susceptibility to be expected on an archaeological site is obtained by multiplying the value of χ_H by the fractional enhancement; Tite suggests 0·25 as a useful typical value, though from Fig. 6.7 we see that the actual value range from 0·02 up to 0·65 for sites intensively occupied over a long period.

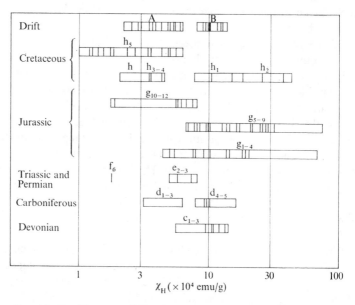

FIG. 6.8. Specific susceptibility (χ_H) of samples of normal agricultural soil after heating in hydrogen at 500°C for several hours (from Tite 1972). Each vertical line represents one sample. The code used for the geological strata is from the Ordnance Survey Geological Map of Great Britain except for A and B which refer to alluvium, river gravels, and glacial deposits from East Anglia and Central England respectively.

The iron oxide concentration corresponding to the range of χ_H shown in Fig. 6.8 is roughly 0·02% to 20%. The highest concentrations are associated with soils from the Middle and Lower Jurassic; this is not surprising since those strata provide the bulk of the iron ore currently being mined in England. It is to be noted that of the sites in Table 6.1, Burrough and Danes Camp lie on these strata.

Anomalies from pits

From the foregoing it is to be expected that for pits of the same size, covered with the same thickness of overlay, the strong anomalies on a site will be from those with a 'ripe' fill—such as might result from the burial of waste food, dead bodies or excreta. Pits left open by ancient man, which have filled by natural silting over the years, will be less strong (unless the surrounding soil happened to have experienced a great deal of burning), and of course a pit that was refilled with the material dug out from it will produce negligible anomaly.

Some idea of the anomalies to be expected from pits of various sizes can be obtained from Table 6.2. This table also gives the measured

TABLE 6.2

Relation of pit anomalies to susceptibility of filling

Site[d]	Dimensions[b] (inches)			Anomaly (gamma)	Susceptibility necessary[c] to account for anomaly (e.m.u. per gram. $\times 10^4$)	Measured[a] susceptibilities of samples from pit filling (e.m.u. per gram. $\times 10^4$)
	a	D	h			
Madmarston	⎰20	15	26	55	18⎱	10
	⎱20	15	35	30	17⎰	
Madmarston	36	24	48	65	23	9, 19
Madmarston	24	36	27	200	33	11, 22
Madmarston	36	60	46	110	22	13
Dane's Camp	26	41	24	125	16	4·6, 4·3, 5·8, 5·4 5·4, 6·3
Dane's Camp	⎰24	60	18	90	8·0⎱	2·4, 1·6, 3·0, 5·0
	⎱24	60	36	45	8·4⎰	

    [a] See note [a], Table 6.1.
    [b] a = mean radius of pit. D = depth of pit below old ground surface, h = height of detector bottle above old ground surface.
    [c] Calculated on 'cylinder approximation' (see text).
    [d] Conditions on these two sites were exceptional and such strong anomalies should not be taken as the general rule.

susceptibilities of samples taken from the filling, together with a rough estimate of the susceptibility calculated as necessary to give rise to the observed anomaly strength. This estimate is on the assumption that the pit is a uniformly magnetized cylinder and only the component of magnetization parallel to the axis has been taken into account. A more precise calculation is neither possible nor worthwhile, since the actual shape is usually irregular and the magnetization far from uniform—particularly if the filling consists of contrasting layers.

In considering anomaly strength it should be borne in mind that a deep, narrow pit is more effective than a wide, shallow one (e.g. a grave). The reason is illustrated in Fig. 6.9, where the magnetization

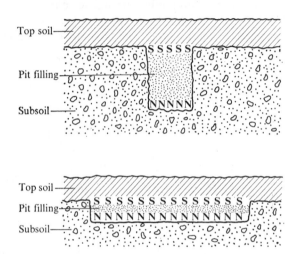

FIG. 6.9. Effect of pit shape. The anomaly from a wide, shallow pit is much smaller than from a narrow, deep one of the same volume. In the former case the induced north and south poles are close together and their magnetic fields tend to cancel.

is represented respectively in terms of long bar magnets and short bar magnets. In the shallow pit, the lines of force on the axis of a magnet near the centre tend to be cancelled out by the return lines of force from adjacent magnets; hence the anomaly is small except near the edges. It is for this reason that an extended layer of uniformly high susceptibility cannot be detected with a proton magnetometer, but only with an SCM-type instrument.

In practice the shape of the anomaly from a deep narrow pit (see Fig. 6.10) is not distinguishable from that of a kiln anomaly. Application reports of surveying for pits on hill-forts in England have been given by Aitken *and* Tite (1962), Tite (1967), and Alcock (1968).

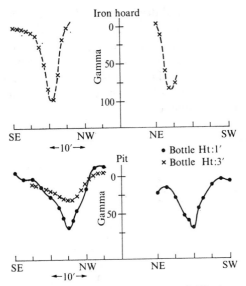

Fig. 6.10. Magnetic profiles—pit and iron hoard. The lower anomaly was due to a pit, roughly hemipherical and 7 ft across. Its top surface was 1½ ft, and its lower limit 4½ ft, below the present ground surface. The filling was very black soil, highly organic. Although the shape of the anomaly differs from those of the kilns in Fig. 6.6, this difference is not characteristic.

The cause of the upper anomaly was a Roman blacksmith's hoard of iron buried 1½ ft below ground level. The magnetic gradient was too strong for the proton magnetometer to function at a lower height than 3 ft—the signal was 'killed'.

Anomalies from ditches

The archaeological circumstances that favour the high susceptibility of pit-fillings do not usually occur with ditches. Some silting of top-soil is likely but, in the main the filling will consist of fall-in from the rampart of the original material excavated from the ditch. Where deliberate refilling of the ditch has taken place before appreciable silting has occurred, the anomaly will be negligible. Because of variation in filling material the strength of the anomaly from a ditch may vary considerably along its length.

Figure 6.11 shows the shape of the anomaly to be expected in a north–south traverse across a ditch running east–west. The reverse (or 'return flux') anomaly on the northern side of the ditch amounts to some 30% of the normal anomaly and this should not be misinterpreted as a road; the greater the depth of the ditch below the detector the greater the northward displacement of the reverse anomaly. For an east–west traverse across a ditch running north–south the normal anomaly is similar in strength to the previous case, but there is no single strong reverse anomaly—instead there are two barely significant ones on either side of the ditch. An advantage of using an instrument of the SCM-type instead of a magnetometer is that there is then no reverse anomaly in either case.

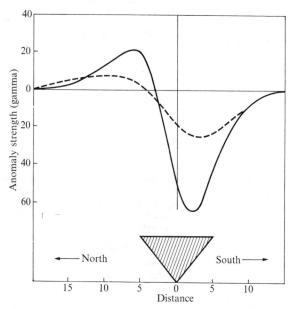

Fig. 6.11. Anomaly from east–west ditch according to simulator measurements (Aitken *and* Alldred 1964). The ditch is drawn to the distance scale indicated on the horizontal axis; the detector heights about the top surface of the ditch were 3 units (full curve) and 6 units (dashed curve). The susceptibility of the ditch filling was 0·001 e.m.u./cm³.

Magnetometer and resistivity traverses across an inner defence ditch at the Romano-British town of Verulamium are shown in Fig. 8.6 (Aitken, 1960, 1961). In a single traverse the anomaly is not unambiguous but the occurrence of the same small peak in successive traverses gives certainty to the presence of the feature. Although the resistivity anomaly was stronger, the greater rapidity of the magnetometer made it the preferred instrument and with it the ditch was followed for over a mile despite the confusion caused by isolated features, both ancient and modern, in its path. This lay through playing-fields and it turned through a right-angle underneath the Corporation cricket pitch—most certainly out of bounds for digging.

Measurement of susceptibility: magnetic viscosity

With soil features we are concerned with the magnetization induced by the earth's magnetic field. On the other hand, for the laboratory measurement of susceptibility it is convenient to use an a.c. method i.e. to apply an alternating magnetic field (at say, 1 kHz) and to measure the alternating magnetic flux induced in the sample by that applied field. For soil, this a.c. susceptibility is usually less than the d.c. value that is relevant to the anomaly produced by the feature. This is because of magnetic viscosity, a phenomenon already discussed in section 4.3, and which will be briefly recapitulated now. If a sample is placed in a d.c. magnetic field, in addition to the instantaneous magnetization induced, there is a slow subsequent growth. Similarly, if the sample is removed from the magnetic field, whereas there is immediate disappearance of the instantaneous magnetization, the viscous component decays away gradually. The growth and decay of this component follow a logarithmic dependence on time, i.e. the change between t and $10t$ is the same as the change between $10t$ and $100t$, and between $100t$ and $1000t$, etc. etc.

The viscosity component included in the susceptibility when measured at 1 kHz is roughly that corresponding to $t \sim 10^{-3}$ second. An alternative, less convenient, method of measuring susceptibility is that used for the data of Tables 6.1 and 6.2 in which the sample was moved into the centre of a coil system and the throw of a ballistic galvanometer observed; this gives the d.c. susceptibility inclusive of a viscous component corresponding to $t \sim 5$ sec. On a range of soils from English archaeological sites the author found that the d.c. susceptibility measured in this way was usually about twice the a.c. susceptibility. Hence for

$$t \sim 5 \times 10^4 \text{ second (14 hr), } \chi_{dc} \text{ should be } 3\chi_{ac}$$
$$t \sim 14 \times 10^4 \text{ hour (16 yr) } \ldots \ldots 4\chi_{ac}$$
$$t \sim 160\,000 \text{ year} \ldots \ldots \ldots 5\chi_{ac}$$

On this basis the susceptibility relevant to anomaly strength will be somewhat greater than $4\chi_{ac}$. On the other hand, Tite (1972a, p. 16) suggests $2\chi_{ac}$.

Such estimates are not easy to check in the field. Certainly measurement of the anomalies from two pits, first before excavation, and secondly one year after excavation, showed a decrease by a factor of two (Aitken *and* Tite, 1962); however, the diminution may have been due to re-arrangement of the soil layers during back-filling, so that the soil of high susceptibility became randomly distributed instead of being concentrated in the upper layers. There is no reason to think that once the chemical conversion mechanism is complete there will be any short-term dependence on climate.

Direct evidence of the viscosity mechanism in soils is afforded by the response to soils of the pulsed induction metal detector described in section 5.5 (Colani *and* Aitken, 1966, 1966a). Although this instrument suffers less from soil background signal than conventional metal detectors, there is nevertheless enough response for detection of shallow soil features. The reason is that the primary transmitter pulse induces a magnetization in the soil which includes a viscous component corresponding to $t \sim \frac{1}{2}$ millisecond (the duration of the transmitter pulse); on cut-off of the transmitter pulse, whereas the instantaneous susceptibility magnetization disappears immediately, this viscous component takes about $\frac{1}{2}$ millisecond. The magnetic field associated with this decay induces a voltage in the receiver coil in the same way as the magnetic field from decaying eddy currents. The two types of response cannot be distinguished except through measurement of the rate of decay and so far this has not proved effective in practice—except as between soil response and a large high-conductivity object, which has a much slower decay.

In the studies on English soils referred to earlier (Tite *and* Mullins, 1971), it was found that the viscous response indicated by a metal detector of this type is roughly proportional to the a.c. susceptibility.

6.5. Walls, roads, and cavities

Except when built of bricks or volcanic rock, wall material is negligibly magnetic. Consequently when soil is replaced by wall material, the main anomaly is a reverse one. In other respects the anomaly is similar to that from a ditch, and Fig. 6.11 is applicable. The relevant susceptibility is that of the soil adjacent to the wall. In general, walls are less easily detectable than ditches; this is because the remains of walls are often fragmentary, the stones having been robbed. However the detection of walls played an important part in the extension campaigns to locate the lost Greek colony of Sybaris in Southern Italy

(Ralph 1964; Rainey *and* Ralph, 1966; Rainey and Lerici 1967; Ralph, Morrison, *and* O'Brien, 1968).

Walls are sometimes shown up by a normal anomaly due to the accumulation of extra thickness of topsoil against one edge. This also applies to roads and paved areas; in general the thickness of these is too small to cause a detectable anomaly. There are exceptions of course, and the roads of the Bronze-Age town at Enkommi, Cyprus showed up clearly for instance (Aitken, 1971); these consisted of 2-metre thick, hard-packed, sun-baked earth and gave normal anomalies ($\sim$10 gamma), with marked reverse ('return flux') disturbances to the north. In England, on the Kentish weald, some Roman roads were made with iron slag and the resultant anomaly is the order of 100 gamma.

An empty tomb cut into sedimentary rock is marginally detectable, but if cut into volcanic rock, there is a reverse anomaly because of the latter's appreciable magnetization. This is the situation at the Etruscan necropolis of Cerveteri, extensively studied by Linington (1961, 1964).

6.6. Iron

The sensitivity to iron is inconveniently high; the advantage of being able to detect archaeological iron objects is more than offset by the interfering effects of iron litter from the present intensive phase of the Iron Age.

Such litter produces characteristically sharp and irregular anomalies, sometimes very strong and usually in both normal and reverse senses. In such circumstances it is impossible to survey for archaeological features, but if the litter is sparse it may be possible to decide which anomalies are due to surface iron and remove them. Although the shape of the anomaly from an isolated iron object may be the same as for a kiln or pit, the width is different. According to rule (b) of section 6.3, the width is equal to the depth of the cause below the detector level; for surface iron this will be equal to the detector height above ground, and, at the usual height of 1 foot, this is likely to be smaller than any detectable archaeological anomalies. If the iron object is buried, then its anomaly is correspondingly wider and it is then difficult to distinguish from a kiln or a pit; however if it is buried then it is much more likely to be a genuine archaeological find and worth excavating (see Fig. 6.10).

An alternative way of identifying surface iron is to use the rate of decay of the proton signal. As mentioned in section 6.2 a magnetic gradient of 200 gamma per metre reduces the proton signal to zero within a second, and such 'fast-decay' is easily noticed on the signal monitor meter; for much stronger gradients the decay may be so rapid that the signal is 'killed' and an obviously spurious reading is indicated. The gradient at a distance x along the axis of a short magnet of moment M producing an anomaly of strength ΔF is given by:

$$\frac{\mathrm{d}(\Delta F)}{\mathrm{d}x} = \frac{\mathrm{d}}{\mathrm{d}x}\left(\frac{2M}{x^3}\right) = -\frac{3(\Delta F)}{x}. \tag{6.2}$$

Thus for $\Delta F = 20$ gamma, fast decay will occur for x less than 0·3 metres (1 foot) whereas for $\Delta F = 100$ gamma it will occur when x is about 1·5 metres. Hence for small anomaly strengths, fast decay is indicative of surface iron, but with strong anomalies the decay may be fast although the cause is buried.

In estimating the likely anomaly strength from a given mass of iron a useful rough rule of thumb has been given by Hall (1966) for use in underwater archaeology. For distances large compared with the dimensions of the object:

$$\Delta F = \frac{10w}{d^3} \times \frac{A}{B}, \tag{6.3}$$

where ΔF is the anomaly in gamma, w is the weight in kilograms, d is the distance in metres, and (A/B) is the ratio of length to breadth. This ratio is relevant because the degree of magnetization is determined largely by demagnetizing effects associated with shape, rather than by the susceptibility. Wide variations about the value predicted by (6.3) are to be expected owing to shape irregularities.

6.7. Field application

Size of measurement mesh

Closely-spaced measuring points are necessary for three reasons:

(i) Many features are only a metre across and the anomaly does not spread much beyond.

(ii) There may be a gradual change in the 'normal' reading in moving across the site, due to geological causes (e.g. depth of topsoil); archaeological effects are distinguishable by a sharp change over a distance comparable with the expected width (or depth) of the feature.

(iii) Even if the survey is for large features, close measurements are worthwhile because they enable surface iron to be recognized; the iron effects only one or two readings (and irregularly) whereas the feature affects many (and smoothly).

For small and near-surface features, a mesh size of 0·2 metre is desirable, but a reasonable compromise between time and efficiency is a mesh of 1 metre with interpolation where disturbances are detected. Excluding interpolation a well-organized team can cover a hectare (2 acres) in 2 or 3 days.

The area is first marked out with stout pegs so as to form a grid of 10 metre squares; it is convenient, but by no means essential, to align the grid within 20° of the points of the compass. Each square is covered in turn by a string net stretched between the four corner pegs. The mesh size of the net is 2 metres, and the middle of each 2 metre length is marked with a coloured tag so that the person moving the detector can judge the additional positions needed by eye. On a 1 metre mesh there are 100 new positions per 10 metre square, i.e. 10 000 per hectare.

Plastic covered string should be used for making the net so as to avoid shrinkage in wet weather. The reeling-out of the net is one of the most skilled operations in the survey.

A sample of a survey is shown in Fig. 6.12. The figures shown are deviations from the average reading calculated subsequent to the survey.

Choice of detector height

With decreasing height the anomaly strength increases, but random variations due to surface irregularities and surface iron are relatively greater. Where the top-soil thickness is 0·3 metres (1 ft) or more, there is not much gain in sensitivity by decreasing the detector height below the standard 0·3 metres; on the other hand the disturbance from a nail on the surface will be more than doubled if the height is decreased to 0·2 metre. If the detector height is made too great, there is more risk that weak features will be masked by irregular transient changes; also, the anomalies due to surface iron become wider and less irregular, so that they are less easily distinguishable from genuine features.

Summary of site hazards

(i) *Transient variations.* Besides currents in the ionosphere, magnetic fluctuations can be produced by power lines carrying d.c., by passing trains, cars, and tractors, by iron in the footwear or clothing of the operator, and by iron components in the plug and socket linking the cable to the detector. The two latter can be eliminated by careful checking whenever a new operator or cable is put into use; an operator, particularly when female, often carries totally unsuspected

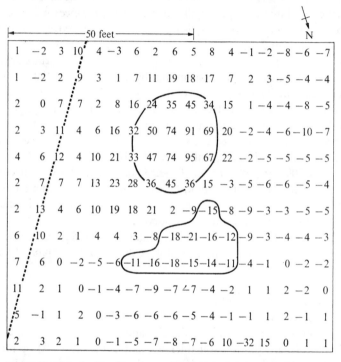

1	−2	3	10	4	−3	6	2	6	5	8	4	−1	−2	−8	−6	−7
1	−2	2	9	3	1	7	11	19	18	17	7	2	3	−5	−4	−4
2	0	7	7	2	8	16	24	35	45	34	15	1	−4	−4	−8	−5
2	3	11	4	6	16	32	50	74	91	69	20	−2	−4	−6	−10	−7
4	6	12	4	10	21	33	47	74	95	67	22	−2	−5	−5	−5	−5
2	7	7	7	13	23	28	36	45	36	15	−3	−5	−6	−6	−5	−4
2	13	4	6	10	19	18	21	2	−9	−15	−8	−9	−3	−3	−5	−5
6	10	2	1	4	4	3	−8	−18	−21	−16	−12	−9	−3	−4	−4	−3
7	6	0	−2	−5	−6	−11	−16	−18	−15	−14	−11	−4	−1	0	−2	−2
11	2	1	0	−1	−4	−7	−9	−7	−7	−4	−2	1	1	2	−2	0
5	−1	1	2	0	−3	−6	−6	−6	−5	−4	−1	−1	1	2	−1	1
2	3	2	1	0	−1	−5	−7	−8	−7	−6	10	−32	15	0	1	1

FIG. 6.12. Sample of magnetic survey in vicinity of pottery kiln. The figures shown are the deviation from normal intensity, in gamma units. On excavation a kiln was found, as expected, a little to the north of the strong anomaly (maximum 95 gamma) and to the south of the reverse anomaly. A ditch was found as indiacted by a line of dots, and the anomaly of −32 gamma was due to a horseshoe close to the surface of the ploughsoil.

sources of iron. The magnetic effect of the current in d.c. electric train lines can be upsetting, even at a distance of several miles from the lines; the effects from the forward and reverse currents should cancel out, but because very large currents are involved (3000 amps or so), a small percentage of earth leakage can give an appreciable unbalance in terms of amps. The effect consists of sharp changes in the reading as trains start and stop *anywhere along the line*.

A differential type of magnetometer (see sections 7.3 and 7.4) eliminates these magnetic variations, as long as the distance of the source is large compared to the separation between the two detectors.

(ii) *A.c. Electrical interference*. This does not affect the actual magnetic intensity, but electromagnetic pick-up by the detector-coil may drown the proton signal and cause the reading to be inaccurate. Power cables are common sources of interference, though as a general rule it is possible to survey within a distance equal to the power-line height. Long-wave radio transmissions can be serious if the frequency is close to the natural resonant frequency of the detector coil (typically about 20 kHz); such interference may occur not only close to the transmitter but also, rather unpredictably, at a considerable distance from the transmitter due to re-radiation from a length of iron railings or mains cables.

A.c. interference can be avoided by use of a toroidal detector coil, or of twin solenoids connected in opposition. Both types are more expensive and heavier, particularly the former. With the usual single coil it is possible to reduce a.c. interference by an order of magnitude by orientating the detector so that flux linkage by the coil is minimized.

(iii) *Instrumental 'noise'*. This is not really a site hazard but it has the same effect on the readings as (i) and (ii). Malfunction of the electronic circuits is an occasional cause, but more frequently it is due to a poor cable connector, or, to an inexperienced operator moving or kicking the cable during the critical half-second following cessation of the polarizing period (see section 6.2). It is distinguishable from (ii) because it cannot be reduced by altering the detector orientation.

(iv) *Igneous geology*. As mentioned earlier, the thermoremanent magnetization of some igneous (and metamorphic) rocks is strong enough to mask archaeological anomalies. This applies particularly to volcanics of the tertiary period and later. The interference from granites may be weak enough to permit surveying.

(v) *Extraneous iron*. In addition to the iron litter to be expected anywhere in the vicinity of present habitation, and also in picnic spots, there is the possibility of water pipes and gas mains. In open country, corrugated iron and wire fences are the most frequent hazards; as a general rule the disturbance from a wire fence is objectionable up to a distance of 5–10 metres. It must not be forgotten that the instrument itself may produce a strong anomaly; unless specially designed so as to be iron-free it should be kept at a distance of 10 metres from the nearest survey point.

(vi) *Trees and undergrowth.* The practical difficulty of moving the cable and the net rules out sites covered in trees and bushes, and less stringently, sites covered in long grass, thistles, and rock debris.

(vii) *Previous excavations.* Irregular ground surfaces, unfilled trenches, and spoil heaps are all liable to produce minor anomalies; in addition, any iron marking-out skewers left behind are certain to cause trouble. It is really only practical to survey over fairly flat undisturbed ground having an unobstructed surface.

General

Despite the discussion of this chapter it is not easy to predict with certainty the efficacity of a magnetic survey on an untried site.

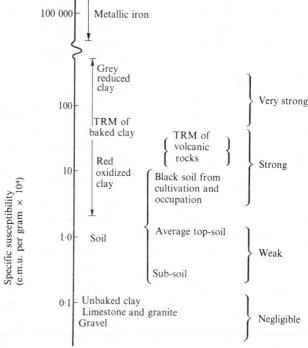

Fig. 6.13. Magnetic characteristics of some relevant materials.

Therefore, before embarking on a large-scale surveying expedition, it is desirable to make a small pilot survey of about an acre ($\frac{1}{2}$ hectare); this should be followed up by test excavations, both on selected anomalies and in anomaly-free regions.

As a preliminary to the pilot survey the geology should be considered and if possible samples of top-soil obtained for susceptibility measurement. Auger soundings can be used to find the depth of top-soil in various regions of the site and this may influence the areas chosen for the pilot survey.

Figure 6.13 gives an order-of-magnitude summary of the relative strengths of magnetization to be expected in various materials.

REFERENCES

AITKEN, M. J. (1959). Magnetic Prospecting—An Interim Assessment. *Antiquity*, **33**, No. 131, 205–207.
AITKEN, M. J. (1960). The magnetic survey. Appendix to S.S. Frere: Excavations at Verulamium 1959, 5th Interim Report. *Antiquary J.*, **40**, 21–24.
AITKEN, M. J. (1961). The magnetic survey. Appendix to S.S. Frere: Excavations at Verulamium 1960, 6th Interim Report. *Antiquary J.* **41**, 83–85.
AITKEN, M. J. (1971). Enkomi-Alasia: The Proton Magnetometer Survey. *Alasia I*, ed. C.F.A. Schaeffer, publication of La Mission Archeologique D'Enkomi-Alasia (Chypre), 1–6.
AITKEN, M. J. and ALLDRED, J. C. (1964). A simulator-trainer for magnetic prospection. *Archaeometry*, **7**, 28–35.
AITKEN, M. J. and TITE, M. S. (1962). Proton magnetometer surveying on some British hill-forts. *Archaeometry*, **5**, 126–134.
AITKEN, M. J., WEBSTER, G., and REES, A. (1958). Magnetic prospecting. *Antiquity*, **32**, 270–271.
ALCOCK, L. (1968). Excavations at South Cadbury Castle, 1967. *Antiquary. J.* **48**, 6–17.
COLANI, C. and AITKEN, M. J. (1966). Utilization of magnetic viscosity effects in soils for archaeological prospection. *Nature*, **212**, 1446.
COLANI, C. and AITKEN, M. J. (1966a). A New Type of Locating Device. II— Field Trials, *Archaeometry*, **9**, 9–20.
HALL, E. T. (1966). The use of the proton magnetometer in underwater archaeology. *Archaeometry*, **9**, 32–44.
HOOD, P. (1973). Mineral exploration: trends and developments in 1972. *Canadian Mining Journal*, **94**, 167–82.
LE BORGNE, E. (1952). Sur la susceptibilité magnétique du sol. *C.r. Acad. Sci., Paris*, **235**, 1042.
LE BORGNE, E. (1955). Susceptibilité magnétique anormal du sol superficiel. *Ann. Geophys.* **11**, 399–419.
LE BORGNE, E. (1960). Influence du feu sur les proprietés magnétiques du sol. *Ann. Geophys.* **16**, 159–195.
LE BORGNE, E. (1965). Les proprietés magnétiques du sol. Application a la prospection des sites archéologiques. *Archaeo-Physika Band 15 der Beihefte der Bonner Jahrbücher*, 1–20.
LININGTON, R. E. (1961). 'Quaderni di Geofisica Applicata, No. 22.' Fondazione Lerici, Milan.

LINGINGTON, R. E. (1964). The use of simplified anomalies in magnetic surveying. *Archaeometry*, **7**, 3–13.

RAINEY, F. *and* RALPH, E. K. (1966). Archaeology and its new technology. *Science*, **153**, 1481–91.

RAINEY, F. *and* LERICI, C. M. (1967). *The Search for Sybaris*, 1960–1965. Lerici, Rome, 313 pp.

RALPH, E. K. (1964). Comparison of a proton and a rubidium magnetometer for archaeological prospecting. *Archaeometry*, **7**, 20–7.

RALPH, E. K., MORRISON, F., *and* O'BRIEN, D. P. (1968). Archaeological surveying utilizing a high-sensitivity difference magnetometer. *Geoexploration*, **6**, 109–22.

TITE, M. S. (1966). Magnetic prospecting near to the geomagnetic equator. *Archaeometry*, **9**, 24–31.

TITE, M. S. (1967). The magnetic survey. Appendix to M. Avery, J. E. G. Sutton, *and* J. W. Banks: Rainsborough, Northants, England—Excavations 1961–5. *Proc. prehist. Soc.* **33**, 296–300.

TITE, M. S. (1972). The influence of geology on the magnetic susceptibility of soils on archaeological sites. *Archaeometry*, **14**, 229–236.

TITE, M. S. (1972a). *Methods of Physical Examination in Archaeology*. Seminar Press, London and New York.

TITE, M. S. *and* MULLINS, C. (1971). Enhancement of the magnetic susceptibility of soils on archaeological sites. *Archaeometry*, **13**, 209–220.

7 Magnetometers

THE standard instrument for archaeological prospecting is the proton free-precession magnetometer; there are several forms—*absolute, differential,* and *gradiometer* (sections 7.1 to 7.4). Two other types of instrument are in use, the alkali vapour *'optical pumping' magnetometer* (section 7.5), and the *fluxgate gradiometer* (section 7.6). All these instruments are either derived or directly borrowed from geophysics, and further information on them will be found in appropriate journals. A general review of such instruments has been given by Stuart (1972).

7.1. Proton free-precession

The free precession in the earth's field of protons in water was first observed experimentally in 1953 (Packard *and* Varian, 1954) the effect having been predicted in 1946 (Bloch, 1946). It depends on the same nuclear properties as nuclear magnetic resonance (n.m.r.), widely used for measurement of strong magnetic fields and the investigation of chemical structure, but, as the word 'free' implies, no resonance is involved in the measurement technique for the earth's field.

Nuclear magnetic resonance experiments are analogous to the measurement of the time of swing of a pendulum by applying to it a periodic force, and finding at what applied frequency the swings are biggest. Free precession corresponds to the simpler method of giving the pendulum an initial displacement from the vertical, and timing a given number of swings with a stop-watch. Thus, in nuclear magnetic resonance measurements, an alternating field is applied to the sample of nuclei and, if the frequency is correct, the nuclei precess in resonance.

With free precession there is no applied frequency, and the signal observed is simply the alternating voltage generated in a coil by the rotating magnetic moment formed by a large number of nuclei precessing in phase. It turns out that whereas the resonance technique is appropriate for strong magnetic fields, for the range of 'weak' field strengths covered by the earth's field the precession technique is necessary.

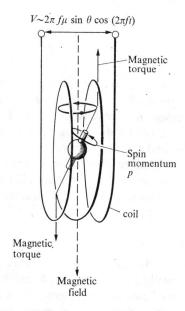

$V \sim 2\pi f\mu \sin \theta \cos (2\pi ft)$

FIG. 7.1. Precession of proton in magnetic field.

The phenomena occur because, resulting from the property called intrinsic spin, the proton has both angular momentum (p) and magnetic moment (μ), both along the same axis. For a proton inclined at an angle θ to the lines of force of a magnetic field F there is a couple $\mu F \cos \theta$ tending to align it along the lines of force but because of its spin it precesses. The frequency of precession (the *Larmor* frequency) is independent of θ and is given by

$$= \frac{\mu F}{2\pi p}.$$

Since μ and p are strictly invariant, this frequency depends only on F. For the proton, the ratio (μ/p) is $26\,751 \cdot 3^{-1}$ oersted^{-1} (Bender *and* Driscoll, 1958), so that

$$f = 4257 \cdot 6 \times F \text{ Hz.} \tag{7.1}$$

Since the range of F over the earth's surface is from $0 \cdot 25$ to $0 \cdot 7$ oersted the frequency is always within the audio range.

Free precession occurs with many other nuclei beside the proton. However, for ease and accuracy of measurement as high a frequency as possible is desirable, and the magnetogyric ratio (μ/p) is highest for the proton. Besides this, protons being the nuclei of hydrogen atoms, a large number per c.c. are conveniently available in a sample of water.

Detection of free precession

If a coil is placed with its axis roughly perpendicular to the magnetic field, the amplitude of the alternating voltage generated in it by a precessing proton is $\mu f \sin \theta$. This is very small and, for detection to be feasible, a large number of protons must be precessing together in phase. To achieve this, the sample is subjected to a strong polarizing field before each measurement.

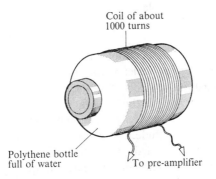

Coil of about
1000 turns

Polythene bottle
full of water

To pre-amplifier

Fig. 7.2. Detector bottle for proton magnetometer.

Figure 7.2 shows a suitable experimental arrangement. The water sample of about 200 c.c. is contained in a polythene bottle, around which is wound a coil of about 1000 turns. This coil serves both for detection and for polarization, by means of suitable switching relays (see section 7.4). During polarization a steady d.c. current of about an amp is passed through the coil, creating a magnetic field of several hundred oersteds along the axis. This tends to align the protons but, because of thermal agitation, the fractional alignment at equilibrium is only ($\mu F/kT$), where k is Boltzmann's constant and T is the absolute temperature. At ordinary temperatures ($T \sim 290$ K), and for $F = 200$ oersteds, this fraction is about 10^{-7}. In 1 cm^3 of water there are approximately 7×10^{22} protons so that since the value of μ is 1.4×10^{23} gauss cm^3 the resulting magnetic moment per cm^3 is $\sim 10^{-7}$ gauss.

When the polarizing current is cut off, this induced magnetic moment gyrates at a frequency of about 2000 Hz (for $F \sim 0.5$ oersteds), thereby generating a voltage in the coil (diameter 5 cm) of amplitude given by

$$V = (2\pi \times 2000) \times (4\pi \times 10^{-7}) \times (\pi \times 2.5^2 \times 1000) \text{ e.m.u.}$$
$$\simeq 3 \text{ microvolts.}$$

This will be detectable after amplification as long as it is large compared to random electrical noise in the coil (assuming there is no external interference in addition). Taking the resistance to be 10 ohms, and the noise factor of the input pre-amplifier to be 10 (20 decibels), the theoretical coil-noise amounts to about 0.02 microvolts for an amplifier bandwidth of 20 Hz. In practice, a signal-to-noise ratio of 50:1 or better is obtainable.

Signal decay

The proton signal does not continue indefinitely. Interfering magnetic fields from neighbouring nuclei perturb the proton gyrations, causing the protons to get out of step so that the resultant magnetic moment slowly decreases to zero; at the same time, gradual alignment with F is occurring. The resultant decay of the signal is exponential, and the time taken for the amplitude to decrease by two-thirds is termed the *relaxation time*. For distilled water this is about 3 seconds. Consequently, the signal is big enough for accurate frequency determination only for a few seconds after each polarizing period.

The relaxation time is also relevant to the duration for which the polarizing field should be applied. The equilibrium alignment of ($\mu F/kT$) is reached only after an indefinitely long polarization; if the duration is made equal to the relaxation time, the alignment is about two-thirds of the equilibrium value, and this is the usual working value. By using a liquid with a short relaxation time, the polarization period can be shortened, and hence the measurement repetition rate increased; however, since the short relaxation time reduces the length of time for which the signal is big enough for frequency measurement, the accuracy is less good. For routine archaeological purposes the compromise between speed and accuracy ordinarily obtainable is quite adequate. When this is not so, a special technique can be used (synchronous polarization), in which the magnetic moment is retained from one polarizing period to the next; in this way a short polarizing period can be used for a long relaxation-time liquid.

Rapid decay of signal can also be caused by an external field gradient. If there is an overall difference of 10 gamma between opposite ends of the sample, the corresponding difference in frequency (according to eqn (7.1)) is 0·4 Hz, and the two halves of the sample will get 180° out of phase, with consequent reduction of the signal amplitude to zero, in just over one second. This corresponds to a gradient of about 20 gamma per metre. Such a gradient is likely anywhere in the proximity of buildings; inside a building the gradients are usually so high that the decay to zero is too rapid for a signal to be observed at all ('killed signal').

Suitable liquids

In general, liquids of low viscosity have long relaxation times. In these, rapid molecular diffusion smooths out the interfering magnetic fields from neighbouring nuclei; on freezing, this effect is lost and the relaxation time becomes very short indeed. The 3-second relaxation time of pure water, combined with a high concentration of protons per c.c., makes it a suitable liquid for many proton magnetometer applications. To achieve the full relaxation time, any dissolved oxygen must be removed, since *free* oxygen is paramagnetic. In pure water the interfering fields arise solely from neighbouring protons; the atomic magnetic moment of free oxygen disappears when it combines chemically, and it has zero nuclear moment.

The removal of dissolved oxygen can be accomplished by bubbling nitrogen through the water for a half an hour, or by distillation in an atmosphere of nitrogen. Distillation has the advantage that other paramagnetic impurities are removed too; for cupric salts the relaxation time is reduced to 0·1 second at a 0·01 molar concentration, and for ferric salts at only 0·001 molar concentration.

The disadvantage of water is that it freezes in cold weather; this temporarily prevents operation because of the short relaxation time of ice but also, because of the expansion of water and ice as the temperature falls below 4°C, there is risk of the bottle bursting. Suitable alternatives are methyl alcohol, hexane, and heptane. It is also possible to obtain a signal from a number of other organic liquids, e.g. domestic paraffin, laboratory alcohol. Benzene has an exceptionally long relaxation time (about 20 seconds) but the signal amplitude is small because of the low concentration of protons per c.c.

Although a relaxation time of about 3 seconds may be desirable for the gradiometer type of instrument described in section 7.4, and for absolute measurements of high precision (which need a longer counting time), a relaxation time of about 1 second is optimum for the rapid measurements at 1 gamma accuracy required in most archaeological applications. A recipe for this (Hall 1962) is 20 c.c. of iron alum solution in 1 litre of methyl alcohol, the strength of the iron alum solution being 15 g per litre of water.

7.2. The proton magnetometer: frequency measurement

A measurement sensitivity of 1 gamma in a total field of 50 000 gamma corresponds to measuring the frequency of 2000 Hz to within 0·04 Hz. Continuous-signal methods of frequency measurement are not applicable because of the decay of the proton signal within a few seconds. In a non-uniform field the decay is quicker still, and the less the time required for measurement, the stronger the gradient that can be tolerated. By using the 'gated oscillator' technique the measurement can be completed in a second or less; essentially this consists of counting the number of pulses of a 100 kHz crystal-controlled oscillator (the 'clock') that occur during the time taken for the proton signal to complete a fixed number of cycles. By having this number around 1000, the number of clock pulses is 50 000 for a field intensity of 50 000 gamma so that a change of 1 unit in the number of clock pulses counted corresponds to 1 gamma. The duration of the measurement is $\frac{1}{2}$ second.

Figures 7.3 and 7.4 refer to the instrument† developed by the Oxford University Archaeological Research Laboratory, which was derived from circuitry designed at the British Signals Research and Development Establishment (Waters *and* Francis, 1958). Further details of suitable input switching circuits are given in Figs. 7.7 and 7.8; for the sake of clarity a simple change-over relay is shown on

† Some commercially available instruments are listed in a footnote to section 6.2.

Fig. 7.3 though this is not satisfactory by itself. The input capacity forms a resonant circuit with the inductance of the detector coil; this has a Q-factor of about 20, and hence the voltage fed to the amplifying circuits is 20 times the voltage of a few microvolts that is induced in the coils by the gyrating protons. After further amplification to several

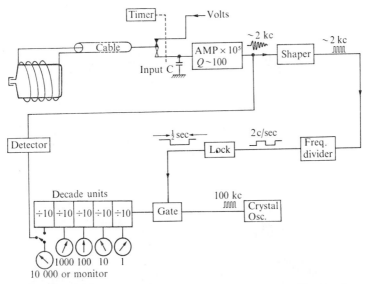

FIG. 7.3. Proton magnetometer: gated oscillator technique. The decade meters record the number of 100 kHz oscillator pulses that pass through the gate while it is held open for the duration of 1024 proton pulses. The lock unit ensures that the gate subsequently remains closed until another polarization has been completed.

volts, the sinusoidal proton signal, which is decaying in amplitude, is shaped to a constant amplitude square wave (of identical frequency). This is frequency-divided by a ten-stage binary chain, so that, since $2^{10} = 1024$, the frequency after the tenth stage is approximately 2 Hz. This is applied to the clock gate via a lock unit, such that the first positive-going edge opens the gate and the next closes it, and the gate then remains closed until the unit is reset. When the gate is open the clock pulses are fed to a five-stage decade chain. The operation of each decade is such that one pulse appears at the output for every ten that enter at the input, and if the number entering is not a multiple of 10, the number remaining after division by 10 is indicated on the

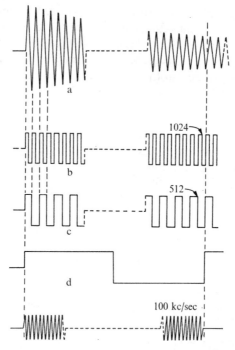

FIG. 7.4. Gated oscillator technique: waveforms (a) Proton signal from amplifier, $f \sim 2000$ Hz. (b) Proton signal after squaring, $f \sim$ 2000 Hz. (c) After frequency division by one binary stage, $f \sim 1000$ Hz. (d) After frequency division by ten binary stages, $f \sim 2$ Hz. (e) Gated output of 100 kHz oscillator.

digital meter for that decade. Thus the five-digit number indicated by these five meters equals the number of 100 kHz clock pulses that get through the gate. Since the gate remains open for 1024 proton gyrations this count is given by

$$n = 100\,000 \times \frac{1024}{f} \tag{7.3}$$

so that from (7.2),

$$F = \frac{24\,051 \cdot 1}{n} \text{ oersted.} \tag{7.4}$$

The crucial factor in precise realization of this relation is the time-accuracy of the base-line crossings of the amplified proton signal at the opening, and at the closing, of the gate (Fig. 7.4(a)). For $F \approx 0.5$ oersted, an error of 1 in n corresponds to an error of 1 part in 50 000. This in turn corresponds to an error of 10 microseconds in the time for which the gate is open, i.e. 1/50 of a proton cycle. This requires that the signal-to-noise ratio should not have decayed to worse than about 16:1 by the time at which the gate closes.

For most archaeological sites there is no point in improving the sensitivity beyond 1 gamma (corresponding to a change of 1 in n) because of the random variations in field intensity arising from top-soil irregularities ('soil noise'). However, should this be required it can be done by counting off more proton gyrations. For $F \sim 0.5$ oersted, using 2048 gyrations gives a sensitivity of $\frac{1}{2}$ gamma and 4096 a sensitivity of $\frac{1}{4}$ gamma. In the latter case the gate remains open for 2 seconds so it is important to use a slow decay liquid (e.g. de-oxygenated methyl alcohol) in the detector-bottle so that the signal-to-noise level is still good at gate closure.

An alternative way of increasing sensitivity is to use a higher frequency oscillator, e.g. 1 MHz. In principle this gives 0.1 gamma sensitivity (for $F \sim 0.5$ oersted) for a gate-open time of $\frac{1}{2}$ second; however, to obtain this sensitivity in practice requires a ten-fold improvement in signal-to-noise ratio. In practical terms this means an increased polarizing power, or, a narrower effective bandwidth (e.g. use of the 'phase-lock' system mentioned below) together with various other sophistications of circuitry.

The *absolute* accuracy of the instrument depends on the calibration of the crystal-controlled oscillator and the accuracy to which the magnetogyric ratio for the proton is known (± 7.5 parts per million). A standard oscillator will remain constant to 1 part in 100 000, over ambient temperature variations between 10°C and 40°C; an order of magnitude improvement can be achieved by means of temperature control.

Direct read-out using the phase-lock system

For archaeological use it is no disadvantage that the reading decreases as the field intensity increases. However, for geophysical application it is more convenient to have the read-out directly in gamma. This can be accomplished as outlined in Fig. 7.5; the sharply-tuned amplifier ($Q \sim 100$) is eliminated and selectivity achieved with the phase-lock system, thereby obviating the need for fine-tuning adjustment. The phase-sensitive detector receives two inputs: one is the proton signal after amplification and shaping, the other is derived, via frequency-division by 128 (2^7), from a voltage-controlled oscillator. The frequency of the latter is adjusted by the d.c. output from the phase sensitive detector until the output of the frequency divider has the same frequency as the proton signal. The frequency of the oscillator is thus exactly 128 times the proton frequency (so that for a

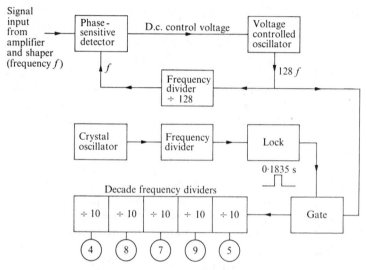

FIG. 7.5. Phase-lock system with direct read-out. The voltage-controlled oscillator forms part of a servo loop such that its frequency is exactly 128 times the proton frequency f. By arranging for the gate to be open for 0·1835 seconds, the indicated digits read the field strength directly in gamma.

proton frequency of 2000 Hz the oscillator frequency is 256 000 Hz). Using eqn (7.1) we see that the field intensity (in gamma) and the oscillator frequency (in Hz) are related by

$$F = 0{\cdot}1835 \times f_{\mathrm{osc}}. \tag{7.5}$$

Hence by arranging for the gate to be opened for 0·1835 second (as timed by the crystal-controlled reference oscillator), the read-out shown by the decades is directly in gamma; if greater sensitivity is required, e.g. so that the last digit represents 0·1 gamma, this can be achieved by opening the gate for longer, or, by dividing the frequency of the voltage-controlled oscillator by a larger factor than 128.

The direct read-out is possible because the proton frequency has been multiplied, and this means that the number of pulses counted in a short time is sufficient to give the required precision. By using a high loop-gain the phase lock system can be made equivalent to a very sharply tuned circuit (though the narrower the effective bandwidth, the longer the delay in 'locking-on'); hence a much higher signal-to-noise ratio can be obtained than is practical when actually using a tuned amplifier. However, in the presence of an interference signal with a frequency component comparable to that of the proton signal there is risk of a false lock-on. Such interference can be guarded against by using a more sophisticated design of detector—either a toroidal coil wound on a toroidal bottle, or, two bottles side by side with their coils connected in opposition. In the latter, the interference is self-cancelling but, because the polarizing fields are anti-parallel, the proton signals add together.

7.3. The differential proton magnetometer

As already pointed out in Chapter 6 use of a differential instrument avoids interference from ionospheric currents (diurnal variation) and d.c. train lines. Although intermittent readings at a fixed point on the site may be adequate to deal with the former (except on magnetic storm days), in the vicinity of the latter, because the changes are irregular and rapid, it is essential to make the measurement at the fixed point simultaneously with the measurement in the roving detector. A dual detector instrument for this purpose has been developed by Scollar (Mudie, 1962; Scollar, 1965). Essentially the instrument consists of two separate amplifying units which feed into a common decade chain, but in opposite senses, i.e. the count from one is automatically subtracted from that for the other, the meters indicating the difference. The increased complexity is considerable, and a particular problem is interaction between the two amplifying units. An additional facility is the availability of the difference readings on punched-tape ready for computer analysis.

Signal mixing techniques

A simpler, though less precise method is to add together the proton signals from the two detector-bottles before amplification; with this system the binary and decade chains are not required. The detectors are fed by a common polarizing current so that, at its cessation, the initial proton signals are in phase. If the detectors are in the same field intensity, then the resultant sum of the two signals has twice each of the individual amplitudes, and decays away to zero in the usual way, as determined by the relaxation time of the liquid. If the detectors are in different field intensities, then there is a difference in frequency between the two signals and, although the initial resultant amplitude is the same as before, the two signals subsequently move in and out of phase. Consequently the resultant amplitude varies between the sum of the individual amplitudes and zero, at a frequency equal to the difference between the frequencies of the two individual signals. This is the well-known phenomenon of 'beats' usually demonstrated with two tuning forks of slightly different frequency. The beat frequency is proportional to the difference in magnetic intensity, 0·2 Hz corresponding to a difference of 5 gamma, i.e. the resultant amplitude first reaches zero after $2\frac{1}{2}$ seconds.

Because the system is more sensitive to deviations from zero difference in field intensities than to changes from a given difference, it is best used in gradiometer configuration, rather than having one detector as a fixed reference. A gradiometer using the simple beat frequency system is described in the next section. As regards the signal mixing technique in general, various interesting sophistications are possible, though as yet not much explored—e.g. frequency multiplication before mixing so that the difference frequency is in the audio range, and, use of a phase-sensitive detector for measuring the relative phase change.

7.4. The proton gradiometer

The detectors are mounted, usually 5 ft apart, on a fibre-glass rod which is held vertically. The lower detector is the standard 1 foot above ground level, and this responds much more strongly to buried features than the upper one; on the other hand a widespread geological change (or distant magnetic interference) affects both detectors equally.

Figure 7.6 shows a block diagram. The two detector-coils are connected in series so that the polarizing current is broken by a single relay contact; besides ensuring that the two proton signals maintain a constant phase relation from reading to reading, the series arrangement accomplishes the addition of the two signals before the pre-amplifier, thus avoiding the need for any special mixing circuit later on.

The multivibrator controls the relay system so that polarizing periods alternate with 'listening' periods as long as the instrument is switched on. At the usual setting the duration of each is 2½ seconds. The amplifier feeding the loudspeaker is operated under 'Class C' conditions so that the signal amplitude necessary to produce maximum intensity (and maximum indication on the meter) is only slightly greater than the threshold signal necessary to produce any note at all. This level is adjusted to be slightly lower than the signal amplitude remaining at the end of the listening period in the case when the detectors are in equal field intensities, i.e. when the decay is determined only by the relaxation time of the liquid. Hence, in equal

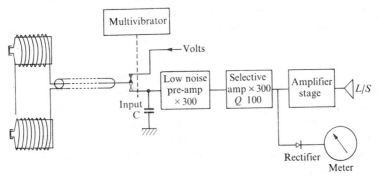

FIG. 7.6. Simple version of proton gradiometer: block diagram.

fields intensities there is a steady 2000 Hz note for the whole duration of the listening period. For a slight difference in intensities, the note ceases before the end of the period (which is indicated by a sharp 'bleep' associated with switch-on of the polarizing current); differences of as little as 1 or 2 gamma can be easily detected. For a difference approaching 10 gamma and assuming the listening period to be set to 2½ seconds, an additional bleep is heard before the one indicating commencement of polarization period; two additional bleeps indicate a difference of 20 gamma etc., hence the names 'Bleeper' and 'Max-bleep'.

Human counting ability limits the maximum measurable difference to 100 gamma, which is not a serious restriction for most archaeological purposes. Electronic circuitry (e.g. Aitken *and* Tite, 1962) can of course be used to count the number of bleeps, or to measure the time taken for the signal to reach 'first zero'; however, field experience indicates that the added complexity is not worthwhile. An additional facility that is worthwhile is a small bias coil (with a ferrox core) positioned on the carrying staff midway between the two detectors; by varying the current through this until the difference in intensity seen by the two detectors is annulled, the polarity of the difference can be determined.

Although the instrument is functionally adequate for archaeological surveys, it is a fatiguing instrument to use for more than a few hours at a stretch. One reason for this is the mental concentration required to interpret the loudspeaker note; this is much more strain than the straightforward reading of digits in the single detector instrument. Another reason is that the extra detector on top of the staff makes the job of the moving operator quite strenuous.

The comparatively simple circuitry of this type of instrument means that it can be built commercially† for a fraction of the cost of a standard absolute proton magnetometer. Its construction is within the competence of a reasonably skilled radio engineer, and suitable circuits details are published from time to time (e.g. Strong, 1968; Harkness, 1969; Huggard, 1970). However, it would be unwise for anyone to embark on it who is not capable of designing suitable amplifier stages (see Fig. 7.5); notes on the construction of the detector bottles and the input switching circuitry are given in the following sub-sections.

The detector bottles

Design criteria and constructional details have been given by Hall (1962). The liquid is contained in a 140 cm^3 polythene bottle, 4·8 cm diameter and 11 cm long. The coil is random wound over a 9-cm length of the bottle, and consists of approximately 1400 runs of 20 SWG synthetic enamelled pure copper wire; the number of turns is adjusted to give an inductance of 0·056 henry and the resistance is about 7 ohms. The coil is terminated in an aluminium socket (brass is unsuitable because of ferromagnetic impurities) and the whole assembly is encapsulated in a casting resin (e.g. Araldite Type CY 212). Aluminium wire can be used instead of copper; this makes the resistance somewhat higher but the reduction in weight is advantageous.

The bottle is filled with pure methyl alcohol through which nitrogen has been bubbled for 20 minutes immediately prior to filling and

---

† e.g. the Elsec 'Max Bleep', the Wardle and Davenport 'Wreckfinder' and 'Skifinder'. Unfortunately none of these are in current production.

encapsulation. This gives a proton decay time of 4 seconds. If the alcohol is left in the bottle without encapsulation the decay time falls, approaching 2 seconds after a few days, due to take-up of oxygen that has diffused through the bottle walls. Distilled water is an alternative to methyl alcohol.

Great care must be taken to avoid magnetic impurities. These can be inherent in the wire or resin, or can get in accidentally during construction. A barely visible speck of iron filing can create such a strong gradient that the decay time is seriously reduced, or even made so short that the proton signal is 'killed'. If the effect is not too acute, the presence of magnetic impurity (as opposed to the short decay time being inherent in the liquid) can be confirmed by testing for 'heading error'. The field resulting from the vector addition of the impurity field to the earth's field depends on the orientation of the detector. Hence if an impurity field is present, different readings will be observed for successive orientations 90° apart. It should be realized that any impurities in the detector construction are subject to magnetization by the polarizing field.

Another possible cause for abnormally short decay is the proximity of metal objects, even though non-magnetic. Eddy currents induced when the polarizing field is switched off may persist long enough to create a disturbing magnetic gradient. In particular, it is impossible to tolerate any form of complete loop around the bottle.

Input switching circuitry

The critical requirement is that the polarizing current should be cut off cleanly and sharply. The final collapse from a few oersted to zero must occur in a time short compared to a millisecond; if this cut-off is slow ('adiabatic') the resultant field changes gradually from along the coil axis to the earth's field direction and the protons follow, instead of being left perpendicular to it. Proton behaviour at cut-off has been discussed by Bullard, Mason, *and* Mudie (1964).

One type of input arrangement is shown in Fig. 7.7. This employs standard relay contacts for breaking the polarization and, although appreciable sparking occurs, an adequate proton signal is obtained; however, it tends to be somewhat variable in amplitude from reading to reading. During the listening period the detector coils form a resonant circuit with the input tuning capacity of 0·05 μF, and the input impedance of the preamplifier must be high enough (say 50 kΩ) to avoid serious loading of this. A Q-factor of 20 is adequate and easily obtainable; too high a Q-factor is undesirable because the resonant currents then flowing in the coil would tend to interact with the gyrating protons and reduce the effective relaxation time.

The sequence of events is as follows:

(i) *During the polarizing period*, RL1 is de-energized and both contacts are closed. Contact 1b feeds power to RL2, which closes 2a and 2c but opens 2b. Power reaches the detector coils via 1a and 2a.

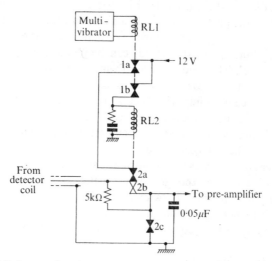

FIG. 7.7. Input relay circuit: early version. During polarization black contacts are closed and white open. During listening period, vice versa.

(ii) *At the conclusion of the polarizing period*, RL1 is energized and 1a opens, thus breaking the current through the coil; although sparking occurs (because of the inductive load) standard heavy-duty contacts stand up to this for a long time. It is important that 1b does not open while sparking persists. The contacts should be bent so that 1a opens just in advance of 1b.

Pre-amplifier overloading is avoided because the condenser–resistance arrangement in parallel with RL2 delays the opening of 2c. During this delay any parasitic ringing in the coils is damped by the 5 kΩ resistor which is effectively across the cable.

(iii) *During the listening period*, the coils are connected across the timing condenser via 2b. At the same time 2a isolates the input from

capacitative pick-up across 1a; such pick-up would come from the
supply voltage which, since it feeds the later amplifying stages, carries
a small ripple at the signal frequency.

An improved circuit is shown in Fig. 7.8. In this the stored inductive
energy in the coils is transferred, at cut-off, to the 32 μF condenser.

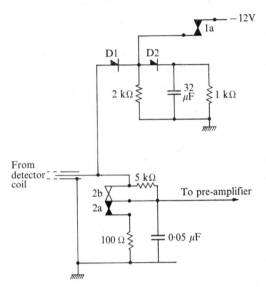

FIG. 7.8. Input relay circuit: improved version. During polarization,
black contacts are closed and white open. During listening period, vice
versa.

Cut-off is initiated by the opening of contacts 1a (which can be a tran-
sistor switch) supplying the polarizing current. The back e.m.f. from
the coils causes the 32 μF condenser to charge up positively via D1
and D2, during which time the polarizing current through the detector
coils falls rapidly and smoothly to zero. At the instant it reaches zero,
D1 and D2 cease to conduct. About 20 milliseconds later (by means of
a delayed relay circuit), contacts 2b close and then contacts 2a open.
The 32 μF condenser is discharged through the 1 kΩ resistor ready for
the next cut-off sequence.

7.5. Optical-pumping: the caesium magnetometer

Given that a nucleus can have both angular momentum and magnetic
moment, the basic operation of the proton magnetometer can be

understood in terms of straightforward concepts from classical physics. For the 'optically-pumped' magnetometer, concepts from quantum physics are needed, and the instrument is altogether more complex. However, the basic measurement is still essentially that of the frequency of precession of a magnetic moment, though the moment is atomic rather than nuclear. However, instead of the simple application of a strong magnetic field, polarization is obtained by means of the ingenious technique of optical pumping; also, resonance is used instead of free-precession, and the resulting forced precessions are detected optically rather than by electromagnetic induction. The development of the technique stems from the work of Kastler (1951, 1954, 1957), of Dehmelt (1956), and of Bell *and* Bloom (1957); there are review articles by Grivet *and* Malnar (1967) and by Stuart (1972).

Magnetometers of this type, specially developed by Varian Associates, have been used for archaeological work by the University Museum Philadelphia (MASCA) since 1964 (Ralph, 1964; Breiner, 1965; Ralph, Morrison *and* O'Brien, 1968). Because of its high sensitivity it is particularly advantageous on sites where the magnetic anomalies are weak and the soil-noise is low; with the Varian model V-4938 a sensitivity of 0·005 gamma is available but for archaeological application there is no point in using an instrument having a sensitivity of better than 0·1 gamma. Its indication is continuous and so it is well-suited to rapid-scan surveys. It should be remembered though that the limitation due to soil noise remains and on many sites this limits the usable sensitivity to 1 gamma.

Suitable atomic transitions for the device are available with various elements; helium, rubidium, and caesium are among these and each has practical advantages and disadvantages. For archaeological application rubidium and caesium have been used, and currently the latter is preferred. The following outline is generally applicable to both but specific quantities quoted refer to caesium.

Optical pumping

The heart of the magnetometer is a cylindrical glass cell, typically 2 cm diameter and 2 cm long, containing caesium vapour plus an inert buffer gas at a pressure of a few mm of Hg. A separate bulb of caesium vapour is excited to fluorescence by a radiofrequency oscillator (100 MHz) and used as a lamp. After filtering out unwanted components the D_1 line (8944 Å) from this is circularly polarized, and passed through the cell. Absorption of this light by a caesium atom causes excitation of the valence electron from the ground state $(S_\frac{1}{2})$ to the first excited state $(P_\frac{1}{2})$, this being the transition corresponding to the D_1 line. Almost immediately the $P_\frac{1}{2}$ state de-excites back to the ground state. However, an incidental effect of this excitation/deexcitation process is a tendency for the atomic magnetic vectors to become aligned with respect to the direction of the light beam. In turn this alignment affects the absorption process, since excitation to the $P_\frac{1}{2}$ state is not possible for an atom that is fully aligned. Thus, in a matter of a second, the absorption coefficient falls from say 50% when the lamp is turned on, to say 40% or less when the pumping regime is fully established.

Magnetic resonance

Similarly to a proton, a caesium atom precesses about the direction of the earth's field, the frequency being determined by the magnetogryic ratio and the magnitude of the field intensity. Atomic magnetic moments are two or three orders of magnitude higher than nuclear ones, and the frequency is correspondingly higher; for caesium in a field of 50 000 gamma the frequency is 175 kHz. If an alternating magnetic field (H_1) is applied to a vapour being optically pumped, it is found that when the frequency of this applied field is made equal to the precession frequency the absorption coefficient increases back towards the value for unpumped vapour. This is because the alternating magnetic field induces transitions from the fully-aligned state to less fully-aligned states.

The absorption coefficient is monitored by means of a photo-cell and by adjusting the frequency of H_1 for minimum signal from the photo-cell, the precession frequency can be found, and hence the value of F. However, for practical application it is more convenient to use the self-oscillating system.

Self-oscillator system

In addition to its de-pumping action the alternating field H_1 also gives phase coherence to the precessing atomic vectors. The motions are modified in such a way that there is a net macroscopic moment that rotates in the plane perpendicular to the earth's field, at the precession frequency, and with a fixed phase lag (90°) with respect to H_1. For practical reasons the direction of H_1 is the same as the direction of the light beam (see Fig. 7.9) and the effect is optimized by having this direction at 45° to the earth's field direction; the effect decreases to zero as either 0° or 90° are approached.

The rotating macroscopic moment is too small to be detected by the voltage it would induce in a coil because the density of the vapour is low (as is necessary to achieve optical pumping). However, it significantly affects the intensity of the light beam reaching the photo-cell. The absorption coefficient depends on the angle between the rotating moment and the direction of the light beam; consequently the light

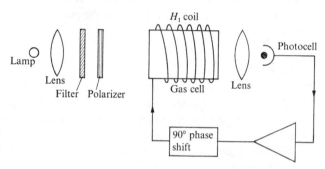

FIG. 7.9. Optical pumping magnetometer: simplified self-oscillator (from Stuart 1972).

intensity goes through a minimum (when the moment has a component parallel to direction of the beam) and a maximum (anti-parallel) once per precession cycle. Hence the signal from the photo-cell is modulated at the precession frequency.

By amplifying this modulation signal, and shifting its phase by 90° a self-oscillator system is possible (see Fig. 7.9). The frequency can be determined either by counting techniques similar to those used with proton magnetometers, or, since the signal is continuous, by mixing it with the output of a crystal-controlled reference oscillator and feeding the difference in frequency to a frequency-to-voltage converter.

Orientation

The optimum angle for self-oscillator operation is with the light beam at 45° to the earth's field direction. When the orientation departs from this optimum there is a fall-off in signal-to-noise ratio, but this is not too serious a difficulty in practice.

Of more concern is the slight change in self-oscillator frequency that may occur if the orientation is changed. This is because there are second-order effects due to the atomic magnetogyric ratio being a combination of the ratios for the nuclear spin momentum, the atomic angular momentum, and the atomic spin momentum. In reality there are a number of closely-spaced precession frequencies rather than a single one. For caesium-133 there are 9, and in a field of 50 000 gamma these have an overall spread of 55 Hz (equivalent to 15 gamma); for rubidium-85 the spread is 210 Hz (38 gamma). In practice each individual frequency has a finite spread too, so that the self-oscillator operates on a frequency characteristic that is a composite of the individual components. Orientation can affect the relative strengths of these components and hence the operating frequency of the self-oscillator.

For archaeological surveying a strong advantage of using caesium rather than rubidium is that the dependence on orientation is much less; even so, for the orientation error to be less than 0·1 gamma the sensor angle must be kept within about 5° of optimum, though if an error of a few gamma is tolerable the angle can be up to about 30° from optimum. In applications where there is no control of orientation such as in rockets, the effect is eliminated by the use of multiple sensors arranged at different angles.

Absolute accuracy

Although this is unimportant for archaeological work, it may be noted that although it has high sensitivity the optically pumped magnetometer does not have high accuracy; for geophysical work absolute calibration is made by comparison with a proton magnetometer. This lack of absolute accuracy is due to the same cause as the orientation effect; it seems that changes in operating conditions (e.g. temperature drift, replacement of lamp) can alter the relative importance of the individual precession frequency components.

Instruments for archaeological use

To make proper use of the 0·1 gamma sensitivity of the type developed for archaeological use it is essential to use two sensors in differential mode; this is because of the diurnal variation, and because of micropulsations; the latter sometimes approach a few gamma in magnitude. The usual practice is to have one sensor in a fixed position and to use the output from this to gate the output of the roving sensor, obtaining direct read-out in tenth gamma units by suitable frequency division circuitry.

A routinely available instrument is the Varian V-4971 Portable Search Magnetometer. This uses a single sensor which is carried at one end of a 2-metre staff, at the other end of which is the electronic package; the batteries are slung around the operator's waist and the overall operating weight is 22 pounds (10 kilograms). There is audio indication of change in magnetic field intensity; this is obtained by listening (in earphones) to the beat frequency between the sensor output and the output of a reference oscillator. The sensor frequency changes by 3·5 Hz per gamma for caesium (4·7 Hz per gamma for rubidium-85); by frequency doubling, the audio tone is made to vary at 7 Hz per gamma.

In one mode of operation the reference oscillator is set to give a difference frequency in the range 10 to 100 Hz and the operator listens for changes in this note—a change of 1 Hz is detectable in a 10 Hz note and 5 Hz in a 100 Hz note.

This mode is used for rapid scanning at one gamma sensitivity. An alternative mode is to adjust the reference oscillator until zero beat frequency is obtained; by noting the reading of the calibrated oscillator control a sensitivity of 0·1 gamma can be obtained. However, as mentioned above, it is not practical to use such high sensitivity for archaeological surveying unless the reference oscillator is replaced by a reference sensor, i.e. a high sensitivity version of the proton gradiometer (section 7.4). Such an instrument has been the subject of a special purpose development by Varian Associates.

7.6. The fluxgate gradiometer

Whereas the preceding magnetometers are based on nuclear and atomic phenomena, the fluxgate depends on the bulk magnetic behaviour of a special alloy. An essential functional difference is that the quantity measured is a component of the earth's field intensity— usually the vertical one—rather than the total intensity. This makes the detecting elements sensitive to angle, which engenders mechanical construction problems. However, the technique has compensating advantages; unlike the proton magnetometer it can operate in strong gradients and it is a continuously reading instrument, making it useful for rapid scanning. Its sensitivity is not in practice quite as good as the proton magnetometer, though it is adequate for the majority of sites. Reports on its construction and utilization for archaeological prospecting have been given by Tite (1961), Alldred and Aitken (1966), Clark and Haddon-Reece (1972), and Philpot (1972). A fluxgate instrument, developed by Plessey Ltd., has been widely and routinely used in Britain for some years by the Ancient Monuments Branch of the Department of the Environment.

Fluxgate detection

The basic mode of action is as follows. A short straight length (say 5 cm) of wire of very high magnetic permeability alloy (e.g. 'mu' metal) is used as the core on which a primary coil and a secondary

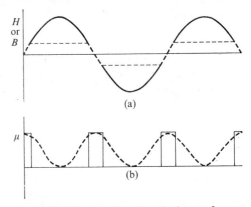

Fig. 7.10. Fluxgate detection: basic waveforms.

(a) Full curve shows the field H produced by the current fed to the primary coil; dashed line shows the flux B induced in the high permeability core.

(b) Full curve shows the effective permeability μ of the core; dashed line indicates the fundamental frequency of this permeability variation. Note that this frequency is twice that of the primary field.

coil are wound. Because of its high permeability, the core is easily driven into saturation, and the magnetic flux induced by a sinusoidal primary field is as shown by the dashed waveform on Fig. 7.10(a). An applied d.c. field has no effect on the flux level during saturation, and hence the core then has zero effective permeability. It is only when changing between positive and negative saturation that the flux in the core is affected by a d.c. field and consequently the effective permeability changes with time as shown in Fig. 7.10(b). Note that the fundamental frequency of the permeability waveform is twice that of the primary waveform.

In the absence of a d.c. field along the axis of the coils the flux induced in the core has frequency components equal to the primary frequency and its even harmonics. There are no odd harmonics because the flux waveform is symmetrical about the zero base line. On the other hand when there is a d.c. field along the axis, flux is induced in the core during times when the effective permeability is non-zero, and from Fig. 7.10(b) we see that this means that it will have a fundamental frequency which is twice that of the primary frequency. Thus, if the primary frequency is 1 kHz, there will only be a 2 kHz component induced in the secondary when there is a d.c. field along the coil axis, and the amplitude of that frequency will be proportional to the magnitude of the field.

Gradiometer configuration

Consider an arrangement in which two fluxgate detectors, with their axes vertical, are fixed at either end of a vertical staff, and with electrical circuitry as indicated in Fig. 7.11. If the characteristics of the

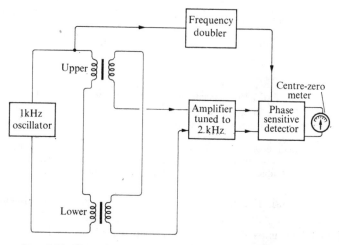

FIG. 7.11. Fluxgate gradiometer: simplified schematic diagram.

two fluxgates are identical then in uniform magnetic field the 2-kHz outputs from the two secondaries will be equal and, because these are connected in series-opposition, there will be no signal indicated on the meter (which is of the centre-zero type). If the device is in a magnetic gradient then the 2-kHz outputs are unequal, and the meter is deflected either to the left or to the right, depending on whether the vertical intensity is stronger at the lower fluxgate or at the upper one.

In practice, in order to correct for inequalities in fluxgate characteristics, d.c. current fed through tertiary windings is used to reduce the field at each fluxgate to near zero, and by differential fine adjustment of this zero meter deflection for uniform field is obtained. Fluxgate elements are usually constructed with two parallel cores; the primary coil is wound around both, but there are two secondaries wound around each individually in opposite senses, so that ideally there is zero output of the primary frequency and its even harmonics.

It is not feasible to use the fluxgate technique for archaeological prospecting except in gradiometer configuration. This is because a slight change in the angle between fluxgate axis and field direction gives a large change in the magnitude of the field component along the axis. Thus with the axis nominally vertical (and in a region where $F = 48\,000$ gamma and $I = 68°$), a departure from verticality of only 0·3 degrees can give rise to a change of 100 gamma. In a gradiometer on the other hand, each fluxgate experiences the same tilt and the effect cancels out; however second-order mismatch and misalignment effects do in fact limit the angle of tilt that can be tolerated. In the instrument reported by Alldred *and* Aitken (1966) the fluxgates are four feet apart on a composite staff mounted on gymbals, and for a tilt of 15° the error signal is not more than two gamma. The rod carrying the fluxgates is mounted on rubber bushes inside an outer tube, and by means of an adjustment mechanism they are precisely aligned at the beginning of a survey. To keep the error signal below 2 gamma the fluxgate axes must be mutually aligned to within 0·06 degrees and this alignment has to be maintained during tilting.

REFERENCES

AITKEN, M. J. *and* TITE, M. S. (1962). A gradient magnetometer using proton free-precession. *J. Scient. Instrum.*, **39**, 625–9.
ALLDRED, J. C. *and* AITKEN, M. J. (1966). A fluxgate gradiometer for archaeological surveying. *Prospezioni Archeologiche*, **1**, 53–60.
BELL, W. E. *and* BLOOM, A. L. (1957). Optical detection of magnetic resonance in alkali metal vapour *Phys. Rev.* **107**, 1559–65.
BENDER, P. L. *and* DRISCOLL, R. L. (1958). A free precession determination of the proton gyromagnetic ratio. *Instit. Radio Eng. Trans. Instrumentation*, **1–7**, 176–80.
BLOCH, F. (1946). Nuclear induction. *Phys. Rev.* **70**, 461–474.
BREINER, S. (1965). The rubidium magnetometer in archaeological exploration. *Science*, **150**, 185–93.
BULLARD, E. C., MASON, C. S., *and* MUDIE, J. D. (1964). *Proc. Camb. Phil. Soc.* **60**, 287–93.
CLARK, A. J. *and* HADDON-REECE, D. (1972). An automatic recording system using the Plessey fluxgate magnetometer. *Prospezioni Archeologiche*, **7**, 107–14.

DEHMELT, H. G. (1956). Slow spin relaxation of optically polarized sodium atoms. *Phys. Rev.* 105, 1487–9.

GARDNER, F. M. (1966). *Phaselock Techniques.* John Wiley & Sons, London.

GRIVET, P. A. *and* MALNAR, L. (1967). Measurement of weak magnetic fields by magnetic resonance. *Advances in Electronics and Electron Physics*, 23, 40–146.

HALL, E. T. (1962). Some notes on the design and manufacture of the detector heads for proton magnetometers. *Archaeometry*, 5, 139–45.

HARKNETT, M. R. (1969). A proton magnetometer with solid state switching. *Archaeometry*, 11, 173–8.

HUGGARD, L. (1970). Proton magnetometer ferrous metal locator. *Practical Electronics*, October 1970, p. 782.

KASTLER, A. (1951). Méthodes optique d'étude de la résonance magnétique. *Physica*, 17, 191–204.

KASTLER, A. (1954). Les méthodes optiques d'orientation atomique et leur applications. *Proc. phys. Soc.* (*London*) A67, 853–63.

KASTLER, A. (1957). Optical methods of atomic orientation and of magnetic resonance. *J. opt. Soc. Am.* 47, 460–5.

MUDIE, J. D. (1962). A digital differential proton magnetometer. *Archaeometry*, 5, 135–9.

PACKARD, M. *and* VARIAN, R. (1954). Free nuclear induction in the earth's magnetic field. *Phys. Rev.* 93, 941.

PHILPOT, F. (1972). An improved fluxgate gradiometer for archaeological surveys. *Prospezioni Archeologiche*, 7, 99–106.

RALPH, E. K. (1964). Comparison of a proton and a rubidium magnetometer for archaeological prospecting. *Archaeometry*, 7, 20–7.

RALPH, E. K., MORRISON, F., *and* O'BRIEN, D. P. (1968). Archaeological surveying utilizing a high-sensitivity difference magnetometer. *Geoexploration*, 6, 109–22.

SCOLLAR, I. (1965). A contribution to magnetic prospecting in Archaeology. *Archaeo-Physica Band 15 der Beihefte der Bonner. Jahrbucher*, 21–92.

STRONG, C. L. (1968). Building a sensitive magnetometer. *Scientific American*, February 1968, p. 124.

STUART, W. F. (1972). Earth's field magnetometry. *Rep. Prog. Phys.* 35, 803–81.

TITE, M. S. (1961). Alternative instruments for magnetic surveying. *Archaeometry*, 4, 85–90.

WATERS, G. S. *and* FRANCIS, P. D. (1958). A nuclear magnetometer. *J. Scient. Instrum.* 35, 88–93.

8 Electrical Resistivity Surveying

8.1. Introduction

ELECTRICITY is conducted through the ground by the process of electrolysis, and the ease with which this occurs depends on the quantity of water retained in the pores of the constituent soil and rocks. Hard, compact rocks such as granite are very poor conductors, while the more porous limestones are much better, though still poor by comparison with soil, sand, and clay. Table 8.1 gives some representative values; the actual resistivities found in practice depend very much on water content.

TABLE 8.1

Electrical resistivities (in Ω m) of rock, soil, and clay: some representative values (after Griffiths *and* King, 1965, p. 10)

Igneous and metamorphic rocks	10^2–10^6
Dense limestone	$>10^4$
Porous limestone	100–1000
Sandstone	100–1000
Sand	50–500
Clay and soil	1–10

While for geological work the variations between rock types are important, for most archaeological applications it is enough to assume that rock and stones have a very high resistivity compared to soils and clays, and that wide variations will be found among the latter according to water content. Consequently for resistivity surveying the archaeological features *par excellence* are stone walls intruding into soil, and earth-filled ditches cut into rock. The detectability of other features is variable, since local conditions, and particularly geological and climatic variations of water content, may easily mask the effect of archaeological features.

For fuller discussion than is given in this chapter the reader should consult articles by two experienced practitioners of the technique: Atkinson (1952, 1953, 1963) and Clark (1969).

Units

Consider a cylinder of cross-sectional area A cm^2 and length l cm, through which a current of i amps flows parallel to the axis. If V volts is the voltage drop between the ends of the cylinder then the resistance is given by

$$R = \frac{V}{i} \text{ ohm} \qquad (8.1)$$

and the conductivity by

$$S = \frac{i}{V} \text{ siemen.} \qquad (8.2)$$

If ρ is the specific resistivity then

$$R = \frac{\rho l}{A}. \qquad (8.3)$$

By inspection it will be seen that the units for ρ are *ohm-metre*. Similarly the specific conductivity σ, which equals ρ^{-1} has units *siemen per metre*. If centimetres are used instead of metres, then

$$\rho_{\text{ohm-cm}} = 100\rho_{\text{ohm-m}}. \qquad (8.4)$$

8.2. Measurement

If two metal probes are inserted into the ground, a few feet apart, and a battery is connected between them (see Fig. 8.1), a small current flows through the ground (of the order of 0·01 amps for a 12-V battery). The presence of material between the probes having an abnormally high or low resistivity will be shown up as an abnormal value of the resistance (V/i) seen by the probes, when compared to adjacent readings.

This simple system is unsatisfactory for a number of reasons:

(i) *Contact voltages.* There will be small d.c. voltages of chemical origin between probes and ground, so that the actual voltage applied to the ground will be different to the measured voltage V. Variations in this contact voltage at each new insertion of the probes are liable to mask the effect of genuine variations in ground resistivity. The effect can be eliminated by using an a.c. voltage source instead of a battery.

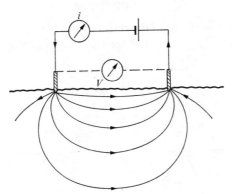

Fig. 8.1. Crude resistivity meter.

(ii) *Contact resistance.* The resistance between each probe and the soil may be larger than the resistance of the earth itself. This can be avoided by watering the soil in the immediate vicinity of the probe, but the measured resistance then depends on the degree of watering. To avoid the effect of contact resistance, separate voltage probes must be used, i.e. four probes in all.

(iii) *Probe polarization.* The measured resistance between the probes will gradually increase with the time for which the current is passed. This is a similar effect to electrode polarization in electrolysis and, as with effect (i), it can be avoided by using a.c.

(iv) *Earth currents.* Natural earth currents arise from chemical potentials developing between different geological strata, and by induction from the transient variations of the earth's magnetic field. These currents are either d.c. or very low frequency, and the effects from them are avoided by using a.c. There are also man-made earth currents arising from power lines etc., and it is important to bear these in mind when deciding the frequency of the a.c. source to be used.

The four probe method

The simplest and most commonly employed version (the *Wenner configuration*) is shown in Fig. 8.2. Although the voltage appearing across the inner probes is only a small fraction of the total applied voltage, the effective resistance defined by

$$R = \frac{\text{Voltage across inner probes}}{\text{Current through outer probes}} \tag{8.5}$$

is a satisfactory measure of the resistivity of the ground beneath the inner probes. As long as the voltage measuring instrument has a high

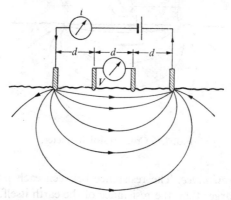

FIG. 8.2. The four-probe method (Wenner configuration).

enough input impedance, the current flowing through the inner probes is insignificant, and so their contact resistance does not matter. The contact resistance of the outer probes affects only the amount of current flowing for a given applied voltage; it does not affect the ratio defined by eqn (8.5).

The main reason for equality of spacing between all probes is ease of practical application in making many readings in a long line; by using five probes, and a rotary switch to move connections along them, the array can be advanced by the movement of the spare probe while a measurement is being made with the other four. Apart from this there is the consideration that if the inner probe separation is made appreciably larger than one-third of the outer-probe separation, the reading obtained becomes significantly dependent on the length of probe inserted into the ground. On the other hand reduction of the inner-probe separation increases the relative effect of errors in probe position. Alternative probe configurations are discussed in section 8.5.

It will be shown later (section 8.4) that for equal spacing the effective resistance, R, is related to the specific resistivity of the ground by the relation,

$$\rho = 2\pi dR, \tag{8.6}$$

where d is the spacing between probes. It turns out that the metre is not a very convenient practical unit of length, and it is useful to remember that if d is measured in feet,

$$\rho = (0.19 \times d_{ft} \times R) \text{ ohm-metre.} \tag{8.7}$$

The value of ρ obtained is a rough average for the ground beneath the inner probes down to a depth of approximately $1.5 \times d$, as long as it is fairly uniform. Where the ground consists of two layers of widely different resistivity, e.g. top-soil above rock, then the lines of current flow are distorted from the paths shown in Fig. 8.2; most of the current will flow along the less resistive top-soil and relations (8.6) and (8.7) are not applicable—though the indicated resistivity is indeed higher because the presence of the rock restricts the cross-section available in the top-soil. As in magnetic surveying the actual value of the reading is not important, it is the fact that by comparison with adjacent readings it is abnormal.

Instruments

The instrument used for the first archaeological trials of the technique in 1946 (Atkinson 1952, 1953) was the Megger Earth Tester,† an adaptation of the instrument commonly used in the laboratory and by telephone engineers, for measuring high resistance. The source of voltage in this is a small hand-turned generator and the effective resistance (as defined in eqn (8.5)) is indicated on a pointer. The applied voltage on open circuit is about 200 V (at 40 Hz), so unless the probe handles are insulated, there is a readily available stimulus for ensuring rapid probe moving!

Compared to the instruments next described, the Megger has the advantage that the operator (in addition to turning the handle) needs only to read the pointer position, and no mental judgement of a 'null' is required. It has the disadvantage that since the detection circuitry

† Manufactured by Evershed and Vignoles Ltd., Chiswick, London.

takes a small current through the inner probes, a high contact resistance can upset the readings; this can be a serious drawback in dry conditions. It is overcome in the Geophysical Megger Earth Tester by using a null technique (see Eve *and* Keys, 1954, p. 119 for details). The null balance technique on which more recent instruments are based is illustrated in Fig. 8.3. The outer-probe current passes through

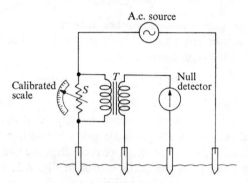

FIG. 8.3. Null balancing circuit. The calibrated rheostat S is adjusted until the voltage across the transformer secondary exactly balances the voltage developed across the inner probes.

a low resistance S, and the voltage developed across S is compared, via the transformer T, with the inner-probe voltage. S is adjusted until the detector deflection is zero, and the setting of S is then a measure of the effective inner-probe resistance as defined in (8.5).

In the '*Tellohm*' *Soil Resistance Meter*†, the a.c. voltage is generated by a reversing-relay (110 Hz) driven from a 30-V dry battery. A second set of contacts on the relay provides synchronous rectification of the difference between the transformer output voltage and the inner-probe voltage so that a sensitive d.c. galvanometer can be used as the null detector. The *Gossen Geohm*‡ is similar to the Tellohm in form and action, but more compact.

The *Martin–Clark Resistivity Meter*§, specifically designed for archaeological work and widely used, employs a transistorized oscillator for the outer-probe current, and meter indication from the

† Manufactured by Nash and Thompson Ltd., Chessington, Surrey, England.
‡ Manufactured by P. Gossen, Erlangen, Bayern, West Germany.
§ Manufactured by Geoelectronics, Chapel Road, Standford-in-the-Vale, Faringdon, Berkshire, England.

rectified output of an amplifier for null detection. The instrument runs from a 4·5-V torch battery and can be held in one hand; the oscillator frequency is 400 Hz.

The preceding instruments have been available at least since 1960; they are reliable and serve their purpose well. A new generation of instruments now appearing employs constant current supply for the outer probes, and ultra high input-impedance circuitry (e.g. ∼100 MΩ) for measurement of the inner-probe voltage, thereby avoiding the tediousness of null-balancing. In the instrument described by Aspinall *and* Picard (1971) the voltage source is a 200-V square-wave generator operating at a frequency of 128 Hz, and the current supplied to the outer probes is electronically controlled to a fixed value irrespective of load resistance variations over a wide range. Braissant *and* Chapellier (1971) revert to a d.c. system but subtract out polarization effects by measurement and storage. Although the instrumental side of measurement is thus being speeded-up, the more serious limitation of probe insertion remains; some of the alternative configurations alleviate this, and there is also the possibility of mechanization (e.g. Hesse 1966). A system has been developed at Bradford University following a design by Mr. A. J. Clark, in which two spiked wheels replace the probe system (the Twin configuration described in section 8.5); these are geared to drive a chart recorder and, using a constant current type of instrument a continuous trace of resistivity is obtained.

8.3. Field application

Procedure

Measurements are usually made along a series of traverses, each 50 to 100 ft long and parallel to one another. The probes are inserted along the line of the traverse (marked out with a measuring tape) and moved along it as the readings are taken. The probe array is moved by a distance equal to the probe separation for each new reading, and in this way a resistivity profile, such as those shown in Figs. 8.4 and 8.5, is obtained. For speed of operation it is advantageous to use the five-probe system mentioned earlier. The probes are all connected into the instrument via a rotary switch, which is advanced by one step before each measurement. Each probe is successively *outer-spare-outer-inner-inner*; in this way only one probe needs moving for each new measurement. Twisting up of the cable does not occur because the switch is a rotary one. A point of detail to be noted when the cable connections to the probes are made by means of large crocodile clips, is that the probes should be kept free from corrosion by the use of emery paper.

The probes themselves are sharpened $\frac{1}{4}$-in to $\frac{1}{2}$-in mild-steel rods, and it is a good idea to have them 'cranked' so that there is a short horizontal section to which the foot is applied during insertion. This horizontal section also defines the depth of insertion; for eqn (8.6) to be reasonably valid, the length of probe in the ground should not be

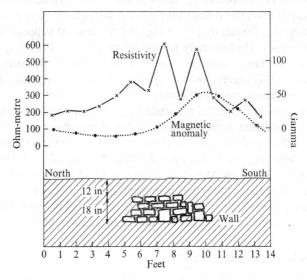

FIG. 8.4. Resistivity traverse across a wall, with magnetic profile for comparison. The resistivity scale is on the right. Resistivity probe separation was 1 ft, and this was also the height of the magnetometer detector above the ground. The southward displacement of the magnetic anomaly is explained in Chapter 6.

more than one-fifth of the probe separation (see section 8.4), but in practice this can be exceeded as long as the length is kept constant. The probe separation should be roughly equal to the expected depth of the feature. If the separation is too great, the feature forms only a small fraction of the volume penetrated by the current; if the separation is too small, very little current will reach the feature. Obviously it is advantageous to make repeated surveys at different probe separations—though time consuming.

Well-trained operators can take about ten readings per minute;

if the time for laying-out traverses is included, the average is about 300 readings per hour. This corresponds to a rate of ground coverage approaching that of magnetic surveying, but it is difficult to keep up top-speed for more than an hour or two, because of the mental strain involved in correct probe-movement and reading-taking (particularly with a null-balancing instrument).

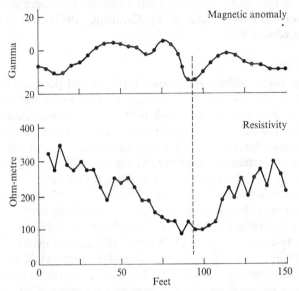

Fig. 8.5. Resistivity traverse across the Inner Fosse at Verulaminum, with magnetic profile for comparison. Resistivity probe separation: 4 ft. Magnetometer detector height: 3 ft.

Examples of resistivity anomalies

Figure 8.4 shows the resistivity profile obtained across a wall, together with the corresponding magnetic profile for comparison. The inverted 'W' shape is characteristic of the Wenner configuration when used with the line of the probes perpendicular to the wall; it is due to distortion of the current path when individual probes are close to the wall (Tagg, 1957).

Earth-filled ditches usually produce a low resistance anomaly (see Fig. 8.5) on account of the dampness of the filling. The effect is greatly attenuated if the filling has dried out so as to acquire a humidity comparable to that of the adjacent strata. If the upper layers of the filling contain an appreciable amount of stone an anomalously high resistance may be produced, particularly when the probe separation is such as to make the sensitivity a lot greater at the depth of the stone layer than lower down. The same considerations apply to pits though, because these are isolated features not showing on successive traverses, their detection is less certain. Empty tombs and caverns show up as a high resistance owing to the absence of a conducting medium. The Etruscan necropoli at Cerveteri and Tarquinia have been mapped in this way (Lerici *et al.*, 1958; Carabelli, 1967; Carabelli *and* Brancaleoni, 1968).

Handicaps

Two geological effects are serious. First, natural pockets of clay or soil in a rocky sub-stratum may easily be mistaken for archaeological features, as is also the case with near-surface streams. Secondly, if the top-soil contains rocky rubble, as frequently occurs on limestone, the random fluctuations of the measured resistance may mask any features. In extremely stony ground the method may be impossible simply because of the difficulty of inserting the probes.

Heavy rain precludes operation because the surface water short-circuits the probes. A moderately damp soil maybe beneficial when looking for walls, but it is a drawback for pits and ditches since the resistivity contrast is reduced. If recent rain has dampened only the upper layer of soil, a greater proportion of the current will travel near the surface thereby reducing the depth of detectable feature. Conversely, a high water-table may attenuate the effect of near-surface features; a subtle way of avoiding this difficulty is to carry out the survey during weather cold enough for the water to be frozen solid (Hampl *and* Fritsch, 1959). It has been observed by Mr. A. J. Clark that the same ditch (dug into chalk) can give a low resistivity anomaly in winter but a high one in summer, presumably because the water content of the looser ditch-fill responds to climatic changes more readily than the close-textured chalk; it follows that there are at least two times per year when there is no anomaly at all.

The way in which recent climate affects the readings has also been studied by Al Chalabi *and* Rees (1962) and by Hesse (1966a, b). The former measured anomalies from filled-in ditches over a period of thirteen months, and noted a variation in average anomaly strength by a factor of four that correlated with net water gain (rainfall minus loss by evaporation and transpiration) over the past few months; if the time period considered was increased above four months, or reduced below one month, the correlation became less good. Presumably the delay in effect represents the time taken by the water to seep downwards; obviously this will vary with type of filling and depth of feature, so that the results for this one site should not be taken necessarily to be applicable in general. More detailed studies by Hesse show that the resistivity is affected not only by wetness but also by temperature—a decrease of about 2% per 1°C increase.

8.4. Theory

As with magnetic location, buried features are revealed by abnormalities in closely spaced readings taken over the area concerned, rather than by theoretical interpretation which tends to be dauntingly complex. However, some acquaintance with the elementary theory is a helpful basis for field experience, and in understanding the alternative probe configurations of section 8.5. For simplicity, the discussion of the present section is restricted to the standard Wenner configuration; for more comprehensive treatment the reader should consult Eve *and* Keys (1954), Griffiths *and* King (1965), or various discussions in geophysical prospecting journals (e.g. Carpenter, 1955).

Single probe

The current from a single probe inserted in ground of uniform resistivity, and maintained at a potential of $+V_0$ by means of a battery for which the earth-return is distant from the probe, flows in straight radial lines as shown in Fig. 8.6. The equipotentials are hemispherical surfaces, so that at a radius r the current crossing unit area of such a surface is given by:

$$j = \frac{i}{2\pi r^2}, \qquad (8.8)$$

where i is the total current leaving the probe. Since j is related to the electrical field E at any point by the relation

$$j = \frac{E}{\rho}, \qquad (8.9)$$

it follows that

$$E = \frac{\rho i}{2\pi r^2}, \qquad (8.10)$$

where ρ is the resistivity.

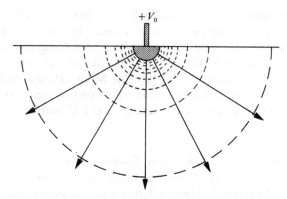

FIG. 8.6. Current flow from single probe. The probe has been idealized by representing it as a hemisphere. In practice the probe ends in a point; this distorts the flow pattern close to it but not at large distances. The dotted lines represent equipotentials.

Hence, by integration, the potential at any radius r is given by

$$V = \frac{\rho i}{2\pi r}. \tag{8.11}$$

If we assume that the end of the probe is a hemisphere of radius r_0, of which the flat surface is flush with the ground, then we must have

$$V_0 = \frac{\rho i}{2\pi r_0}. \tag{8.12}$$

Since this relates the current flowing to the applied potentials, it defines a probe resistance equal to $(\rho/2\pi r_0)$.

Two probes

The flow of current between two probes, differing in potential by V_1, may be considered as the superposition of the flow patterns for two isolated probes at $+\frac{1}{2}V_1$ and $-\frac{1}{2}V_1$ respectively, as long as r_0 is negligible compared to the distance between the probes. The actual current at any point is the vector resultant of the individual currents (see Fig. 8.7), and the potential is the algebraic sum of the individual potentials. In this way the current patterns of Figs. 8.1 and 8.2 may be derived.

All the current flowing into the earth from the positive probe flows out of the earth at the negative probe, so that from eqn (8.12) the resistance between the probes is given by

$$R_1 = \frac{\rho}{\pi r_0}. \tag{8.13}$$

Although R_1 is independent of the distance between the probes, this is not a good method of measuring ρ for three reasons. First, in practice a variable contact resistance will be measured in addition.

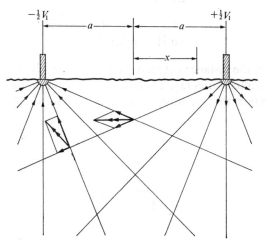

FIG. 8.7. Current flow from two probes. The magnitude and direction of the current at any point is obtained by vector addition of the currents that would flow from a positive probe and a negative probe independently of each other (see Fig. 8.6).

Secondly, it has been assumed that the probes have hemispherical ends just protruding into the ground—an impractical arrangement. Thirdly, the main part of the resistance measured is that of the ground very close to the probes.

When using the four-probe method, R_1 is nevertheless of interest in determining a suitable value for the output impedance of the power source used. In practice the portion of the probe in the ground is not hemispherical, but consists of two or three inches of rod ending in a point. In this case one can define an effective radius r_0' which when substituted in eqn (8.13) gives the observed value for R_1. It was found experimentally that for $\frac{5}{16}$ inch-diameter rod, r_0' is about 2 cm for

2 inches of rod in the ground, and 4 cm for 6 inches. These figures do not increase much if $\frac{1}{2}$ inch rod is used instead.

Voltage variation between two probes

The potential on the ground surface along the line joining the two probes, at a distance x from the mid-point, can be obtained from eqn (8.11) and is given by

$$V = \frac{\rho i}{2\pi} \left\{ \frac{1}{(a - x)} - \frac{1}{(a + x)} \right\}$$

$$= \frac{\rho i}{\pi a} \left\{ \frac{x/a}{1 - (x/a)^2} \right\}, \tag{8.14}$$

where $2a$ is the distance between the probes. This is shown in Fig. 8.8; the potential varies rapidly in the vicinity of the probes, but in the central section the variation is small and uniform. The potential

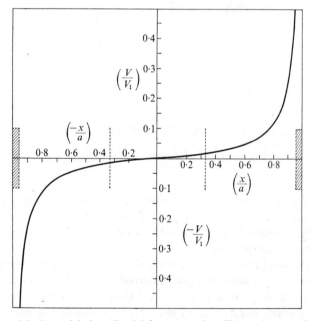

FIG. 8.8. Potential along line joining two probes. The probe potentials are $+\frac{1}{2}V_1$ and $-\frac{1}{2}V_1$ respectively. The separation is $2a$. V is the potential at a distance x from the mid-point. The probe ends are assumed to be hemispherical and of radius $r_0 = (a/20)$.

difference V_2, between two inner probes placed at $x = +b$, and $x = -b$, is given by

$$V_2 = \frac{2\rho i}{\pi a}\left\{\frac{b/a}{1-(b/a)^2}\right\}. \tag{8.15}$$

Thus the inner probe resistance, defined as (V_2/i), is given by

$$R_2 = \frac{2\rho}{\pi a}\left\{\frac{b/a}{1-(b/a)^2}\right\}. \tag{8.16}$$

Although the actual magnitude of the current flowing will depend very much on the resistivity of the ground close to the outer probes, the value of R_2 is mainly dependent on the region below the centre probes, down to a depth somewhat greater than the inner-probe spacing.

If b equals $(a/3)$, the probes are equally spaced, and on substituting d for the inter-probe distance we obtain the relation quoted in section 8.2,

$$R_2 = \frac{\rho}{2\pi d}. \tag{8.6}$$

Reciprocity of current and voltage probes

It follows from a generalized form of Helmholtz's reciprocal theorem (Searle, 1910) that for ground of uniform resistivity, interchange of function between inner and outer probes does not affect the value of R_2. This has no practical application in respect of the Wenner array but it is useful to bear it in mind when considering some of the alternative configurations of section 8.5.

Error due to fine probe insection

The foregoing assumes that the length of probe in the ground is negligible. Wenner (1916) has shown that for probes inserted to a depth h, but insulated except at their ends, the inner-probe resistance is given by

$$R_2 = \frac{\rho}{4\pi d}\{1 + 2(1 + 4h^2/d^2)^{-\frac{1}{2}} - (1 + h^2/d^2)^{-\frac{1}{2}}\}. \tag{8.17}$$

The practical case, in which current can leave the probes all along the length inserted, will be intermediate between (8.6) and (8.17). Since the difference between these is less than 7% as long as h is less than one-fifth of d, the effect may be neglected except when the inter-probe spacing is down to 1 ft, and even then for comparative purposes it is unimportant as long as h is kept fairly constant.

Using an inter-probe separation of 1 ft and $\frac{5}{16}$-in diameter probes, it was found by experiment that the measured resistance decreases by 10% on increasing the length inserted from 2 in to 6 in. With an inter-probe separation of 2 ft, the corresponding decrease is less than 2%.

Errors due to inaccurate probe spacing

It follows from eqn (8.16) that a certain percentage error in the inner-probe separation produces the same percentage error in R_2, and that the same percentage error in the outer-probe separation produces an error in R_2 of double that percentage, but in the opposite sense. Hence, when the nominal inter-probe distance is only 1 ft a positive error of 1 in in the inner-probe separation will cause R_2 to be too high by 8% and a positive error of 1 in in the outer-probe separation will cause R_2 to be too low by 5·5%. For a nominal inter-probe distance of 2 ft, the corresponding figures are 4% and 3%. When using the smaller spacing, the probes must be inserted to within $\frac{1}{2}$ in of their correct position in order to keep the total error in R_2 below 14%.

Errors due to lateral displacement from being in a straight line are comparatively unimportant.

Capacitative effects and phase shifts

By a similar analysis to that used to derive R_2, an estimate of the inner-probe capacity can be obtained: it is

$$C_2 = \frac{\rho\varepsilon_{\mathrm{r}}}{R_2} \times 8{\cdot}85 \times 10^{-12} \text{ farad,} \qquad (8.18)$$

where ε_{r} is the relative permittivity (dielectric constant) of the soil. Hence if θ is the phase lag of the inner-probe voltage behind the outer-probe current,

$$\tan\theta = f\rho\varepsilon_{\mathrm{r}} \times 56 \times 10^{-12}. \qquad (8.19)$$

Taking $\rho = 1000$ ohm-metre, and $\varepsilon_{\mathrm{r}} = 5$, we see that θ is negligible for the range of frequencies commonly employed in soil resistivity measurements; it is not until f reaches the order of 1 MHz that significant phase shift is liable to occur.

8.5. Alternative probe configurations

Figure 8.9 shows various configurations that have been used archaeologically of which (a), (b), (d), and (h) are scaled-down versions from geophysical prospecting.

The comparative responses of types (a), (b), and (d) have been

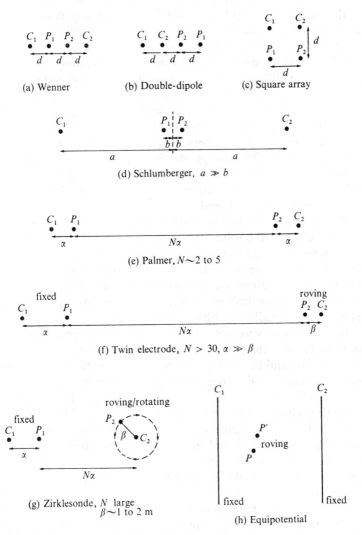

FIG. 8.9. Types of probe configuration.

evaluated by Carabelli (1967) using laboratory models. One reason for changing from the usual Wenner system is the complexity of anomaly shape (e.g. the inverted W shape mentioned earlier). Rearrangement of probe functions into the *Double-Dipole* system ('Eltran') avoid this, and also gives stronger indications—at any rate in the case of cavities —though the fall-off with increasing depth of feature is more rapid.

The *Square Array* (Clark, 1968) is a particularly compact and convenient arrangement since the probes can be built into a rigid framework (with suitable insulation) and used to form the legs of a small table which carries the instrument and recording pad. Also, by use of a suitable switch the functions of the probes can be swopped around, and a pair of readings is taken for each position: C_1 is moved to the probe previously used for C_2, and C_2 to the probe previously used for P_2. Because of its composite structure the array can be moved from place to place by one person and a reading rate of 5 pairs per minute achieved, 1200 pairs per day being possible 'with no unusual fatigue'. In the model described by Clark the side of the square is 0·75 metres and the probes are made from Dexiom steel angle which is squeezed flat and sharpened.

The *Zirkelsonde* (Schwarz, 1961) is also a one-man instrument and is most suited for following along a linear feature. The V_2 probe is a heavy wheel (5 kilogram, diameter 0·4 metres) which is connected by an insulated axle, one or two metres long, to a vertical stake which forms the C_2 probe. Features are detected by variations indicated as the wheel makes a circumferential traverse, rather than by comparing point-to-point readings as with the other systems.

In the *Schlumberger* arrangement, much used in geophysics, the distance between the voltage probes is small and a detector of good sensitivity is required (see Fig. 8.8). As used in the survey of a Roman villa site (Dunk, 1962; Rees *and* Wright, 1969) the current probe spacing was 8 ft and the voltage probe spacing 6 in; to achieve accurate positioning the array was carried on a hinged board.

In the *Palmer* arrangement, C_1 and P_1 are close together and can be mechanically linked, and likewise $C_2 P_2$. Like arrangements (*a*), (*c*), and (*d*), the Palmer system gives rise to the inverted W type of response but with the added disadvantage that the separation between the two peaks is greater.

In the *Twin Electrode* system (Aspinall *and* Lynam, 1970), N is made sufficiently large for the measured resistance to be independent of N. Increasing N from 30 to 300 causes an increase of only 3% in the measured resistance on uniform ground. Consequently C_1 and P_1 can be fixed, and the survey carried out with C_2P_2. Because of the strong gradient of voltage near C_2 the measured resistance is most influenced by the ground in the vicinity of P_2; the background resistance due to the whole region between P_1 and P_2 is minimized by making $\alpha \gg \beta$. Because C_1 is far distant, the current flow around C_2 is roughly that of a single probe (Fig. 8.6), and consequently the orientation of the C_2P_2 pair is unimportant. Because the detection is effectively by means of the electrode-pair C_2P_2 there is no inverted W effect and the clarity of indication is as good as with the Double-Dipole system. However, a disadvantage is that the percentage change due to a feature is lowest of all the principal configurations; Schlumberger is best in this respect, followed by Wenner and Palmer.

In the *Equipotential* method, the current electrodes consist of a number of probes linked together. These are positioned on either side of the survey area and the ground in between is investigated by a pair of roving probes connected to earphones, equipotential lines being plotted out. So far only one archaeological usage has been reported (De Terra *et al.*, 1949).

REFERENCES

AL CHALABI, M. M. *and* REES, A. I. (1962). An experiment on the effect of rainfall on electrical resistivity anomalies in the near surface. *Bonner Jahrbücher*, **162**, 266–71.
ASPINALL, A. *and* LYNAM, J. T. (1970). An induced polarisation instrument for the detection of near surface features. *Prospezioni Archeologiche*, **5**, 67–75.
ASPINALL, A. *and* PICARD, K. (1971). A direct-reading earth resistance meter. *Prospezioni Archeologiche*, **6**, 21–24.
ATKINSON, R. J. C. (1952). Méthodes électriques de prospection en archéologie. In *La Découverte du Passé* (ed. A. Laming), pp. 59–70. Picard, Paris.
ATKINSON, R. J. C. (1953). *Field Archaeology*, 2nd edn. Methuen, London, p. 32.
ATKINSON, R. J. C. (1963). Resistivity surveying in archaeology. In *The Scientist and Archaeology* (ed. R. Pyddoke), pp. 1–30, Phoenix House, London.
BRAISSANT, P. *and* CHAPELLIER, D. (1971). Le potentiomètre Braissant. *Prospezioni Archaeologiche*, **6**, 25–28.
CARABELLI, E. (1967). Ricerca sperimentale dei dispositivi più adatti alla prospezione electtrica di cavità sotterranee. *Prospezioni Archaeologiche*, **2**, 9–21.
CARABELLI, E. *and* BRANCALEONI, F. (1968). Rilievo electtrico di tombe a camera con dispositivo a doppio dipolo. *Prospezioni Archeologiche*, **3**, 55–60.
CARPENTER, E. W. (1955). Some notes concerning the Wenner configuration. *Geophysical Prospecting*, **3**, 388–402.
CLARK, A. J. (1968). A square array for resistivity surveying. *Prospezioni Archaeologiche*, **3**, 111–14.
CLARK, A. J. (1969). Resistivity surveying. In *Science and Archaeology*, (ed. Brothwell, D. *and* Higgs, E. S.), pp. 695–708. Thames and Hudson. London.

DE TERRA, ROMERO, J., *and* STEWART, T. D. (1949). Tepexpan man. *Viking Fund Publications in Anthropology*, No. 11, New York.

DUNK, A. J. (1962). An electrical resistance survey over a Romano-British villa site. *Bonner Jahrbücher*, **162**, 272–6.

EVE, A. S. *and* KEYS, D. A. (1954). *Applied Geophysics*, 4th ed. Cambridge University Press.

GRIFFITHS, D. H. *and* KING, R. F. (1965). *Applied Geophysics for Engineers and Geologists*. Pergamon Press, Oxford.

HAMPL, F. *and* FRITSCH, V. (1959). Geoelektrische Messungen in ihrer Anwendung für die Archäologie, *Technische Beiträge zur Archäologie, Mainz*, **1**, 116.

HESSE, A. (1966). Perfectionnement des applications archéologiques de la prospection électrique. *Bulletin de la Société Prehistorique Francaise* LXIII.

HESSE, A. (1966a). The importance of climatologic observations in archaeological prospecting. *Prospezioni Archeologiche*, **1**, 11–13.

HESSE, A. (1966b). *Prospections géophysiques à faible protondeur. Applications à l'archéologie*. Dunod, Paris.

LERICI, C. M., CARABELLI, E., *and* SEGRE, E. (1958). Prospezioni geofisiche nella zona archeologica di Vulci. *Quaderni di Geofisica Applicata* XIX.

PALMER, L. S. (1960). Geoelectrical surveying of archaeological sites. *Proc. Prehist. Soc.*, **XXVI**, 64–75.

REES, A. I. (1962). Electrical prospecting methods in archaeology. *Antiquity*, **36**, 131–4.

REES, A. I. *and* WRIGHT, A. E. (1969). Resistivity surveys at Barnsley Park. *Prospezioni Archeologiche*, **4**, 121–4.

SCHWARZ, G. T. (1961). The Zirkelsonde a new technique for resistivity surveying. *Archaeometry*, **4**, 67–70.

SEARLE, G. F. C. (1910). On resistances with current and potential terminals. *The Electrician*, **66**, 999–1002.

TAGG, G. F. (1959). A resistivity survey in the Wash area. *J. Instn elec. Engrs.* **3**, 5.

UHLIR, A. (1955). The potentials of infinite systems of sources. *Bell System Technical Journal*, **34**, 103.

WENNER, F. (1916). A method of measuring earth resistivity. *Bull U.S. Bur. of Stand.* **12**, 469.

Subject Index